PHYSICAL EDUCATION, SOCIAL ATTITUDES AND LEADERSHIP QUALITIES

PHYSICAL EDUCATION SOCIAL ATTITUDES AND LEADERSHIP QUALITIES

By

DR. V. SATYANARAYANA
B.Sc., M.A., M.P.Ed., Ph.D.
Department of Physical Education
Osmania University
Hyderabad-500 007
Andhra Pradesh

Editor

DR. DIGUMARTI BHASKARA RAO
M.Sc., M.A., M.A., M.Ed., Ph.D.
R.V.R. College of Education
D-43, S.V.N. Colony,
Guntur-522 006
Andhra Pradesh

DISCOVERY PUBLISHING HOUSE
New Delhi

First Published - 2001
Reprinted - 2016

ISBN: 978-81-7141-593-9

Physical Education Social Attitudes and Leadership Qualities

Published by:
DISCOVERY PUBLISHING HOUSE PVT. LTD.
4383/4B, Ansari Road, Darya Ganj
New Delhi-110 002 (India)
Phone: +91-11-23279245, 43596064-65
Fax: +91-11-23253475
E-mail: discoverypublishinghouse@gmail.com
sales@discoverypublishinggroup.com
web: www.discoverypublishinggroup.com

Printed at:
Infinity Imaging Systems
Delhi

PREFACE

Physical education as an integral part of the total education process becomes a basis for the development of physically, mentally, emotionally and socially fit citizen. It helps in the development of a well-balanced, well-integrated and vitally alive human personality. It inculcates the habits of self-discipline, self-control, tolerance and forbearance, fortitude and spirit of sportmanship that enable a person to withstand life's setbacks and shocks, and brave all risks and hazards with a smiling face and quiet graceful demeanour. It also contributes to the development of desirable social attitudes and appropriate leadership qualities which are required for efficient citizenship.

Considering the role of physical education in human life, a study was taken up to study the relationship of physical education with the development of social attitudes and leadership qualities. The subjects felt that the participation in games and sports generally helps in the formation of desirable social studies and desirable leadership qualities. It is necessary to conduct a thorough probe which would highlight the sluggish growth of leadership qualities among sports personalities at the highest levels of their participation.

Grateful thanks are extended to Prof. Parmaji Sabinkar, Prof. Ramesh Ghanta, Prof. E. G. Parameshwaran, Prof. K. Ravi Chandra, Dr. N. R. Kishan, Dr. S. M. Reddy, Smt. V. L. Devi, Dr. K. Anjaiah, Mr. P. Ramchander and Mr. P. Sunderesh for their masterly guidance and friendly cooperation.

Dr. V. Satyanarayana

Dr. D. Bhaskara Rao

CONTENTS

1

INTRODUCTION

1.0.0 INTRODUCTION—BACKGROUND

Today games and sports have become an important part of human culture throughout the world. Stone (1962) stressed that life must be viewed as a continuous socialization for the child and the adult, and that life is a series of careers with each critical turning point marked by a definite change, the new upcoming game being rehearsed immediately prior to entry upon the appropriate field of play. Personality traits and the sportsman spirit are highly correlated with each other. An eminent education thinker, Froebel said, 'Sports or play is the highest phase of child development. Play is the purest, most spiritual activity of mankind at this stage, and at the same time, typical of human life as a whole of the inner hidden natural life in man and all thing.' It is full of pleasure, freedom, peace and mental as well as physical activity. According to Stern (1976) 'Play is a voluntary self contained activity.' Sportsman spirit is a natural and universal phenomenon. It is an essential part of the adolescent's personality. It helps the individual in moulding his personality towards appropriate future life; Educationists have since long been interested in the phenomenon of sports as a means for personality development. Sports reduces emotional as well as mental tension. It aims the mind and provides better physique to an individual.

Education to be complete must have five principal aspects relating to the five principal activities of the human being: the physical, the mental, the social, the emotional and the spiritual. Usually, these phases of education succeed each other in a chronological order following the growth of the individual. This however, does not mean that one should replace another but that all must continue, complementing each other, till the end of life.

Physical education is an essential part of an ideal educational system. For even a highest and complete education of the mind is not enough without the education of the body. But this aspects of education has been overlooked in many developing countries of the world including India. During the early years of this century, Sri Aurobindo pointed out the need for rigorous physical education.

Sri Aurobindo (1948), said that 'We must organise physical education all over the country and train up the rising generation not only in the moral strength and courage for which Swadeshism has given us the materials, but in physical strength and courage and the habit of rising immediately and boldly to the height of even the greatest emergency'.

'Perfection, the true aim of all culture . . ., if our seeking is for a total perfection of the being, the physical part of it cannot be left aside, for the body is the material basis, the body is the instrument which we have to use.'

It is true that (in the past) the body has been regarded by spiritual seekers rather as an obstacle, as something to be overcome and discarded than as an instrument or spiritual perfection and a field of the spiritual change.

In fact, whatever type of body a man may have, he must accept as a starting point and bring out, by a concentrated effort and an appropriate training, the possibilities it contains and make it into a fit instrument for as perfect a life as possible.

Physical education is one of the aspects of education. 'Physical education is an integral part of the total education process and has as its aim the development of physically, mentally, emotionally and socially fit citizens through the medium of physical activities which have been selected with a view to realizing these outcomes.' - Bucher, Charles (1958)

Physical education is that sum of those experiences which come to the individual through movement.

Physical education is that field of education which deals with big muscle activities and their related responses.

The old concept of physical education as mere drill or series of regulated exercises has been rejected. It includes all forms of physical activities which promote the development of the body and mind.

There has been a tendency in various schemes of physical education in the past to emphasize only the physical fitness value of physical education and ignore its educational value. The concept of physical education has been broadened, as it should contribute not only to physical fitness but also to physical efficiency, mental alertness and the development of certain qualities like perserverance, team spirit, leadership, obedience to rules. Moderation in victory, and balance in defeat, Social Attitude formation etc.

Need and Importance of Physical Education

To highlight the significance of Physical Education some thoughts of great philosophers are quoted in the following paras:

Socrates: 'What a disgrace it is for a man to grow old without even seeing the beauty and the strength of which his body is capable of.'

Swami Vivekananda: 'What India needs today is not the Bhagawad Gita but the football field.' .... 'Our men must be strong, religion comes next. Be strong my young friends, you will be nearer to heaven through football than Gita and you will understand Gita better with your biceps.'

Ryburn: 'We need in India, education, a general physical education—we need a conception of education in which physical education takes its rightful place, in which its vital importance is recognised.'

A properly directed physical education should result in health, happiness, efficiency and character.

Froebel: 'If we wish to develop the whole being, we must exercise the whole human being.'

Rousseau: 'It is the sound constitution of the body, that makes the operation of the mind easy and certain.'

Physical education takes care of the most vital aspect of human life which is the very basis of human existence and strength. It is basis of a healthy, happy and harmonious life. It helps in the development of a well-balanced, well-integrated and vitally alive human personality. It inculcates the habits of self discipline, self control, toleration and forbearance, fortitude and spirit of sportsmanship, that enable a person to withstand life setbacks and shocks and brave all risks and hazards with a smiling face and quiet graceful demeanour.

Definition of Physical Education

'Physical education is an integral part of the total education process and has its aim the development of physically, mentally, emotionally, and socially, fit citizens through the medium of physical activities which have been selected with a view to realizing these outcomes'—Bucher. Charles (1958).

Aims of Physical Education

The aim of physical education is development of effective citizenship and social efficiency. The object of physical education is to help in the production and maintenance of health in body and mind. The aims of physical education are not different from those of education. The subject teacher is merely contended with discussing the theory and imparting knowledge whereas the physical education teacher makes a ceaseless and untiring effort to achieve these aims through muscular activities.

The following are the aims of physical education:

(a) Development of well-built and strong bodies. Conservation of health.

(b) To keep children fit and in trim form during school life and ultimately make them into well-developed, full fledged, wholesome personalities.

(c) To develop in them the sense of personal hygiene, social hygiene, mental hygiene, moral hygiene and sex hygiene.

(d) Development of regular habits of exercise, cleanliness and play and of healthful living.

(e) Development of personal qualities like, self-reliance, endurance, self-control, courage, initiative, steadiness of purpose, and resourcefulness.

(f) Development of social qualities like obedience, cooperation, fellowship.

Objectives of Physical Education

Brownell and Hagman (1951) have given four general objectives:

1. Objectives related to the development of Physical Fitness.
2. Objectives related to the development of Social and Motor Skills.
3. Objectives related to the development of Knowledges and Understandings.
4. Objectives related to the development of Habits, Attitudes and Appreciations.

Clarke (1950) has given the following three objectives of Physical Education:

1. Objective of Physical Fitness.
2. Objective of Social Efficiency.
3. Objective of Culture.

Cowell and Hazelton (1955) have classified the general and specific objectives of Physical Education into five groups:

1. Organic Power, the Ability to maintain adaptive effort.
2. Neuromuscular development.
3. Personal-social attitudes and adjustment.
4. Interpretive and intellectual development
5. Emotional responsiveness.

Hetherington (1922) listed five fold classification of Physical Education objectives; viz.,

1. The immediate objectives
2. The remote objectives
3. The objectives in development
4. The objectives in social standards
5. The objectives in the control of health conditions

Irwin (1951) has classified the objectives of Physical Education into five categories, namely,

1. The Physical objective
2. The Social objective
3. The Emotional objective
4. The Recreational objective
5. The Intellectual objective

LaSalle (1946) listed five classifications of objectives of Physical Education, viz.,

1. The objectives of organic aspects of development
2. The objectives of neuromuscular aspects of development
3. The objectives of emotional aspects of development
4. The objectives of social aspects of development
5. The objectives of intellectual aspects of development

Nash (1948) had classified objectives of physical education in four categories, namely,

1. Organic development
2. Neuromuscular development
3. Interpretive development
4. Emotional development

Sharman (1934) had classified the objectives of Physical Education into two, namely;

1. Educational objectives
2. Administrative objectives

Oberteuffer (1951) listed several immediate and long-range objectives or outcomes towards which physical educators should direct their efforts. The first group of these outcomes includes those which are immediate, easily recognized, and may be gained by the individual through participation. They are, (1) skill in an activity, (2) organic value and (3) fun and amusement. The second group consists of those outcomes which, although frequently seen, are more difficult to achieve. These are psychological characteristics and social controls. The third and last group is composed of those outcomes which have outstanding value but which are very difficult to produce. However, their achievement is possible, and any physical education programme designed to make the greatest contribution to the individual and to society will reach these goals. They are a deeper understanding of human nature and human relations, an understanding of the democratic way of life, and practice in reflective thinking.

The preceding discussion covering the meaning and definition of Physical Education, the need and importance of Physical Education according to some philosophers and theoreticians and the aims and objectives of Physical Education has an integral undercurrent which highlights a plethora of aspects that are likely to get developed through Games & Sports activities. It would be appropriate to scan the reseaches undertaken so far covering the aspects specified. It may be that some aspects have received appropriate research attention and some because of various reasons could not get the needed research attention.

An analysis of previous reseaches done would highlight the thrust areas. With this objective, the research reviews are presented in the following paras.

1.1.0 PREVIOUS RESEARCHES: REVIEW

The review of research literature normally provide a backdrop to the research. It identifies the thrust areas needing immediate research attention. It even classifies researches done in each thrust area in its dimension-wise.

But the pioneering researches in the areas, where sufficient number of researches have not been conducted, find it difficult to classify and present the relevant researches to provide the needed backdrop.

The research under report is one such pioneering work and so the researcher could not find out sufficient number of researches covering the sub-dimensions of the research.

So an attempt is made to cover only the main dimensions i.e., the Social Attitudes and Leadership Qualities. The researches reported in various research journals and in the books covering conceptual theory are reported in the following paras chronologically highlighting the sub-areas whenever possible.

The review of researches covering Social Attitude is presented under caption 1.1.1 and the review of research covering Leadership Qualities under caption 1.1.2.

1.1.1 SOCIAL ATTITUDES: REVIEW OF RESEARCHES

The researches covering Social Attitudes are classified under the following headings:

1. Identification of Variables/Dimensions
2. Formation of Social Attitudes
3. Social Attitudes in relation to other variables

1.1.1.1 Identification of Variables/Dimensions:

The main aim of education is to modify the behaviour of the child according to the needs and expectancy of the society. Behaviour is composed of so many attributes. One of these important attributes is attitude. One's behaviour, to a great extent depends upon one's attitude towards the things—idea, persons or object, in his environment. The entire personality and development of the child is influenced by the nature of his attitudes. Leaning of a subject and acquisition of habits, interests and other psychophysical dispositions are all affected by his attitudes. Therefore, it is important for a teacher to understand the meaning and nature of attitudes, the factors responsible for their formation and development and techniques of their measurement.

Attitude (Dictionary Meaning)

A more or less stable set, or disposition of opinion, interest or purpose, involving expectancy of a certain kind of experience and readiness with an appropriate response; sometimes used in a wider sense, but rather less definitely, as in Aesthetic Attitude, in the sense of tendency to appreciate or produce artistic results, or Social Attitude in the sense of being sensitive to social relations, social duties or social opinions: attitude scales and attitude tests are scales and tests devised to throw light on temperament and personality traits—Harvey Wallerstein (1952)

A learned predisposition to react consistently in a given manner (either positively or negatively) to certain persons, objects or concepts. Attitudes have cognitive, affective and behavioural components—B.B. Wolman (1973). An attitude directed to inter-individual or inter-group relations—B.B. Wolman.

An opinion shared by many people—B.B. Wolman

Attitude towards the community and other members of the community—H. Wallerstein.

Meaning of the Term 'Attitude'

Attitude represents an individual's feeling towards something for or against (in modern psychological literature).

So an attitude is thus one's mental disposition or degree of acceptance directed towards an object, which may either be concrete or abstract. The object may be real object like church, school, parliament, institutional practices like teacher education, punishment, vocational training, co-education, etc.

Explaining the term "Social Attitude"

Social attitude plays an important part in directing man's social behaviour. Man's behaviour is influenced by his beliefs, assumptions and decisions. All these are affected by the individual attitude towards different persons and objects. They are the motivating forces. Hence, it is only natural for the individual's social behaviour to be influenced by these attitudes.

The child develops in a social environment. In this social environment he gains the experience of different objects, individuals, institutions and associations, etc. With different experiences he formulates different types of attitudes towards them. In this development of attitudes there is some contribution of beliefs, decisions and assumptions. In this manner, by the time he attains adulthood his attitudes become quite firm and these also direct his social behaviour. In this way, it is evident that Social Attitudes play an important role in social behaviour. Hence, the social behaviour of the individual is better understood if prefaced by an understanding of these social attitudes. But there is also limit to the accurate prediction of the social behaviour of the individual on the basis of the knowledge of his social attitudes, because, for one, it is difficult to know an attitude in its entirety and secondly, attitudes also keep on changing.

The Importance of Social Attitudes

Probably no branch of social psychology has received more attention than this problem of social attitudes since 1920. It is looked upon as the central problem in social psychology. The net product of the socialization process is the formation of the attitudes among individuals. These attitudes are reflected by the words and deeds of an individual. In his interaction with other persons and groups, in his dealing with the cultural products, in all these we see the influence of the Social Attitudes. It is by forming the appropriate Social Attitudes that one become a Hindu or Muslim or a Christian: a Congressman or a Socialist, or a Communist: a Capitalist or a labour leader. Nobody is born one way or the other. He becomes one by the formation of the appropriate social attitudes. In the last 60 years, considerable work has been done regarding the formation, the change and the measurement of Social Attitudes. Studies have been made about the way in which groups of people, incline towards the church, the social, the political party, the economic programmes, war and such other institutions.

Definitions of Attitude

Various authors have defined attitude in the following ways:

Allport (1935): 'An attitude is a mental and neural set or readiness, exerting a directive dynamic influence upon the individual's response to all objects and situations with which it is related.'

The definition reveals the following facts concerning attitude:

a. Attitude is the mental or neural state of readiness.

b. Attitude influences the reactions of the individual.

c. Attitude changes the reactions of the individual.

From its foregoing definition, it is evident that attitude is a mental or neural set of readiness, system or disposition in which the motivational, affective, perceptual and throughout processes are included and due to which the individual's positive or negative activity is directed to the subjects, individuals and groups surrounding him.

Travers (1973): 'An attitude is a readiness to respond in such a way that behaviour is given a certain direction.'

Mckeachi and Doyle (1966): 'We define an attitude as an organisation or concepts, beliefs, habits and motivates associated with a particular object.'

Sorenson (1977): 'An attitude is a particular feeling about something. It therefore involves a tendency to behave in a certain way in situations which involve that something, whether persons, idea or object. It is partially rational and partially emotional and is acquired, not inherent, in an individual.'

Whittaker (1970): 'An attitude is a predisposition or readiness to respond in a predetermined manner to relevant stimuli.'

According to the Traver's definition attitude is responsible for behaving in a particular and definite way. If one keeps a positive and favourble attitude towards an object, he will be attracted towards it, he will admire it and try to achieve it. On the other hand if one has a negative or unfavourable attitude one will try to avoid it and even feel hostile to it. For example, a person having positive attitude towards democracy will respond positively to democratic practices and institutions and negatively to authoritarian procedures. His behaviour will speak out of his attitude.

The Mckeachie's definition takes into account all of the concepts, beliefs, habits and motives associated with the object. The concepts and beliefs associated with an attitude are often referred to as the cognition component of the attitude, the habit as the action component, and the motives as the affective component. In this way all what one thinks, feels and how does he react expresses one's attitude towards an objects. For example, if we take attitude towards a political party, the formation of favourable or unfavourable attitude will be the result of his thinking and feeling towards that party and it will be exhibited overtly through some act tendencies like heated discussion with associates or strangers, casting a vote in favour of the party candidate or doing active party work during the election campaign.

The Sorenson's definition explains why an individual behaves in a certain way when he is needed to respond to a particular object for which he has developed a positive or negative attitude. He has somewhat a definite set of feelings, likes or dislikes for that object which partly stands on rational and partly on emotional footings. But in all cases, they are acquired and learned through varying experiences. One's attitude towards one's religion is an acquired tendency or disposition. He is not born with enthusiasm or apathy for this particular religion. He has developed a sort of attachment or favourable feeling towards his religion due to his own experiences from his early childhood. His feeling is party rational and partly emotional. He may be able to give very good reasons for advocating and appreciating his religion but their basis is partly beneath conscious reasoning.

Whittaker's definition accepts attitude as a predisposition or tendency to behave in a particular and definite way to a particular situation. One's attitude decides one's response to a particular stimulus. For example, in responding to all stimuli related with the congress party one has a predisposition or tendency to act in a certain way if one has developed an attitude towards the party.

In this way attitudes are, to a great extent, responsible for the particular behaviour of a person about an object, idea or person. But by this conclusion it should not be taken that one's behaviour is an absolute function of one's attitude. Behaviour by all means is a function of both characteristics of the behaving person and the situations in which he behaves. Hence, a person may hold strong attitude and yet, under certain circumstances may behave in quite contradictory to those attitudes. In this way one's behaviour towards object related to a particular attitude cannot be safely predicted through that attitude but it can be safely said that it makes the individual respond in a particular way to the particular stimuli.

Therefore, we may understand attitude as a determining acquired tendency which prepares a person to behave in a certain way towards a specific object or class of object subject to the conditions prevailing in the environment.

A variety of patterns are included in an individual's attitudes. There are attitudes towards health, life, death, people, new situations, music and art, work, play, government, religion, and many more than are of like importance. These attitudes have been influenced by the educative process through planned and random experiences. Since creating and shaping attitudes is one of the most important functions of the school, attention should be given to a study of their genesis, nature, and dynamic aspects.

1.1.1.2 Formation of Attitudes

Attitude could be formed to social as well as non-social aspects of the environment. We are now concerned only with Social Attitudes, i.e., attitude formed in relation to social stimulus situations. Thus, social attitudes may be formed towards persons or groups of persons; or towards the products of human interaction. These products of human interaction may be material like the technological devices or they may be non-material like the values or norms of a group.

Attitudes are learned or acquired dispositions. How Social Attitudes are formed, has been a question for investigation to the psychologists. Based on the opinion of Allport, Stagner have suggested that attitudes have formed under one of the following conditions:

1. *The integration of experiences*: The accumulation and integration of a number of related experiences about an object gives birth to an attitude towards that object. Attitude of Hindus towards Muslims or vice versa has been formed in this way.
2. *The Differentiation of Experiences*: When the new experiences are acquired, they are differentiated or segregated from the already acquired experiences. This segregation or differentiation may tend to make certain attitudes more specific.

3. *Trauma or dramatic experience*: Attitudes are formed with greater speed and intensity on account of the suddenly unusual, shocking and painful experiences. A shopkeeper whose shop has been burnt by the striking students may develop intensely negative attitudes towards all students.

4. *The adoption of the available attitudes*: A large number of attitudes are acquired in a ready made fashion by simply following suggestions or examples of friends, teachers, parents or adopting the mores and traditions of the community or society. Negative attitude of the children of Tamilnadu towards Hindi has been formed through the process of adoption, rather than as result of first hand experience.

Attitudes are formed in the context of the individual's wants, information, group affiliation and responsibility development.

Factors Influencing the Formation or Development of Attitudes

Attitudes are unquestionably an acquired disposition and therefore conditioned by learning or acquisition of experiences. Heredity factors do not play any role in the formation of development of attitudes. Environmental forces help an individual to form and develop various attitudes. An attitude at any stage is essentially a product of the interaction of one's self with one's environment. Therefore the factors influencing the formation and development of attitudes can be divided into two parts as follows:

A. Factors within the individual himself.

B. Factors within the individual's environment.

A. *Factors within the individual himself*

All individuals do not respond similarly in identical situations. The effect of environmental stimuli in acquiring some predispositions is very much conditioned by the growth and development pattern of an individual child. Let us try to emphasize these developmental factors.

1. *Physical Growth and Development*

In the development of attitude physical growth and development plays a significant role. Poor physical health, low vitality and undeveloped somatic structure is responsible for poor emotional and social adjustment and poor social adjustment inevitably exercises an important effect on the formation of attitudes in many different directions. A crippled and undersized girl of fifteen years is unlikely to form the same attitudes as those formed by another girl of fifteen who is tall, well proportioned and charming for her age. Even the colour of the skin, weight of the body or biochemical changes in the body tissues and fluids, for example sex hormones have a vital effect on the development of attitudes through its connection with social adjustment.

2. *Intellectual Development*

Development of attitudes is conditioned by the growth of intelligence. The components of intelligence like memory, understanding, thinking and reasoning play a significant part in attitude formation as they help in gaining perceptual experience. Due to his limited intellectual capacities a young child is incapable of forming attitudes about remote or complex abstract things. His attitudes are always of a particular kind that are related to his own immediate problems and experiences. With the growth of intellectual capacities an intelligent adult is capable of having more abstract and generalized attitudes.

3. *Emotional Development*

Emotional development also affects the formation of attitudes. Emotions play a dominant role in overt or covert behaviour manifestation and behaviour is related to attitudes. As the child develops with age and growth the capacity for varied emotional experiences and attitudes is gradually developed. Emotional maturity helps in social adjustment and seeking social approval. In turn it makes an individual to develop numerous attitudes through his direct or indirect experiences.

4. *Social Development*

Attitudes are rarely individual affairs. Social interaction and group processes are the key of attitude formation at any stage of human development. Children having poor social adjustment are much more likely to have antisocial attitudes and are less subject to group influences in the formation of other attitudes. Children with healthy social adjustment easily pick up social attitudes from their respective groups.

5. *Ethical and Moral Development*

Each individual develops certain ideals, values and a concept of self in which he has pride. For enhancing his feeling of self-esteem one tries to develop those attitudes that suit his values and ideals. A student who values historical events or objects will have a favourable attitude towards the subject of history. A man who thinks that God is one and will not have unfavourable attitude towards the persons belonging to the religions other than his own.

B. *Factors within the individual's environment*

Leaving aside the individual variations shown through their various personality characteristics on account of the pattern of their growth and development, attitudes are largely borrowed from the groups within one's environment to which one owes one's stronger allegiance. It has now been firmly established that the environmental forces, in the shape of the social groups, institutions and community cast a strong influence shaping the beliefs and attitudes of an individual. Let us try to understand a few important environment factors.

1. *Home and Family*

In attitude formation home and family environment plays a leading role. The child by identifying himself with his parents and other members of the family picks up their attitudes. The family, more or less, defines for the child the expected roles which he must play in various situations and thus initiates the formation of specific attitudes. The healthy family environment and positive attitudes of the parents and family members bring desirable impact on children in picking up desirable attitudes while parental negative attitudes for example of hostility and rejection lead them to imbibe ascendant and aggressive attitudes. In the similar way many antisocial attitudes are said to be the product of the faulty upbringing and uncosequential environment of the home and family.

2. *Social Environment*

Where the family and home environment plays its role in the formation of early attitude, the contact with the people in neighbourhood, school, community and society and mores and traditions of the community to which one belongs casts strong influence in reshaping early attitudes and acquisitions of many more new attitudes. As the child grows older and has wider social contacts he is influenced by so many social institutions and groups and as a result he tries to pick up attitudes of those groups for which he has stronger allegiance or that suits much to his own nature and motives.

In school, the factors like teachers and their behaviour, classmates or school-mates, and their behaviour, the teaching method, curriculum, general tone and discipline of the institution, all contribute towards attitude formation.

The religious groups, social clubs or constitution where one learns or earns has a definite set of emotional and intellectual environment with the result that the members of the group tend to pick up the characteristic attitudes of the group and in this way social groups play a leading role in attitude formation.

Mass media in the form of newspapers, in radio, and television, moving pictures, propaganda literature and advertisements also play a key role in shaping and reshaping the attitudes. Individuals tend to identify them with the views expressed through these agencies. Thereby heroes and heroines of the screen and radio programmes, attractive figures shown in the advertisements and slogans of a popular leader prove a potent source for the formation of attitudes.

1.1.1.3 Social Attitudes in Relation to Other Variables

In their most primitive form attitudes exist as simple pleasant or unpleasant states of the infant. Some of these feelings or results of satisfied or unsatisfied biological needs. Others are produced by pleasurable or unpleasurable responses from mother, father, or siblings. Whenever an infant eats, excretes, sleeps, cries, and moves about he is interacting with its surroundings, both animate and inanimate. This interaction produces sensory stimulation and feeling-tones of a general nature. As growth and development occur in the infant a changing array of needs brings new reactions to objects and situations. An infant gains pleasure from being helped and protected, whereas a child in the early period of walking is likely to resent and reject the helping hand. Taking in food through the mouth, sucking, and other receptive oral activities provide obvious pleasure for the infant, but the child who is teething finds the mouth a source of pain and discomfort. Developmental changes of this kind produce tremendous changes in the child's relationships with objects and situations.

Despite apparent incongruity the orderly and sequential development of the total organism results in threads of continuity of feeling. Ordinarily a satisfying state of affairs over an extended period of time produces a positive feeling in the child for the object or ability involved. As the child's perpetual field expands, some generalization of response becomes possible. An infant who has experienced general pleasure at the breast or bottle is likely to anticipate pleasure from eating other foods. Continued dissatisfaction and unpleasantness during nursing are likely to create a negative feeling about eating. Eating problems are frequently found in young children who have experienced disagreeable or unsatisfying feeding of significant duration or intensity during infancy. As the psychological life of the child becomes more complex and some of its needs directly oppose others, feelings are not so simple related to external situations. This is illustrated in the very young child who learns that attention can be gained more readily from mother and father by doing something that is forbidden and to which they respond with displeasure. A continuing need for attention that is stronger than the need for a pleasurable response from the parent reinforces the child's undesirable behaviour. Youngsters who want to be punished because of their feelings towards their parents may seek unpleasant responses from them.

A child's attitude towards authority figures is obviously an important element of socialization and determines much of his behaviour in school. Early experiences involving the child and his parents are responsible for the beginnings of this attitude. A rebellious attitude towards authority figures (teacher, principal, leader and others) may spring from a conflict with someone in authority, usually a parent or parent substitute. Itkin (1955) in a study involving 400 students and their *parents,* found a very significant relationship (one per cent level) between both male and female students 'attitudes towards the father figure and the father's acceptance-rejection of the child. This relationship was not the result of dominance or laxity of the parent but simply the kind of feeling between father and child. Another important element in the early development of a child's attitude towards adults is the satisfaction or dissatisfaction derived from the child's dependency upon parents, particularly the mother figure'. Spitz and Ribble (1944) have contributed significantly to this subject. Their findings seem to be well expressed by Roudinesco (1952) in the remark that 'any separation from the family, and especially from the mother, is for a young child a painful and distressing experience which is not tolerable before he has acquired the concepts of time and space. Such an experience in children under three years of age usually brings a change in their relationship with adults." Separation over a period of time accompanied by deprivation of needs is likely to produce an incapacity to achieve close and intimate human relationships. Koch (1955) in her study of 384 children five and six years of age, found that the child's attitude towards the teacher was *strongly* influenced by the following elements of the mother-child relationship:

1. Satisfying experiences with mother.
2. Mother's experiences and what she expected of the child.
3. Mother's attitudes towards other children in the family.

Other attitudes of children have their origins in the family relationships in the home. A detailed study of parent-child relationships was conducted by Baldwin (1949) and others at the Fels Institute. Several syndromes of parent attitudes toward children were discovered and explored. The parental attitude of 'acceptant-democratic' seemed to facilitate growth and development more than the others. Children from the home atmosphere of warmth and equality had an accelerated intellectual development were more original, indicated more emotional security and control, and were less excitable than children from other homes. In school these children were popular, friendly, and non-aggressive leaders. A later report Lasko supports these findings and points out that warmth, democracy, and indulgence seem to typify three types of home environment encountered in her study. Of these the democratic atmosphere was most important in accounting for the observed variations in behaviour. Evidence from these studies suggests that the parent' acceptance of the child and the autonomy that the child experiences in daily contacts in the home are strong determiners of later behaviour in a school situation.

Certainly the other members of a family constellation play an important role in shaping early attitudes of the child. Such factors as the child's place in the chronological order of the family and the sex of sibling have been explored as possible determiners of attitudes. Koch (1955) found significant relationships between these factors and certain attitudes in her study of 384 five and six years old children from two child families. More signs of stimulation or stress were noted among members of opposite-sexed pairs of sibling than among like-sexed pairs. When an age difference of two to four years existed between these opposite-sex pairs, they were found to be 'more self-confident, more cheerful, active, healthy, less vacillating, and more inclined to recover poise readily than the children whose sib was like them in sex'. This study indicated that age spacing is more closely associated with such things as confidence, emotional intensity, excitability, moodiness, anger, decisiveness, alibiing, projecting of blame and indirection. Differences in attitudes were not significantly related to simple sex differences.

Attitudes developed during the preschool years are associated with the general culture in which the child is reared as well as the direct influences of family relationships, Playmates, neighbours, members of other culture groups, physical surroundings, economic conditions of the family, and various other factors influence the child directly and indirectly. These factors place a limit upon the child's experiences and establish the nature of the environment. Day-to-Day experiences and the child perception of them have a strong influence in establishing the pattern of feelings developed in the child about objects, activities and situations. A study of responses of 4,360 people to a questionnaire led sister Mary Charleen (1950) to feel that children bring to school prenomic status. Her data indicates that teachers must be prepared to receive these different attitudes as early as kindergarten and first grade. Direct experiences were responsible for many of these attitudes, but a strong factor in their development must have been the indirect influence from older persons such as parents and siblings. Allport (1935) points out that, in addition to the reactions to direct experiences, attitudes are taken into the child through the process of identification and interjection. A child is likely to internalize the attitude of people whom he desires to be like or to please. It is likely that the attitudes of persons whom the child dislikes will be rejected along with them.

This discussion has brought us to that period in child's life when the school becomes a very important factor in shaping existing attitudes and creating new ones. Teachers and others who attempt to fulfil this important role of dealer-in-attitude should be acquainted with their dimensions as well as their development.

1.1.1.4 A Review of the Existing Literature

Prabhat, Gurnam Singh (1973) made a comparative study of the Social Attitudes of the Physically Handicapped and normal children studying in secondary schools in Punjab.

He made the comparative study with the following objectives:

To verify whether Physically Handicapped and normal children show any differences in their Social Attitudes.

To study the direction of Social Attitudes of normal children.

To study the direction of Social Attitudes of Physically Handicapped children.

To determine the differences, if any, between the Social Attitudes of different types of Physically Handicapped children, specially visually impaired, crippled and speech defective ones.

To study the sources of Social Attitudes.

The researcher had picked up 309 pairs of children studying in 8th, 9th and 10th classes in secondary schools of Punjab including two equally matched groups of Physically Handicapped and normal children covering an equal number from each class for the sample.

The findings of the study were as follows:

Both Physically Handicapped and normal children have positive attitudes in all the five areas i.e., Religion, Peers, School, Country and Family.

Physically Handicapped and normal children do not differ with respect to their attitudes towards religion.

The visually impaired children have a less positive attitudes towards family as compared to the normal group of children.

The sources of attitudes of the Physically Handicapped and normal children are the same.

Hardev Singh (1978) studied the attitudes of post-graduate students towards religion. The main objective behind his study was to examine the attitudes of post-graduates studying in the Universities of Punjab.

The study was conducted on 500 students (male, female, arts and science students) of different universities.

The following conclusions were reported out of his study.

Female students have a favourable attitude towards religion irrespective of their subjects of study.

Arts and Science students do not differ significantly in their attitude towards religion.

Dhillon, G.K. (1979), conducted a comparative study of the personality characteristics, adjustments and motivation level of non-participant and participant children of secondary schools in physical activities.

The major objectives of the research were:

To study the differences on personality dimensions, school adjustment, achievement motivation and academic achievement between participants and non-participants in sports at district level.

The study was conducted on 800 students of secondary schools of Punjab.

The major findings of the study were as follows:

Participants are high on extroversion and neuroticism in comparison to non-participants.

In all the spheres of school adjustment, academic matters, with school-mates, school administration, teacher, self and over all school adjustment, participants are higher than non-participants.

Participants have more achievement motivation than non-participants.

Academic achievement of participants in higher than non-participants.

Among the participants, non-participants and the total sample, overall school adjustment scores and academic achievement scores of female are higher than that of males.

Banga, U.S. (1982) studied the impact of Teacher Training programme in Physical Education on Physical Fitness, Personality, Adjustment and Motivity of Student Teachers.

The objectives of the study were:

To measure the changes in physical fitness, personality characteristics, adjustment and motivity in student teachers caused as a result of undergoing a one year training in Physical Education.

To identify the areas in the training programme in which improvement in needed.

The following findings were observed:

The training programme is a useful and a modifying experience for trainees and improves their personalities and physical fitness.

The impact is significant and positive for boys. The girls do not gain much in personality, adjustment, physical fitness and motivity.

The programme of training needs to be modified and enriched.

Male dominance in it has to be balanced and such elements which act negatively have to be eliminated and substituted with components which have positive effects.

Darshan Singh (1982) made an attempt to construct an

attitude scale towards sports on Higher Secondary School Children with the following objectives:

To find out the concept help by the higher secondary students regarding sports.

To find out the concepts and values of sports held by the students through various sources.

To construct and standardize an evaluation scale to be used by the physical education teachers/coaches/physical directors for measuring the attitude of higher secondary students towards sports.

The data was collected on 800 high/higher secondary school students of Punjab state.

The following findings were observed:

HSSATSS inventory is highly varied and reliable, easy to administer and score.

Higher secondary male students have a more favourable attitude towards sports than female students.

Higher secondary students of rural areas have a less favourable attitude towards sports than the students in privately managed schools.

Rao, P.S. (1984) conducted a study on changing attitudes in Urban Secondary School Students—Techniques and Effects.

The objectives of the study were:

To construct valid scales for measuring attitudes towards manual work, casteism and family planning.

To design educational treatments employing three distinct communication strategies—verbal visual communication, dramatized communication and combination of the two.

To study the separate and relative effectiveness of the three treatments in producing changes in attitudes in urban secondary school students.

To relate the initial attitudes and changes (gains) in the attitudes produced by the treatment to sex and SES of the subjects.

The sample consisted of class IX students from five schools located in Visakhapatnam. Each treatment group in each school included 30 students. Hence the total sample was 450. The investigator constructed and validated three attitude scales. The split-half reliability coefficient values were 0.949, 0.909 and 0.907 in case of attitude to manual work, casteism and family planning respectively. A 3 × 3 rotation design, with pooling of five institutional groups, and with a pre-test/post-test, was adapted for this study. Three treatment strategies and materials were developed. All the three strategies consisted of four kinds of treatment which took 45 to 50 minutes and the rest of the time was used for rapport, establishing pleasant roles, summing up highlights, etc. At the kind of the treatment programme on each attitude, the post-test was administered. SES data were collected on a personal data blank. Two-day Anova and Anacova were the statistical techniques used to examine the hypotheses.

The major findings of the study were:

All the mean differences between the final and the initial scores were positive and significant in all the nine cases.

All treatments produced clear attitudinal changes in desired direction in the subjects.

There were no significant differences among the three treatments in respect of the effect produced in terms of gains or changes in the three attitudes.

There was no clear unidirectional relationship between SES and Attitudes.

There did not seem to any significant difference between boys and girls on the one hand, and among the SES groups on the other in respect of the positive changes produced in the attitudes.

Paramjit Kaur (1984) attempted a study on attitude of boys and girls studying in professional and non-professional colleges towards marriage and family size.

The main objectives behind the study were:

To find out the attitude of professional and non-professional college students towards marriage.

To find out the difference in attitudes of professional and non-professional students towards marriage and delayed marriages, inter-caste marriage, love marriage and family size.

To examine the sex differences in attitudes of college students towards marriage, delayed marriage, inter-case marriage, love marriage and family size.

To explore the differences in attitude towards family size among different group i.e., Arts group, B.Ed., Medical and Engineering Groups.

Nearly 800 boys and girls (professional and non-professional) were interviewed.

The conclusions made were as follows:

There is no difference between professional and non-professional colleges regarding their attitude towards delayed marriage, love marriage, and family size. But differences exist towards marriage and inter-caste marriage.

There is no difference between boys and girls regarding their attitude towards marriage, delayed marriage, inter-caste marriage, love marriage and family size.

There is no difference between different groups i.e. Arts, B.Ed., Medical and Engineering groups regarding their attitude towards marriage.

Baljit Kaur (1984) conducted a studied on Attitude towards School of IX grade boys and girls in relation to Achievement Motivation.

The objectives for the study were:

To know the attitudes towards school of IX grade students.

To find out the sex differences in attitude towards school.

To find out the attitudes of IX grade students in relation to achievement motivation.

To find out the attitudes of students towards school in relation to the level of achievement motivation.

To find out the effect of the level of motivation on attitude towards school.

To find the relationship between attitude towards school and level of achievement motivation.

The study was conducted on 600 students of IX grade high school students.

The findings are:

There is no sex difference between boys and grls regarding their attitudes towards school.

High motivated students have a more favourable attitude as compared to low motivated students.

Achievement motivation does not influence the attitude of boys towards school.

Students having high achievement motivation have a more favourable attitude towards school as compared to those who have low achievement attitude.

Mathur, V. (1985) conducted a study on political attitudes and alienation among female college students.

The objectives of the study were:

To ascertain the process of crystallization of political attitudes among the females who are non-participants either at the ideological opinion level or at the behavioural level.

To explore the interactive influence of the estrangement of alienation factor and political ideological formation factor resulting in the crystallization of definite patterns of political attitudes.

To ascertain the influence of affiliation as measured by five sub-components (loyalty towards friends, parental attachment, attachment to neighbours, attachment to off-spring and home, affiliation for social customs) to the formation of political attitude among females.

A sample of 300 female students of first, second and third years from a girls, college of Jaipur was selected. The age of these students ranged between 17 and 19 years. All of them were dwellers coming from middle income families.

The findings of the study were:

The female college students, when they came into first

year had more of parental attachment, greater attachment to home, and also to social customs. However, after exposure to college life for a couple of years, these attachments gradually diminished.

The alienation scores at the point of entry in the educational institutions at the first year level were enhanced the point of exit, that is, at the third year level.

The degree of estrangement among college students were enhanced by the process of meaningless drift during college life, but by the time female students was about to leave college, a sense of purposefulness of life had developed.

The pressures and pupils exerted by the bi-polar poles of alienation and affiliation did not yield at 'G' factor to prove that political attitudes were pervaded and predetermined by the strong general factor.

Two factors came our implicitly from the data and these were labelled 'Social Affiliation for Home' and 'Affiliation for Social Customs'. These two factors were separate sub-dimensions and significant discriminant indices of affiliation.

The three criteria measures (affiliation, alienation and attitude) did not induce a compounded interactional effect. Each of the criteria measure influenced the other two in an independent and orthogonal order rather than obliquely.

Rizvi, S.A.H. (1986) conducted a study of attitudes towards religious education in relation to certain value orientation.

The objectives of the investigation was to study students' attitudes towards religious education in relation to the value system and to know whether they regarded religious education as useful in life.

The data was collected from 200 post-graduate students of the Hindu and Muslim communities studying in Aligarh Muslim University, Aligarh.

The major findings of the study were:

A majority of students held moderate attitudes towards

religious education, but the students of the Hindu and Muslim religious groups were found to hold different attitudes towards religious education.

Favourable attitudes towards religious education were found to be associated with such values as helpfulness, preserving traditions and adoption to nature. In this respect sex, socio-economic status and religious group differences were not found.

Irrespective of the difference in their sex, socio-economic status, and religion, students held similar views with respect of the association between attitudes towards religious education and conservative liberal and scientific-fatalistic value dimensions.

Faimal Singh (1986) conducted a study on 540 Physical Education Teachers to find out the relationship between anxiety, adjustment and attitude towards teaching the secondary grade students.

The objectives behind the study were as follows:

To find out the relationship between anxiety and attitude while teaching.

To study the relationship between the adjustment and attitude while teaching.

To find out the inter-relationship among the variables, anxiety, adjustment and attitude towards teaching.

The findings of the study are:

The measures of anxiety and adjustment cluster in specific constellations with the criterion measure of attitude towards teaching to explain common factor variance.

All the five factors of anxiety are negatively correlated with attitudes towards teaching in most of the cases.

Home adjustment, health adjustment, emotional adjustment and occupational adjustment are correlates of teacher effectiveness.

Sukvir Kaur (1989) studied attitude of women towards small family size in relation to education level and socio-economic status.

The main objective of the study was to know the attitudes of women towards small family size in relation to their educational level and socio-economic status.

The study was conducted on 500 women of Chandigarh District.

The following conclusions were made:

The attitude towards small family size norm of matriculates, graduates, post-graduates and highly qualified women is more positive than primary pass women.

The attitude towards small family norm of graduate, post-graduate and highly qualified women is positive than metric pass women and similarly attitude towards small family norms of highly qualified women is more positive than graduate and post-graduate women.

Sardari Lal (1990) studied physical fitness in relation to school adjustment, emotional stability, socio-economic status and sex of players and non-players.

The objectives of the study were:

To explore the relationship between (i) Physical fitness and school adjustment, (ii) Physical fitness and emotional stability, (iii) Physical fitness and socio-economic status of secondary school students.

To differentiate playing and non-playing secondary school students with regard to physical fitness, emotional stability, school adjustment and SES.

To find the sex differences in respect of their physical fitness, emotional stability, school adjustment and SES.

Six hundred (600) students from high and higher secondary schools of Hoshiarpur and Patiala districts were used for the purpose.

The following conclusions were made:

There is a positive relationship between socio-economic status and physical fitness of students.

There is positive relationship between school adjustment and physical fitness of students.

There is significant and negative relationship between emotional maturity scores and physical fitness scores of students.

High physically fit students, male players, male non-players, female players and female non-players have higher scores on socio-economic status scale than low fitness groups.

Highly adjusted students in school situation are more physically fit as compared to low adjustment group.

Emotional maturity is a determinant of physical fitness of subjects.

1.1.2 LEADERSHIP QUALITIES: REVIEW OF RESEARCHES

The researches covering Leadership Qualities are classified under the following headings:

1. Leadership—Identification of Variables
2. Development of Leadership
3. Theories of Leadership
4. Types of Leadership
5. Leadership Qualities as an independent variable.

1.1.2.1 Leadership—Identification of Variable

'The speed of the boss is the speed of the team.'

Ralph Also Emerson (1942) perceptively remarked: 'An institution is the lengthened shadow of one man.' History tells us that whenever a leader has achieved extraordinary success, he has gathered his team first—he has inspired them, set course, provided the momentum and steered them in profitable directions.

A leader is a person who directs, commands or heads a group, an organization or a nation. The word 'Leader' has originated from 'Lord' which in the old Nordic language meant the course or path of a ship at an area. The leader was the captain, who, in olden times, was usually the steersman and navigator as well.

The pre-Independence era in India saw the emergence of a galaxy of men and women who were 'leadership material'. These leaders were loved, respected and admired by the Indians. Gopala Krishna Gokhale, Lokamanya Tilak, Mahatma Gandhi, Jawharlal Nehru, Sardar Patel to name a few. One felt that the nation was in safe hands and these 'captains' were capable of steering the country through the troubled times it was passing through.

In present day India, however, the situation is far from satisfactory. What was the aura of magic, dynamism and magnetic appeal which the leaders of yester years seemed to radiate? Why is it that we have not been able to produce a leader of the caliber of Mahatma Gandhi again?

Leadership is a spontaneous social interaction between individuals and groups. It is defined as the influence or act of influencing people so that they will strive willingly towards achievement of group objectives. Leadership qualities are the result of inborn qualities (personality make up) and also nurtured by optimum environmental conditions.

A famous Sanskrit proverb runs as follows, (Yatha Raja, Tatha Praja—As the ruler, so the ruled). The underlying message of this maxim is that a leader should serve as a role model for his people. 'A true leader is a person who knows the way, shows the ways and goes he way.'

Dictionary Meaning

The exercise of authority in a social group; the quality or qualities upon which such exercise of authority depends, varying with the nature of the social group and the circumstances in which leadership is displayed or established—Wallerstein, Harvey

Explanation of the term

In every society, there is a great demand for leaders. Every society, for its survival, asks for more and better leaders. The insistence on the demand for leaders is evidently due to the pressing needs of the environment. There needs to be talent for leading everybody cannot lead. Every person can not effectively handle organized human relationships. Keeping this is view, leadership problem is a matter that concerns every member of society. Leaders try to influence the behaviour of others for attainment of some specified goals and objectives. Leadership behaviour is in demand in various fields of life situations—social, political, cultural, educational, sports, etc., leadership is therefore, a very important feature of many spheres of human activity. Leadership can have far reaching effect on the zeal and activities of the group, industries, sports and games and politics.

The word 'leadership' is most talked about the least understood phenomena in the world. By 'leadership' a majority of people bring to their mind a number of leaders who have had direct or indirect impact upon them and upon their world. While talking on leadership almost invariably the attributes and the methods of the famous leaders were discussed. These leaders may include individuals limelighting themselves in any area—model, a moral or immoral: benefactors or malefactors of humanity; persons who regard human beings or reject them outrightly.

Various thinkers have defined the world leadership in a functional as well as behavioural manner. Terry (1960) writes that 'leadership' is the activity of influencing people et. al. (1961) define it as 'interpersonal influence exercised in a situation and directed through the communication process, towards the attainment of a specialized goal or goals.' Stogdill (1950) takes leadership as 'the process of influencing activities of an organized group in its efforts towards setting goal achievement.' These definitions are more concerned with the actions which are required by the group in various conditions if they are to achieve their goals. Leadership is the performance of those acts which help the group to achieve its preferred outcomes. The preferred outcomes naturally differ from situation to situation. There is an innumerable variety of situations calling for leadership but all these situations do comprise certain relations, in which leadership is exerted. Leadership and isolation are incompatible. While sitting by himself, a leader may feel loneliness but it is only through relationships and effective communication that he can exercise his leadership.

The statement by Cartwright and Zender (1968) needs mention here. They consider leadership consisting of 'such actions by group members as those which aid in setting group goals, moving the group towards its goals, improving the quality of the interactions among the members, building the cohensiveness of the group, and making resources available to the group. In principle, leadership may be performed by one or many members of the group.'

Definitions

'A leader may be defined as person who influences the activities of the group to which he belongs and who plays a central role in defining group goals and in determining the ideology of the group.'

There are a number of features in this definition which called for further elaboration. First of all, it must be noted that the leader is part of the group. There is always a leader-follower relationship which underlies the concept of leadership and its effectiveness. Secondly, the leader's role is central, in the sense that his presence in the group is decisive and significant. All the members of a group influence one another and, in this sense, everybody has in himself a potential degree of leadership, what makes the leader a special type of member in the group is the value of his influence: significant at all times; decisive at critical junctures. Thirdly, the leader's influence on the activity of the group may be direct or indirect. It is this last aspect of the leader's influence on group members that determines the various types of leadership.

Sprott (1952): 'Any one, who acts as model to others is often called a leader.'

Lapiere Fransworth: 'Leadership is a behaviour that affects the behaviour of other people, more than their behaviour affects that of a leader.'

Pigor: 'Leadership is a concept applied to the personality, environment relation to describe the situation when a personality is so placed in the environment that is well, feeling and insight direct and control others human energy in the pursuit of a common cause.'

Britt (1942): 'Leadership is the process of mobile stimulation of reciprocal reinforcement which by the successful interplay of relevant individual differences control human energy in the pursuit of a common cause.

MacIver & Page: 'By leadership we mean to keep to persuade or to direct man, that comes from personal qualities apart from face.'

Kimball Young (1948): 'What is popularly called leadership is the more accurately to be discussed in terms of dominance.'

Seeman & Morris: 'Leadership acts or presents which influence other persons in a direction.'

Robert Tanneubuam (1961): 'Leadership is defined as into personal influence, exercised in situation and directed through the communication process, towards the attainment of specified goal or goals. Leadership always involves attempts on the part of a leader (influence) to affect (influence) the behaviour of a follower (influence) or followers' situation.

Stogdill (1950): 'Leadership may be considered as the process (act) of influencing the activities of an organized group in its efforts towards goal setting and goal activeness. The definition of leadership relates it directly to the organized group and its goal.'

Reuter: 'Leadership is an ability to persuade or direct man without use of prestige or power of formal office or external circumstances.'

Bass (1954): 'Leadership in group discussion is the assumption of the task of initiating, organizing, classifying questioning, motivating, summarising and formulating conclusions.'

Sanford: 'The leader is that person who is identified and accepted as such by his followers.'

Hamons: 'Leader is the man who comes closest to realising norms, the group values highest, this conformity gives him his high rank which attracts people and implies the right to assume control of the group.'

Beak: 'The leader is one who initiates and facilitates member inter-action'.

Dubin: 'Leadership is the exercise of authority and the making of decision.'

Cattle (1946): 'Leader is the person who creates the cost effective change in group performance.'

Cowley: 'Leader is one who succeeds in getting others to follow him.'

Pigor: 'It is a process of mental stimulation which, by the successful interplay of relevant individual differences, control human energy in the pursuit of a common cause.'

Ordway Tead (1935): 'Leadership is the activity of influencing people to cooperate towards one goal which they find desirable.'

Hemphill (1954): 'Leadership is the initiating of acts which result in a consistent pattern of group interaction directed towards the solution of the problems.'

Fiedler (1967): 'Leader is the individual in the group who gives the task directing and coordinating task-relevant group activities or who, in the absence of a designated leader, carries the primary responsibility for performing these functions in the group.'

1.1.2.2 Leadership Development

Ideas about leadership have changed considerably in recent times. People today are better educated and more articulate. They can no longer be commanded in the same way as before. In industry, trade unions are certainly more vigilant and often more militant. There needs to be much more involvement or participation at work—everyone recognizes that fact. But to achieve these ends industry has to see its managers more as leaders. Indeed, every kind of working enterprise has acknowledged that it needs more and better leadership at all levels. How can it be developed?

There is general agreement in the literature that leaders are made, not born. But not everyone is or can be a leader—there are some innate attributes of character and temperament that are starting points for the development of leadership potential. It is difficult to teach courage, integrity, risk taking, creativity or innovativeness—attributes commonly associated with leaders. One might even say that it is too late to teach these at commonly associated with leaders. One might even say that it is too late to teach these at all to adults, since their characters already are well formed and subject to only marginal changes.

But the characteristics of leaders are by no means the only

important factors in leadership. The principal leadership task can be learned through a variety of experiences. In many cases, the leader or would be leader is the driving force in the learning experience—reflecting on leadership, watching and analyzing other leaders, finding mentors, and seeking out opportunities for growth.

Colleges and universities, as educational organizations and as employers, have a special role to play in fostering leadership by creating an environment that encourages its faculty, administrators and staff to realize their potential and be active contributors to the life of the institution.

Leadership development encompasses many activities and experiences that enhance the ability of individuals to make a difference, to shape the direction of their institution or unit, and to bring others along in sharing and implementing goals. It is identifying new leaders, providing people with opportunities to grow and learn, to affirm their beliefs and values, to expand their understanding of issues and people, and to improve their management skills. Leadership development may be formal or informal structured of unstructured, deliberate or serendipitous. Management development is a narrower term and refers to activities that improve management skills such as decision making, planning, budgeting, and supervision. Professional development is also a narrower concept than leadership development and focuses more on enchancing job effectiveness, honing job skills, and preparing individuals for future responsibilities.

In summary, leadership development is a broad concept that includes but goes beyond teaching skills and enhancing career mobility. While individuals must create opportunities to develop themselves, institutions must help them to do so by effectively managing human resources, by establishing a climate that encourages participation and innovation, and by actively promoting leadership development.

Leadership Development is a Shared Responsibility of the Institution and the Individual : Ultimately, people must take responsibility for their own learning and growth. The must seize and create opportunities, no one else can do it for them. Yet the institution has a responsibility to create a climate that fosters professional growth and to view leadership development as a responsibility of leaders and an effort that is integral to institutional planning and development, because the benefits of leadership development accrue to both the individual and the institution, it is fitting that the beneficiaries share the responsibility.

Leadership Development is Ongoing and Often Not Deliberate: It is entirely possible to be engaged in leadership development without having deliberately embarked on a course to do so. Most learning occurs on the job—through relationships with peers and mentors, new assignments and exposure to new ideas. Such experiences can be even richer if they are deliberately assigned or structured to be growth experiences. A faculty member who becomes the chair of committee charged with revising the general education requirements can, with the help of a supportive dean, use the opportunity to attend national workshops, read and write on the topic, and deliberately develop a new expertise that will become a source of personal satisfaction and a resource for the institution.

Origin and development of leadership: Various factors are responsible for the origin and development of leadership. Various social thinkers and sociologists have put forward their views in this regard. Some of them consider the origin of leadership as a matter of divine origin while others feel that it is the result of certain social phenomenon. The theories in regard to the origin and development of leadership as given by different sociologists and psychologists are enumerated below.

Origin and development of Leadership as given by psychoanalysis: Psycho-analysts have held out the view that for the origin of leadership, desire sex feeling, failures, greediness, desire to acquire prestige, repression, family experiences and such other qualities are necessary. This school of the social thinkers is of the view that it is these psychological traits that contribute to the origin and development of leadership. They lay greater stress on 'feeling sex' and put forward the view that leader tries to sublime this desire by assuming the role of leader. Several studies were carried on the basis of the theory, and the results arrived at by many psychologists corroborate that family quarrels, sex, depression, guilt feeling, power seeking, inferiority complex are responsible for leadership. These studies were carried by Lasswill (1965).

This does not mean that only unhealthy psychological traits are responsible for the origin and development of leadership.

Erickfrom made a study of the life of Hitler and came to the conclusion that he grew to be a leaders as a result of frustration. He was also dadistic and masochiotic and because of this he became a dictator.

Criticism—This theory of the psychoanalysis has been criticized by psychologists of other schools of thought. They have held the view that it is wrong to say that only unhealthy traits or repression and frustration or power seeking are the only traits that bring about the origin and development of leadership. Many of the leaders are very pious and possess high values. They also belong to a good family and social background.

Origin and development of leadership as given by Bogardus (1947)—Bogardus, the well known social thinker has laid down the following three as prominent factors responsible for origin and development of leadership.

(*a*) ***Hereditary***: According to Bogardus, every individual can not become a leader. Inspite of helpful and proper social environment he has to make certain innate qualities which are a gift of heredity.

(*b*) ***Social stimulations***: Social stimulations or social environment brings about not only the origin but also the development of leadership. Constantly social stimulations, takes a person constantly forward. In other words, it is a social environment that is very necessary for origin and development of personality.

(*c*) ***Personality***: A person may have hereditary traits to become a leader, he may get consgenital social environment but if he does not possess good character, intelligence and physical capacity to influence others, he can not become a leader. In other words personality is a must for origin and development of leadership.

Other factors responsible for origin and development of Leadership—Leadership originates and develops on account of various factors. Some of these factors have been enumerated above. Apart from these factors, culture, social values, social objectives and certain other traits are also responsible for the origin and development of leadership. A leader has to possess not only hereditary qualities and guide proper social stimulation, but he has to possess certain other traits, apart from an attractive personality. Several other factors also contribute to origin and development of leadership.

1.1.2.3 Theories of Leadership

Various theories have been advanced on leadership behaviour. These theories can be classified into the following broad headings:

1. Interaction Theory
2. Classical Theory
3. Times Theory
4. Psychoanalytic Theory

A brief description of each of the above theories is given in the following lines:

1. *Interaction Theory*

This theory considers leadership as a group function. Leadership is expected to emerge in a group as part of a more diffused differentiation or roles by which group members try to achieve group goals and try to satisfy their individual group-invested needs. Leaders in the group are those persons who are perceiving most frequently to perform those roles or functions which initiate and control behaviour of others towards achievement of group goals. Quality of interaction is clearly emphasized in this theory. In international process, two primary aspects are important : (1) Cognitive perception and conceptualization, (2) Attachment of aversion. They orientate the leaders and followers in the group. The leaders tries to affect the dynamics of the group. He tries to polarize and energize the group towards the group goal.

The important features of the international theory of leadership as described by the Gibb (1969) are as follows:

1. Groups are mechanisms for achieving individual satisfaction and, conversely, persons interact with other persons for the achievement of satisfaction.

2. There is role differentiation in leadership and this differentiation help in the satisfaction of needs of individual members.
3. There is interaction between two or more persons. These persons act with each other in the pursuit of common ends.
4. There is integration of cognitive perception of the leader with the group.
5. Complex emotional relationships are established among group members which in turn define a variety of leadership relations.

In International theory, the leaders and the group the intimately connected with each other. Interaction of the leader, who has personal attributes, with group determines efficient functioning of leadership roles. Leadership has to take into account the specific requirements imposed by the nature of the group. Both characteristics of the leader and the characteristics of the group are important in leadership roles.

In international theory, there are lots of 'pull' and 'push' aspects in leadership phenomena. In 'pull' type of leadership there is someone in the first and others follows. In the 'push' type of leadership, there are some who dominate and others who submit. Leadership within such dominance-submission relationship may be characterized as the 'push' type.

2. *Classical Theory*

In this type of theory the basic leadership is explained in terms of great man theory. According to this theory, it is asserted that particular individuals are naturally endowed with characteristics that cause them to stand out from the many others. These intellectually and socially gifted people are able to lead, guide and direct the majority. They belong to the class of divine rights theory of beings. On the basis of this theory, leaders are endowed with insight and unusual foresight by virtue of which they bring social and intellectual changes in the society. Nature brings such intelligent people into society and it is their responsibility to lead their society.

3. ***Times Theory***

According to 'times' theory a leadership behaviour is a function of the given social situation. In each society, at a particular time, there are needs, aspirations and problems which have to be fulfilled. A leader in such a society has to take the responsibility of fulfilling the needs, aspirations and problems of the group. Such leadership role emphasises certain qualities in the personality of a leader who can take the leadership at the critical time. Such a leadership will be valid and good only for that particular situation. The unique needs of the group are met by the unique qualities of the individual.

4. ***Psychoanalytic Theory***

Psychoanalytic psychologists have advanced their own theory on leadership behaviour. They treat leaders as the father-figures for the individual members. The figure has energy, strength and vitality. It has power and force. The leader serves as a perfect focus for the positive emotional feelings of the individual. All members try to identify themselves with this father-figure. Leader is treated as the ideal object for father-figure. For transference also he is an ideal figure. People try to submit themselves before the leader. This submissiveness is born out of the feeling of emotional surrender towards the leader.

Father-figure is not usually associated with parental figure. People want to experience in the leader an emotional experience which is satisfying to them. At times, they may add magical charms to the leader and it may end in many ritual practices of implicit obedience in the leadership of the leader. The follower may try to identify with the individual beliefs and expectations of the leadership. These leaders get tremendous powers and following. However, the leader has to be really great to sustain expectations in people for a long time. Leaders can have tremendous powers for a short time in special group circumstances. Examples of Roosevelt and Hitler are illustrative.

1.1.2.4 Types of Leadership

Leadership is an ambiguous concept. Its exact meaning depends on the types of relationship that is established between the leader and the followers. Tricket has suggested classification in terms of traditional, situational and behavioural approaches.

(a) Traditional: The traditional approach is based on the 'charismatic' explanation of leadership as a person superior to and better than his followers. In this context, leadership appears as the art of imposing one's will upon others in such a manner as to comman their obedience, their confidence, their respect and their loyal cooperation.

(b) Situational: The situational approach emphasizes the social conditions as determinants of leadership. Stcdgil (1948) states: 'The qualities, characteristics and skills required in a leader are determined to a large extent by the demands of the situation in which he is to function as a leader.'

Krech, Crutchfield and Ballachey (1948), seem to suggest a similar approach to the problem by stating that 'the emergence of leadership: increase in the size of the group and in the complexity of its organization; obstacles in the achievement of group goals, external and internal threats confronting the group in crisis; and the presence of members with strong motivation to come forward and attempt leadership.'

(c) Behavioural: The behavioural approach does not differ very much from the situational in practice. It looks upon leadership as an interaction process in which the leader influences the follower in a situation. Tannenbaum and his colleagues (1961) have defined leadership as 'Interpersonal influence exercised in a situation and directed, through the communication process, towards the attainment of a specific goal or goals'. The basic difference between the behavioural and the situational approaches lies in the emphasis of the behavioural approach on the communication process between leader and follower, or on the personal interaction between the two sets of individuals involved; the leader and the followers.

Stripped to their essentials, these three types of leadership may be characterized as follows: the traditional approach is based on a person to person interaction; the situational approach is based on a social set of forces which give rise to the emergence of a leader, who takes up the challenge; the behavioural approach emphasizes both the personal and the social by drawing attention to the personal interaction in the context of a concrete social situation.

We should guard against any confusion of the concept of leadership with the concepts of popularity, or unattended social contagion, effects of automatically performed conditioned reactions, or influence exerted on the behaviour of others through mass media of communication.

Different social thinkers have given different classifications of the Leadership. These classifications are based on different traits and purposes.

Martin Convay's classification of leadership

Martin Convay has enumerated the following fourfold classification of leadership:

1. Crowd compeller
2. Crowd exponent leader
3. Crowd representative leader
4. Group originator

Bartlett's classification of leadership

The well-known social thinker Bartlett has given following three types of leadership:

1. Institutional Leader
2. Dominant Leader
3. Persuasive Leader

Nafe's classification of leadership

Nafe has given the following two kinds of leadership:

1. Static Leadership
2. Dynamic Leadership

Bogardus's classification of leadership

Bogardus has given the following kinds of leadership:

1. Direct and indirect leadership
2. Social, executive and mental leadership
3. Autocratic, paternalistic and democratic leadership
4. Partisan and scientific leadership
5. Specialists in leadership

Classification or kinds of leadership on various basis: Apart from the classifications of the leadership given by various scholars and thinkers, leadership has also been classified on various bases.

(a) Relationship between the leader and led

(b) Origin

(c) Purpose

(d) Nature

(a) Relationship between the leader and led

The classification of leaders are given by Bartlett is as follows:

1. Institutional Leader
2. Persuasive Leader
3. Dominant Leader
4. Expert Leader

Classification of the leadership of the basis of the origin

1. Self appointed leader
2. Group appionted leader
3. Executive appointed leader

Classification of the leadership of the basis of purpose

1. Executive leadership
2. Artistic leadership
3. Intellectual leadership

Classification of leadership on the basis of nature

Every leader has his own way of exercising his influence over his followers. Some of the leaders persuade them while others make them agree to accept their views. From this point of view the leadership is usually under the following three heads:

1. Authoritarian leadership
2. Democratic leadership
3. Laissez Faire leadership

1.1.2.5 Leadership Qualities as an independent variable

Good leadership is a prime necessity for the promotion and enhancement of Physical Education in educational institutions. An institution may possess all the other facilities but if there is no adequate leadership and supervision, it will be like a Ship without a Captain, a Factory without a Manager, a Rest-house without a Care-taker, and a Temple without a Priest. Leadership is therefore the main-spring for the proper conduct of the coordinated programme of Physical Education, Health Education and Recreation—Thirunarayan (1966).

A good leader should

a. be a good follower himself.

b. be honest, truthful, sincere and pious.

c. have a degree of refinement.

d. have a well-groomed appearance.

e. have primitive and executive ability.

f. have a sense of humour.

g. have a sympathetic and friendly attitude and at the same time avoid undue familiarity.

h. have self-confidence and courage of his convictions.

i. have the capacity to lead the group democratically.

j. have a healthy, alert, vigorous and trained body, abounding in vitality.

k. have a knowledge of human psychology with adequate Educational and Professional background.

U.S. Army has carried out a number of studies on leadership qualities. They have come to the conclusion that leaders should have the following characteristics:

1. Perform professional and technical speciality,
2. Know subordinates and show consideration for them,
3. Keep channels of communication open,
4. Accept personal responsibility and setting an example,
5. Initiate and direct action,

6. Train men and a team, and
7. Make decisions.

Other studies carried out by the American Institute for Research have discovered the following qualities in leader:

1. Should have supervising personnel,
2. Should have planning, initiating and directing action,
3. Should handle administrative details,
4. Should accept personal responsibility,
5. Should show group belongings and loyalty to the organization, and
6. Should perform professional or technical speciality.

A number of studies on leadership qualities have been conducted. From the studies undertaken, three factors have been identified:

1. Intellectual Penetration,
2. Strength of will, and
3. Soundness of feeling.

1.1.1.6 A Review of Existing Literature

Kurt Lewin (1939) and his co-workers conducted a series of experiments to study the various aspects of leadership behaviour using the experimental procedures. Later on in 1952, the two investigators, Lipitt and White have summarized the results of these studies. They studied the behaviour of 10 to 11 years old children who had belonged to a children's club, by submitting them to an alteration of authoritarian, democratic Laissez-Faire leadership patterns. The leaders in the authoritarian role were coached to give orders and avoid explanations. Those in the democratic role were trained to discuss problems with the group and obtain group decisions for action. The leader in the laissez-faire role was almost entirely passive and never tried to influence the members of the group in any manner. Three groups of boys were used in the experiment and each group was exposed to each of the three groups of leadership.

The results were extremely complex. It was found that in a democratic atmosphere there was more ego-involvement and the group used the words 'we', 'us', and 'ours' more often than in the group under the authoritarians atmosphere. The children in the Laissez-Faire atmosphere spent great deal of time playing, but co-ordinated action of the group was difficult.

The autocratic group showed two kinds of reactions; either the children were cowed down into apathy or they responded with aggressiveness. It was also found that the apathetic group showed marked aggressiveness when the atmosphere changed to the democratic or to the Laissez-Faire variety. The results provided evidence for the hypothesis that the conduct of the group is a function of its structure. Aggressiveness was very low under the democratic leadership. It was also found that some boys preferred the autocratic to the democratic order.

Bird (1940) examined 20 enquires and found 79 traits. However, he found that 51 traits or 65 per cent of them were mentioned only once: 20 per cent were mentioned two times; 5 per cent of them three times and another 5 per cent four times. Among the traits mentioned only two times are aggressive, ascendant, dignified, expansive friendly, honest, just, reliable, self-composed, self-controlled, sociable, suggestable, talkative, vigorous. The four qualities mentioned only three times among the 20 enquired are courageous, original, self-reliant and tactful. Those mentioned fourtimes were enthusiastic, fair, self-confidence and sympathetic. The two qualities extroverted and sense of humour, were given in five enquiries while initiative was given six times and high intelligence ten times.

Bird (1940) points out that in all these studies, 'instead of defining the field of leadership in which the traits are manifest only the lists are given'. Obviously, the person who becomes a leader among the boy scouts in a school, the young man who becomes the editor of the college newspaper, the person who becomes the captain of a football team, the adult who becomes the leader of a gang of thieves, all these cannot be said to have the same traits.

Bavelas (1942) conducted a research on Training for Leadership. Six urban project play ground leaders rated as 'mediocre' were used as subjects. Three of the subjects served as experimental leaders, and the other three (matched for age, sex, rated skill, and length of service) were used as control leaders.

The six leaders had been rated by observers 'on the job' who recorded their actual behaviour with children. The experimental leaders were subsequently given three weeks of intensive training aimed at broadening their goals, restructuring their approach, and developing new techniques. They did, however, continue to work on the playground with the children during their training sessions. After four weeks the trained and non-trained leaders were observed again by the same method used at the beginning of the experiment. Untrained leader B persisted in using an authoritarian approach to the children (80 per cent of the time), while trained leader A (who used to display the same characteristics in the pre-training period-dropped from 77 per cent of the time to 4 per cent, whereas his democratic behaviour increased from 5 per cent to 73 per cent. Groups led by the trained leaders were characterized by their attraction to the children (the groups increased in size), the enthusiasm of their members, the 'holding power' of the group over its members, efficiency in organization and task, high degree of self-discipline, and the quality of work output. These characteristics were attributed to the effect of training in as much as no such pattern occurred in the groups led by untrained leaders.

To study the effects of three types of leadership, Lippitt and White (1943) undertook an experiment in which school boys of about ten years of age were asked to volunteer to attend an after school club at which they would be able to carry out various handicrafts such as model making, designing toy aeroplanes and so on. They were divided into four groups of five boys. These groups were subject in turn to three different types of leadership, designated as 'democratic', 'autocratic' and 'laissez-faire'.

In the results, it was noted that autocracy provoked one of two reactions, submission or aggression which might amount to open rebellion. Group morale, in the sense of spontaneous cohesion or thinking was highest in the democratic group and lowest in the submission autocracy. The democratic group was the most contented and friendly, but autocratic leadership seemed to inhibit the normal free and easy sociability of the laissez-faire group was dissatisfied with their own level of efficiency and their behaviour showed the vicious circles of frustration-aggression-frustration. The best work was done in the democratic group, who took pride in their work in marked contrast to the lack of case shown by the autoractic group.

Peak (1945) in his study of Nazi membership observes: 'person reared in the authoritative family, which is common in Germany, typically find the greatest security and satisfaction where they are dominated by superior authority. On the one hand and where they can, on the other, "Lord it over" some one else of lower status'. Thus, the background in which people are brought up is a factor of considerable importance which determines the way in which people respond to the authoritarian or democratic leadership.

There have been many investigations regarding the relationship between leadership and intelligence.

Cattell (1946) had shown, 'general mental capacity' as one of the 12 primary source traits of personality.

Intelligent -Wise - Emotionally Mature - Reliable - Independent - Thoughtful - Deliberate-Not Frivolous - Persevering - Pains-taking - Mentally alert and Vigorous - Conscientious having intellectual and wide interest.

These traits included by Cattell in the general mental capacity are obviously of very great value to be a successful leader.

Stogdill (1948) reviewed 124 studies of the characteristics of leaders and found that an average person occupying the position of leadership had some qualities which exceeded an average member of his group to some degree. The qualities, characteristics and skills required in a leader are determined to a large extent by the demand to the situation in which he is to function. Intellectual fortitude and personal integrity are positively related to leadership in adult groups whereas there tends to be very little relationship of leadership with age, height or appearance. It seems clear that leadership cannot be discussed adequately apart from the situation in which it operates.

Merei (1949) observed preschool children for 35 to 45 minutes each day for a period of two weeks after having been placed in day nurseries. The children were especially, chosen for this experiment. Homogeneity was maximized by matching them for sex, age, liking, and 'average capacity for leadership.' At the end of the observation period those children who were rated as not displaying leadership behaviour (e.g., imitation outnumbering being limited, or following orders more than giving orders) were selected for the experiment. Divided into 12 groups, they spent 30 to 40 minutes together each day for 3 to 6 days, until they had formed their own 'institutionalization' (or 'culture' permanent seating order, permanent division of toys, group ownership of certain toys, ceremonies connected with the use of certain toys, expressions of belonging together, returning to certain activities, group jargaon, etc. A 'leader' was then placed in each group. He was not appointed, but was older, had displayed leadership qualities during the preliminary observation period, and was domineering and aggressive in general. In all but one group, the leader was forced to adopt the traditions of the group. However, he was still managed to play the role of the leader by adopting certain strategies. The order giver, who began to boss the children around and was completely ignored and fitly changed his tactics and during the second meeting ordered them around in tasks 'they would have done anyway,' in line with their traditions. The proprietor followed the children's tradition: despite the fact that his suggestions were rarely accepted, his implicit authority was recognized, as witnessed by the fact that 'the children gave him every object, without his asking.' The diplomat upon being rebuffed on the first day ostensibly followed the group's tradition, but gradually put in his own suggestions.

Cattell and Stice (1954) found that the trait H (adventurous, friendly, out going, cooperative) differentiates four types of leaders from non-leaders, while the traits F differentiates problem solving leaders. Commenting on this, Gibb Wonders whether 'a sergeant personality for the formally recognised and elected leader', while such is not the case with 'power behind throne'.

Bass (1954) found a low correlation (0.30) between F scale authoritarianism and leadership performance in leaderless groups. That is highly authoritarian rigid and conservative personalities displayed little leadership. He also found that the extremely equalitarian personalities also displayed poor leadership. Neither highly authoritarian nor highly equalitarian personalities show good leadership. It is the moderately equalitarian personalities who were more successful.

Studies with leaderless group discussion (L.C.D.) deal with the problem of participating in which there is no designated leader. Heinicke and Bales mentioned that L.G.D. is one of the technique used by the Army selection board to assess leadership among candidates.

One of the earliest studies conducted with Leader Behaviour Description Questionnaire was by Hemphill (1955) who undertook a study to know the association of leadership behaviour of 22 department chairmen with their administrative reputation. It was concluded on the basis of his study that older and matured faculty members had a large proportion of reputation information than younger or new members of the faculty. Besides, larger departments tend to have better administrative reputation than the smaller ones.

Halpin (1955) made a comparative study of the leader behaviour and leadership ideology of educational administrators and aircraft commanders. The results of this study revealed that both sample leaders were found to have low relationship between their belief in how they should behave and their behaviour as described by their group members. This study shows that the LBDQ can be successfully used in any situation to study leadership behaviour.

Moser (1959) undertook a study with regard to stages of leadership, in which he involved 12 superintendents and 24 principals of 12 school districts. The subjects answered the interview questions which were designed to stimulate their own leadership ability and that of others. In this study, Moser identified three styles of leadership: (i) the nomothetic dimension characterized by goal accomplishment in terms of the institution; (ii) the idiographic dimension characterized by behaviour of the individual self; (iii) the transactional dimensions characterized by elements of both nomothetic and idiographic. Among the findings, these were the principals emphasized idiographic behaviour in dealing with teachers, and nomothetic behaviour in their relations with the superintendents. Superintendents who professed nomothetic behaviour, indicated the highest level of personal satisfaction and were given the highest ratings by the principals. This study points out the different styles of leadership.

Mann (1959) found that inner personality is indeed a condition of leadership. Thus, people with high intelligence who are well adjusted personally and who tend towards extroversion are more likely than others to become leaders; also, to be popular in the group and to contribute positively to the group activity.

Lewis (1959) conducted a study to discover how 300 selected high school principals in 11 western states functioned in their offices. This study gives clear indication that a majority of the principals responding felt that they would be performing superior services if they spent a much larger percentage of their time and effort in such functions as evaluation and reorganization of curriculum, supervision of instruction, selecting competent staff members, managing the school building, including the testing programme and establishing good staff relationships.

Kumar, P. (1964) attempted a Personality Study of Student Leadership. The enquiry aimed at studying certain personality variables associated with student leadership. It was hypothesized that certain personality variables would be found significantly needed for the enactment of a leadership role in the situation under study; and that the perceptions of the two groups the leader and non-leader, would show an agreement as to the ideal and the perceived leadership qualities. It was also hypothesized that certain personal factors would show a significant relationship with the leadership.

The study was conducted on a sample of 50 student leaders and 50 non-leaders. Sinha@W.A. Self-analysis Form. Eysenck's Short Questionnaire, the Ascendance Submission Study, the Revised Adjustment Inventory the Test for Rigidity and Ambiguity Tolerance and the Allport, Vernon Value Scale were used for collecting data. Chi-square, critical ratio and correlation techniques were used for analysing the data.

The findings were:

Age, caste and length of stay in the university were found significantly related to student leadership.

The leaders tended to be more anxious and more dominating than the non-leaders.

Extroversion, neuroticism, adjustment, rigidity and ambiguity-tolerance failed to give any relationship.

Leaders were higher on social and economic values, and lower on theoretical and religious values. Aesthetic and political values failed to discriminate significantly between the leaders and the non-leaders.

Leadership was ideally imaged as responsible, hard-working, social, honest and helping. But the actually perceived leadership image deviated greatly from the ideal. It was perceived as ambitious, emotional, social, dominating and tactful.

The inter-group analysis of the ideal and perceived leadership images failed to give a positively significant relationship. There was agreement that the student leaders did not possess qualities ideally required for the fulfilment of a leadership role in the given situation.

Gross and Herriott (1966) conducted a study on 175 elementary school principals to study their executive professional leadership. The result indicated that the principals varied greatly in their conformity to a professional leadership definition of their role. The study suggests that the characteristics requiring more consideration in appointing elementary school principals are: a high level of academic performance in college, a high order of interpersonal skill, the motive of service, the willingness to commit off-duty time to their work, and relatively little seniority as teachers. The findings of the study are of immense value for those who are engaged in the business of appointing principals.

Employing the Leader Behaviour Description Questionnaire (Form XII), Garrison (1968) studied the relationship between the leadership behaviour and innovation. The criteria of innovativeness was determined by the number of innovations reported by Oklahoma School Principals in the North Central Association of College and Secondary Schools Commission on the Secondary Schools study of innovativeness. The results indicated that high scores on the dimensions of the LBDQ were directly related to innovations in the schools. High innovative principals tended to be effective leaders when working with their staff, but less effective while working with their superintendents. The opposite was also true of the low innovative principals. The superintendents appeared to value principals who were administrators rather than leaders. This study reveals an interesting fact why *a* principal is rated differently on his leadership behaviour by his faculty members and the superintendents.

Meade (1967) conducted a study to determine the effect of authoritarian and democratic leadership on productivity and morale in the atmosphere of a boys' club in India. Authoritarian or democratic types of leadership were taken as the two conditions of independent variables.

The results showed that the morale was higher under the authoritarian leadership atmosphere than the democratic leadership atmosphere. The productivity was also higher under the authoritarian leader than under the democratic leader. The quality of work done under the authoritarian leader was judged to be superior.

Gibb (1969) reports that less than one per cent of the candidates selected for officer training in the military were below the estimated population mean. This, however, should not be taken as an indication that the most intelligent man in the group is best fitted to be the leader of that group.

Gibb concludes 'that though leaders are more intelligent than followers, they must not exceed the followers by too large a margin, great discrepancies between the intelligence of leaders and followers militate against the emergence of the leadership relation, presumably because such wide discrepancies render improbable the unified purpose of the individual concerned.'

O'conner (1969) felt that one of the important reasons for students' and teachers' strike is the principal's failure to be an effective leader. Teachers look to a principal for leadership and when he fails to provide, it results in militancy and strikes. He made an attempt to study the positive characteristics that teachers identify with an effective principal. The data collected from 443 teachers indicated how an effective principal should behave: (i) he should attend national principal's meetings; (ii) be a man rather than a woman; (iii) have strong interests in humanities; (iv) abide by the decisions of the majority when an issue is subject to vote; (v) perform his duties as he believes it should be done regardless of public opinion; (vi) attend national subject area meetings; (vii) make a thorough study of the faculty opinion before taking a decision; (viii) use latest automation equipments and services; (ix) be well groomed and dressed in the latest fashion; (x) back up a teacher in his use of discipline; (xi) compliment a teacher on specific work well done; and (xii) encourage the teachers to use new methods of teaching. An administrator should reflect such behavioural characteristics and there should be no place for apathy in him or the faculty members.

Nolan (1969) used the Leader Behaviour Description Questionnaire and involved 97 superintendents, 105 elementary school principals, 98 teachers and 72 presidents of parent organizations to study the leadership behaviour and administrative action patterns of principals of public elementary schools of the state of New Jersey. The behaviour was studied and four dimensions: (i) Initiating structure; (ii) Consideration, (iii) Role assumption; and (iv) Tolerance of freedom. The Principal's profile developed at the University of Georgia and modified by James B. Kiney was used to evaluate the administrative action patterns. The findings of this study revealed a marked degree of agreement as to what kind of leadership was expected by the superintendents, the teachers and the presidents of parent organizations. Further, it was found that principals's appraisal of their own leadership was realistic in view of the comparison of their role with perceptions of the superintendents, teachers, and presidents of parent organizations. The study supports the trend towards increased professionalization of administrators.

Norman (1970) studied the leadership behaviour of 40 women working in various areas namely, law, administration, public education, government, business, higher education, fine arts (music and literature), and civic wor p 3Xk p 2X She found personality traits associated with leadership behaviour. The women in leadership positions were found to be womun o ff high intelligence, confidence, self-assured, composed, conscientious, persevering, experimenting, liberal, self-sufficient, resourceful, temperamentally independent, uninhibited, able to work without fatigue, socially precise, with a strong self-image, imaginative, self-motivated, creative, shrewed, and calculating with an intellectual approach to situations. Those women who had the ability to initiate structure in an organization were considered in taking to account regard for well-being. They could tolerate uncertainty and postponement, and reconcile conflicting demands. They could maintain cordial relations with superiors. Contrary to many studies, this establishes that personality is related to leadership.

The leader behaviour of 15 men and 15 women principals was compared by Morsink (1970) using the Leader Behaviour Description by Morsink. On the basis of the data, he reported that there is no justification in the argument that men behave more appropriately than women as school principals. This study points out that no discrimination would be done on basis of sex without any sound reason. Women should also be allowed to contribute their talent in the development of the nation.

Mahajan (1970) undertook a study to examine critically the supervisory role of principals of Delhi Higher Secondary Schools.

Some of the important findings of the study are:

Government schools are better places as a whole in respect of principal-teacher relations and academic leadership though the differences are not statistically significant. Government girls' schools have better facilities and academic leadership than the government boys' schools.

The principals in many cases prefer that teachers should confine themselves to the use of chalk and blackboard rather than the enthusiastic to use methods, albums and other teaching aids;

The principal-teacher relations, on the whole, have been satisfactory.

Staff meetings, individual conferences, orientation and induction as instruments of teachers growth and specific in service education techniques such as action research, inter class visitation, inter school visitation, seminars, workshops at school level, find little place in school life.

Most of the principals fail to play an effective leadership role in the academic field in the schools because of limitation of time and energy.

Vats (1972) worked on a study keeping in mind the following objectives:

To portray the leadership behaviour patterns of educational administrators and to assess their relevance and efficiency for implementation of educational policies and programmes.

To identify differences in self role perceptions of educational administration vis-a-vis the role expectations of teachers or observers.

To pinpoint the inadequacies in the existing leadership role of educational administrators and to suggest the directions for improvement.

The major observations were as follows:

The most important aspect of career development was an officers' own motivation and his effort for self-development. New stresses and strains had developed within the administrative system, hence there was a need for improvement of personnel efficiency, discipline and personnel system, methods and practices. In India, there has been some movement in this direction. In the education department of Punjab, there was hardly any provision for professional or in-service training of officers expect by way of seminars, conferences, etc., at the time of this study.

The expansion of education demanding increasing responsibility and functional competence at the lower sector highlighted the necessity for more managerial expertise on the part of the administrators so that they were able to energies the administrative organization to full action.

As regards institution building, more than 60 per cent leaders at all levels had said that there was practically no attraction for developing new ideas and new programmes.

Singh (1975) undertook a study to find out some aspects of local leadership as modes of leader origin, factors responsible for leadership and problems experienced by leaders. He selected 75 local leaders from 10 tribal villages of Bihar, M.P. and Orissa States, out of a list of one of the local leaders. These modes of origin of leadership were found, viz., (a) Election, (b) Appointment, (c) Sociometric choice. An election leader is one who assumes leadership position with the consent of members of social system. Voting is the common system for elective leaders. An appointed leader is a person chosen by government or other agency to perform the leadership role. A 'sociometric choice leader' is one to whom people go for guidance and help. He plays an important role in influencing opinions and actions of the people.

Information regarding the origin and problems of leaders was collected and the following results were concluded. In tribal areas, a good number of leaders are of 'sociometric choice' type who have intimate contacts with the people. Leadership position of relatives, better financial and family status and urban contacts tend to influence favourably an individual's choices of becoming a leader. Village factions, inadequate finances for programmes, lack of incentives, lack of interest on the part of people and overwork tend to be the major problem of local leadership, so local leaders must be helped to overcome these problems.

Singh (1978) worked on the leadership behaviour of the heads of secondary schools in Haryana. He compared the headmasters@leadership behaviour with that of some other professional leaders and notes the relationship of variables such as personality factors, sex, age, teaching and administrative experience with leadership. Five teachers from each of 100 schools of Haryana state were selected. Thus, 100 heads as known by their 500 teachers constituted the sample. Seven factory managers, 7 army officers, 7 college principals and 7 municipal committee presidents were included in the sample for the study of leadership. The study tools were the Leadership Behaviour Description Questionnaire and Cattell's 16 PF Inventory. It was found that the leadership behaviour was significantly related to the four personality factors i.e., outgoingness, intelligence, emotional stability and assertiveness. Headmasters were in the 3rd position in leadership scale out of 5 professional leaders. The head's leadership behaviour was not related to his age (between 25 years to 62 years). Post-graduate heads were significantly better than graduate heads but total leadership behaviour was neither related to academic qualifications or related to their teaching experience (between 6 years to 35 years).

Jugal (1982) conducted a study of Socio-psychological Make-up Student Leaders of Kumaun University in relation to Their Liking for Involvement in College/University Administration.

The objectives of the study were:

To find out the liking for involvement of student leaders in their college or university.

To find out the association of liking for involvement in college/university administration of student leaders with their sociological make-up.

To explore the relationship between sociological variables and liking for involvement in college/university administration of student leaders who were differentiated on the basis of Cattell's Four Secondary Personality Factors, viz., (i) high anxiety vs. low anxiety; (ii) Introversions vs. extroversion, (iii) tend-minded emotionally vs. alert poise, (iv) subduedness vs. independence.

To study the linking for involvement of student leaders in college managed by university government and private bodies.

The following non-parametric methods were used for drawing inferences: (i) The Mann Whitney U-Test, (ii) the chi-square tests, (iii) the median test, (iv) point biserial coefficient of correlation. Cattell's Sixteen Personality Factors Questionnaires, Socio-economic Status Scale by S. P. Kulshreshtha, Deva's Social Adjustment inventory, Student Looking for involvement in College/ University Administration Scale and Cheklist for determining the type of management of various colleges under Kumaun University were used. The population for this study consisted of 175 subjects who were members of the executive committee or student unions during the session 1980-81. The majority of the subjects in the sample were from governmental colleges of the Kumaun region. The purposive sampling technique was adapted.

The conclusions drawn from the study were:

Socio-economic status and sociometric status were significant determinants of a looking for involvement in college/university administration of student leaders.

Social adjustment and emotional adjustment were not significant correlates of liking for involvement in college/ university administration but social maturity of leaders was significantly related with liking for involvement in college/ university administration.

The personality traits of extroversion and alert poise were significantly related with liking for involvement in college/ university administration.

Anxiety and independence were not related with liking for involvement in college/university administration, when socio-metric status was not considered.

When socio-metric status was controlled, high anxiety among isolated leaders influenced their liking for involvement.

Low SES leaders having introversion had higher liking for involvement than high SES introvert leaders.

Type of management did not have significant bearing upon looking for involvement in college/university administration of student leaders.

Despande, S. (1983) attempted an Analytical Study of Leadership Qualities in Junior College Students in Vidarbha Region.

The main purpose of the study was to identify leadership qualities among junior college students in the Vidarbha region of Maharashtra State.

The sample consisted of 1046 boys and girls of class XI and XII from 22 junior colleges in eight district of Vidarbha. The tolls used for the study were: (i) questionnaire for the students, (ii) interview schedule for the teachers, and (iii) sociometric scale of selecting the leaders. Statistical techniques were used for (i) ranking leadership qualities percentagewise, (ii) for calculating the coefficient of correlation, and (iii) in preparing diagrams and graphs were used.

The following were some of the major findings of the study:

Twenty-four leadership qualities were identified in the junior college students.

There was no relationship between parents education and students@leadership qualities.

There was no relationship between parents' political or social status and student leadership qualities.

There was no significant relationship between parents' economic status and student leadership qualities.

There was no significant relationship between parents' occupation and students leadership qualities.

The student leaders mentioned reading and games as their hobbies.

The student leaders had good and cheerful nature, honesty, good conduct, punctual, cooperativeness, industriousness and good study habits, in the opinion of the lecturers.

The students leaders possessed self-confidence, discipline, cooperativeness, love for knowledge and industry.

The student leaders liked doing social work, social service and other social activities in the course of their college career.

Mulia, R.D. (1986) made an investigation into the Leadership Behaviour of Students in the context of Some Psycho-socio Factors.

The objectives of the study were:

To construct a reliable and valid leadership scale.

To study the leadership behaviour of higher secondary students of science, commerce and arts streams.

To study the leadership of higher secondary students of different age groups.

To study the leadership of higher secondary students in the context of sex.

To study the leadership of higher secondary students in the context of their SES, IQ, achievements and social maturity.

To study the leadership of higher secondary students in the context of some personality traits and adjustment.

A leadership behaviour scale was constructed by adopting a mixed Thurstone and likert model, initially, 97 statements on the aspects of (i) organization, (ii) policy making, (iii) expertise, (iv) group representation and (v) example setters were prepared and finally 50 statements were selected keeping in view the t-values, chi-square and Q values. The reliability of the scale was established by various methods. It ranged between 0.72 and 0.88. The congruent and concurrent validity were established. It was found to be 0.60 and 0.67 respectively. Percentile norms for boys and girls of different streams were fixed on sample of 1000, SES Scale by B. V. Patel and I.A. Vora, a Social Maturity Scale by J.I. Vora, a Non-verbal Test of Intelligence by Tarulata Shah, a Personality Inventory by A.S. Patel and an Adjustment Inventory by J. C. Parikh and M. T. Patel were used for collecting data. 3×2×2 factorial design and analysis of variance technique were used for testing the hypotheses.

The major findings were :

The students of the science stream had higher leadership behaviour than students from the commerce and arts streams.

Girls were superior to boys in leadership behaviour.

Age ranging between 15 and 21, had no significant relationship with leadership behaviour.

The SES variable had no effect on leadership behaviour.

There was no interaction between sex and stream.

The I.Q. showed a positive relationship with leadership behaviour. The students with high I.Q. had a higher level of leadership behaviour than those with low I.Q.

The mean obtained on the leadership behaviour scale by students belonging to the high educational achievement groups as higher than that of lower achievement group.

The means obtained on the leadership behaviour scale by pupils belonging to the high social-maturity group.

The students with high self-sufficiency dependency had a higher level of leadership traits than the low self-sufficiency group.

A person having an extrovert trait of personality had a higher level of leadership behaviour than the introverts.

The students of the science stream with radical traits of personality were superior in leadership traits.

The mean obtained on the leadership behaviour scale was significantly in favour of a high level of emotional stability.

Sex, stream and emotional stability interacted with each other.

The neuroticism variable was not related with leadership behaviour.

The mean obtained on the leadership scale of students belonging to a high level of social adjustment was higher than that of students of the low adjustment group.

The vocational adjustment variable had a poor positive relationship with leadership behaviour.

Students with high educational adjustment had higher levels of leadership trait than those with low adjustment.

Students with high family adjustment had higher levels of leadership than those from the low adjustment group.

Students with high personal adjustment had higher levels of leadership traits than those with low adjustment.

There was no interaction between stream and sex. Both operated independently.

Researchable Areas

Various researches studies show that leadership remains comparatively an ignored area in educational research in India. Researchers have done very little to unfold the mysteries of leadership and to know the various variables related to it.

Leadership may be researched in the context of the following thrust areas:

(a) Leadership and its various dimensions—Do the emerging situations demand revised dimensions of leadership behaviour?

(b) Leadership and organizational health.

(c) Leadership and staff morale.

(d) Leadership and its various styles.

(e) Training of leaders at various levels.

(f) Leadership and its correlates like age, sex, areas of adjustment, teaching experience and administrative experience.

(g) Leaderships and its various models.

(h) Moral leadership.

(i) Leadership among teachers, students and non-teaching employees.

(j) Leadership and institutional planning.

(k) Role performance of leaders at various levels.

(l) Leadership behaviour and systems approach.

1.2.0 THE PROBLEM

The review of research literature presented has highlighted a significant association between the pupils studying at various levels of education i.e., school, junior college and degree college and the general attitudes formed. But the only study presented in the reviews was on the formation of social attitudes between physically handicapped and normal children. But no study has concentrated its effort on the students' participation in games & sports and the formation of Social Attitudes. Similarly, the reviews presented focused on the leadership development among student leaders, political leaders, administrators, principals and other labour leaders. But no study has concentrated its effort on the student participation in games & sports and development of Leadership Qualities.

So, there is a greater need to highlight the participation of games & sports and the formation of Social Attitude and the development of Leadership Qualities.

The present research is designed to study the impact of physical education in the formation of Social Attitudes and the development of Leadership Qualities. It further studies the inter-relationship between these two variables i.e., Social Attitudes and Leadership Qualities.

Thus the study is undertaken to find out the answers to the problem focused.

1.3.0 STATEMENTS OF THE PROBLEM

The study has been undertaken to find out the answers to the following posers:

1. Is there any association between physical education programmes offered (participation in Games & Sports) and the formation of Social Attitudes?
2. Is there any association between physical education programmes offered (participation in Games & Sports) and development of Leadership Qualities?
3. Is there any inter-relationship between the formation of Social Attitudes and the development of Leadership Qualities?

1.4.0 SIGNIFICANCE OF THE STUDY

Social Attitudes and the Leadership Qualities are the attributes that are basic to the development of any society, particularly when the society is a developing one.

The most striking feature of the present Indian Scenario is the crisis of Leadership. During the freedom struggle the movement which was a sustained one and which was fought on high moral groups, had thrown out world class Leadership—a leadership which any country in any era could be proud of. Each leader was excelling the other in personal integrity, self negation, commitment to the society—nay, humanity as such. Leaders like Mahatma Gandhi and Jawaharlal Nehru, Swami Vivekananda and Aurobindo, Raja Rammohan Roy and Rabindranath Tagore etc. etc., guided the destinies of the nation. They were the models for emulations for the younger generations.

But alas! presently there appears to be none who could be regarded as a father figure, or a model for emulation or a friendly philosopher who can extricate one from the morass and guide in the right direction.

Thus the crisis in leadership highlights the need for the systematic grooming and training of the leaders particularly in the absence of a movement.

Likewise, people seem to become exceedingly selfish, self-centered, asocial and some times anti-socials getting isolated from the social moorings. A need is there to sencitize the future citizens towards the social needs and integrating them deep with the society so that an individual feels that he is a part of the society; wherein his future is predicated on the development of the society.

How to develop the Leadership Qualities and Social Attitudes?

One possible way of building the Leadership Qualities and Social Attitudes in men and women is by providing situation where Leadership attributes and Social Attitudes get formed and developed. It is possible that a situation of Games & Sports provides the needed milieu for the development of the said attributes.

But it is hypothetical that a situation of a Games & Sports develops in the participants the attributes of Leadership Qualities and Social Attitudes. It is to be established to what extent the Leadership Qualities and Social Attitudes get formed and developed through Games & Sports activities. If any research highlights the connection between Games & Sports and Leadership Qualities and Social Attitudes, we need to include in our school agenda the Games & Sports Activities which inter-alia develop the Leadership Qualities and Social Attitudes. The research findings can demand a pride of place for the Games & Sports in such a situation.

Thus the findings of the research, if they go on the expected lines can transform the educational system by altering the existing scheme of priorities by putting a premium on Games & Sports Activities.

1.5.0 OBJECTIVES OF THE STUDY

Now the present study seeks to work with the following objectives:

1. To find out the association between the levels of participation of pupils in games & sports and social attitudes formed at various levels of education i.e., school, junior college and degree level.

2. To find out the association between the levels of participation of pupils in games & sports and leadership qualities formed at various levels of education i.e., school, junior college and degree level.
3. To find out the inter-relationship between the developments of Social Attitudes and Leadership Qualities at various levels of education.

1.6.0 HYPOTHESES

1. There will be a positive association between the participation in games & sports, and Social Attitudes formed.
2. There will be a positive association between the participation in Games & Sports, and Leadership Qualities formed.
3. There will be inter-relationship between the developments of Social Attitudes and Leadership Qualities among pupils at various levels of education.

1.7.0 OPERATIONAL DEFINITIONS

The definitions of the terms used in the thesis are given in the following paras:

1. Participants in Games & Sports (PAG)

The students who had participated in the Games & Sports at school level, junior college level and degree level are named as participants in Games & Sports.

2. Non-Participants in Games & Sports (NPAG)

The students who had not participated in the Games & Sports at school level, junior college level and degree level are named as Non-participants in Games & Sports.

3. Social Attitudes

'An Attitude is one's behaviour towards the community or society and other members of the community or society'. (given by the researcher).

4. Leadership Qualities

'A person who is a good follower of himself is called a leader'. (given by the researcher).

1.8.0 LIMITATIONS OF THE STUDY

This study was undertaken in schools, colleges, play fields of district sport centres of various towns i.e., Warangal, Hyderabad, Adilabad, Khammam and Karimnagar.

The sample had been selected among the participants in Games & Sports and non-participants in Games & Sports from the different levels of education i.e., school, junior college and degree college, in the districts, Warangal, Karimnagar, Hyderabad, Tirupati, Ananthapur, Rajahmundry, Khammam and Adilabad.

For the sake of convenience in the data collection, the Physical Education Common Entrance Test (PE-CET-95) conducted at different centres of State like, Warangal, Rajahmundry, Ananthapur, Tirupathi was considered for the study as the researcher faced a hard time to trace the participants in Games & Sports especially at inter level. The Inter completed students appearing for the PE-CET for admission into Under Graduate Diploma (UGD) course in Physical Education and the Degree completed students appearing for the B.P.Ed. Entrance Test at PE-CET-95 were selected as participants in Games & Sports.

The non-participants in Games & Sports at School, Junior College and Degree College level from the educational institutions of Warangal, Hyderabad, Karimnagar and Khammam were considered for present study.

2

METHODOLOGY

2.0.0 INTRODUCTION

In the preceding Chapter, the researcher has presented the review of related literature, focussed the problem, discussed the significance of the problem, stated the objectives and formulated the hypotheses. The limitations of the study were specified.

In the present Chapter, the discussion of the methodology of the research is proposed to be presented. This chapter discusses the design of the study, sample considered, tools used, the methods followed for data collection and finally the statistical techniques adopted.

As mentioned earlier this research is intended to find out the impact of physical education programmes (participation in games & sports) in the formation of Social Attitudes and the development of Leadership Qualities among students at various levels of education.

The research was intended to find out the differences, if any, between participants in games & sports and non-participants in Games & Sports in relation to the following variables:

1. Education level and formation of Social Attitudes and development of Leadership Qualities.

2. Sex and formation of Social Attitudes and development of Leadership Qualities.
3. Community background and formation of Social Attitudes and development of Leadership Qualities.
4. Age and formation of Social Attitudes and development of Leadership Qualities.

The variable i.e., the intensity of participation in games & sports and its relationship with the Social Attitude formation and Leadership Qualities development is also studied under this chapter.

In order to highlight effectively the impact of physical education on these two variables i.e., Social Attitudes and Leadership Qualities separately, a research design depicting the impact of participation is presented in the Figure 2.1.0

2.1.0 DESIGN OF THE STUDY

A schematic representation of the design of the investigation carried out is given in the Figure 2.1.0

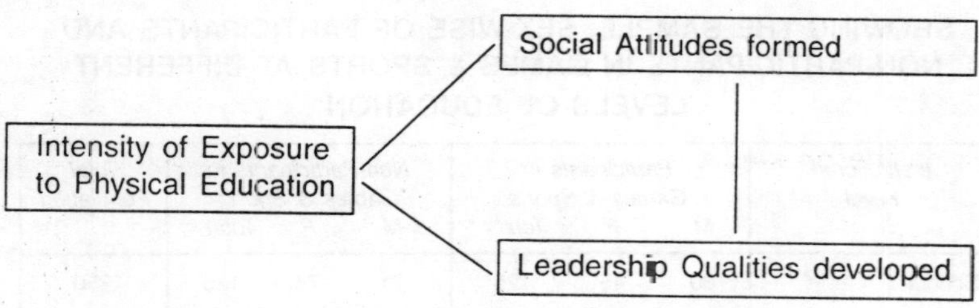

FIGURE 2.1.0: SCHEMATIC REPRESENTATION OF THE DESIGN

2.2.0 SAMPLE OF THE STUDY

A sample of 690 pupils, participants in Games & Sports and non-participants in Games & Sports studying in schools, junior colleges and degree colleges was selected for the study.

The sample considered for the study was education level-wise, sex-wise, community Background-wise and age-wise among participants in Games & Sports and Non-participants in Games & Sports as shown in the following table.

TABLE 2.2.1
SHOWING THE SAMPLE EDUCATIONAL LEVEL-WISE OF PARTICIPANTS AND NON-PARTICIPANTS IN GAMES & SPORTS AT DIFFERENT LEVELS OF EDUCATION

Institutional Level	*Participants in Games & Sports*	*Non-Participants in Games & Sports*	*Total Population*
School	125	125	250
Junior Colleges	110	110	220
Degree Colleges	110	110	220
Total at three levels of Education	345	345	690

Table 2.2.1 reveals that in all the total sample consisted of 690 pupils. Out of which 345 pupils were participants in Games & Sports and 345 pupils, non-participants, studying at three levels of education i.e., School, Junior College and Degree College.

The sex-wise sample is shown in the following Tables, 2.2.2 (a) and 2.2.2 (b).

TABLE 2.2.2 (a)
SHOWING THE SAMPLE, SEX-WISE OF PARTICIPANTS AND NON-PARTICIPANTS IN GAMES & SPORTS AT DIFFERENT LEVELS OF EDUCATION

Institutional Level	*Participants in Games & Sports*			*Non-Participants in Games & Sports*			*Total Population*
	M	*F*	*Total*	*M*	*F*	*Total*	
School	80	45	125	71	74	125	250
Junior Colleges	85	25	110	80	30	110	220
Degree Colleges	98	12	110	62	48	110	220
Total at three levels of Education	263	82	345	213	132	345	690

Table 2.2.2 (a) clearly shows that the total number of male participants in Games & Sports were 263 in number (School-80; Junior College-85; Degree College-98) and the female participants in Games & Sports were 82 in number (School-45; Junior College 25; Degree College-12). The male non-participants in Games & Sports were 213 in number (School-71; Junior College-80; Degree College-62) and the female non-participants in Games & Sports were 132 in number (School-54; Junior College-30; Degree College-48).

TABLE 2.2.2 (b)

SHOWING THE TOTAL STUDENTS (PARTICIPANTS) AND NON-PARTICIPANTS SAMPLE, SEX-WISE AT DIFFERENT LEVELS OF EDUCATION

Institutional Level	*Male Pupils*	*Female Pupils*	*Total Population*
School	151	99	250
Junior Colleges	165	55	220
Degree Colleges	160	60	220
Total at three levels of Education	476	214	690

Table 2.2.2 (b) shows that a total of 476 male pupils (School-151; Junior College-165; Degree College-160) and a total of 214 female pupils (School-99; Junior College-55; Degree College-60) formed the sample of the study.

The Community Background-wise sample is shown in the Tables, 2.2.3 (a) and 2.2.3 (b).

TABLE 2.2.3 (a)

SHOWING THE SAMPLE, COMMUNITY BACKGROUND-WISE OF PARTICIPANTS AND NON-PARTICIPANTS IN GAMES & SPORTS AT DIFFERENT LEVELS OF EDUCATION

Institutional Level	*Participants in Games & Sports*			*Non-Participants in Games & Sports*			*Total Population*
	R	*U*	*Total*	*R*	*U*	*Total*	
School	84	41	125	94	31	125	250
Junior Colleges	76	34	110	75	35	110	220
Degree Colleges	62	48	110	61	49	110	220
Total at three levels of Education	222	123	345	230	115	345	690

Table 2.2.3 (a) clearly reveals that the total number of rural participants in Games & Sports were 222 in number (School-84; Junior College-76; Degree College-62) and the urban participants in Games & Sports 123 in number (School-41; Junior College-34; Degree College-48). The rural non-participants in Games & Sports were 230 in number (School-94; Junior College-75; Degree College-61) while the urban non-participants in Games & Sports were 115 in number (School-31; Junior College-35; Degree College-49).

TABLE 2.2.3 (b)

SHOWING THE TOTAL SAMPLE OF STUDENTS (PARTICIPANTS AND NON-PARTICIPANTS IN GAMES & SPORTS) COMMUNITY BACKGROUND-WISE AT DIFFERENT LEVELS OF EDUCATION

Institutional Level	*Rural Pupils*	*Urban Pupils*	*Total Population*
School	178	72	250
Junior Colleges	151	69	220
Degree Colleges	123	97	220
Total at three levels of Education	452	238	690

Table 2.2.3 (b) shows that a total of 452 rural pupils (School-178; Junior College-151; Degree Colleges-123) and a total of 238 urban pupils (School-72; Junior College-69; Degree College-97) formed sample of the study.

The age-wise sample is shown in the following Table 2.2.4.

TABLE 2.2.4

SHOWING THE AGE OF PUPILS IN COMPLETED YEARS, SEX AND COMMUNITY BACKGROUND-WISE AND PARTICIPANT IN GAMES & SPORTS-WISE AT DIFFERENT LEVELS OF EDUCATION

Institutional Level	*Rural*		*Urban*		*Total Population*
	Male	*Female*	*Male*	*Female*	
School					
AGE/PAG	15(56)	14(28)	15(24)	14(17)	(125)
AGE/NPAG	14(56)	14(38)	14(15)	14(16)	(125)
Junior College					
AGE/PAG	21(66)	19(10)	21(19)	20(15)	(110)
AGE/NPAG	19(57)	18(18)	19(23)	18(12)	(110)
Degree College					
AGE/PAG	24(58)	23(04)	25(40)	22(08)	(110)
AGE/NPAG	23(38)	22(23)	23(24)	22(25)	(110)
Total at three levels of Education					
AGE/PAG	20(180)	19(42)	20(83)	19(40)	(345)
AGE/NPAG	19(151)	18(79)	19(62)	18(53)	(345)

Pag : Participants in Games & Sports

Npag : Non-Participants in Games & Sports

( ) : Indicates total number of pupils

The Table 2.2.4 gives a clear presentation of the ages of the pupils in years at all levels of education.

The age of the participants and non-participants in Games & Sports at School Level was almost equal. The average age was 14 years except in the case of male pupils (participants) including both rural and urban students who were 15 years old.

At inter level the age of Male Participants in Games & Sports (Rural and Urban) was recorded as 21 years. But the female rural participants in games & sports were 19 years old and the female urban participants in games & sports were one year older than the female rural participants. The age of the female urban participants in games & sports was 20 years.

Similarly the male non-participants in games & sports (Rural and Urban) and female non-participants in games & sports (Rural and Urban) were placed in the same age group i.e., 19 years and 18 years respectively.

Contrarily at Degree level the ages differed at every stage among participants in Games & Sports. For example while the average age of male rural pupils was 24 years that of male urban pupils was 25 years and that of female rural pupils and female urban pupils were 23 and 22 years respectively. But in the case of non-participants in the games & sports the male pupils (Rural and Urban) were similar in age i.e., 23 years and the female urban students were also similar in age i.e., 22 years.

Interestingly the total 345 pupils from different levels of education who participated in games & sports were of the same age i.e., Male participants (rural and urban) were aged 20 years and female participants (rural and urban) aged 19 years.

Likewise, the total 345 non-participant pupils in Games & Sports were also similar in age i.e., the male (rural and urban) students were 19 years old and the female (rural and urban) students were 18 years old.

Finally, it is very clear from the tables presented that the participants in Games & Sports (sex and community background-wise) were older in age than the non-participants in Games & Sports at three levels of education.

The average age of the total participants in the Games & Sports (345 pupils) was recorded as 19.5 years, while the average age of the total non-participants in games & sports (345 pupils) was recorded as 18.5 years.

The average age recorded for the entire population (690 pupils) was 19 years.

2.3.0 TOOLS USED

It is obvious that all students are not exposed in equal measures to physical programmes in the educational institutions. But a few students are exposed to physical education programmes at school level alone, some at junior college level and others at degree college level, while others are exposed throughout. Among these participants in physical education programmes, some of them get the honour for national level participation, others for inter-versity level participation, state level participation, inter school and junior college level participation and district level participation. So the participants in Games & Sports are exposed in different measures and at different stages of their education to Games & Sports. Hence, it is assumed that these differences in exposure would result in differences in Social Attitudes and Leadership Qualities formed.

Hence, the research involves the assessment of both Social Attitudes and Leadership qualities developed among the participants in Games & Sports and non-participants in Games & Sports at various levels of Education.

The following three types of tools were used to measure the impact of physical education in developing Social Attitudes and Leadership Qualities:

(i) Tool to measure the intensity of participation of pupils in Games & Sports.

(ii) Tool to measure the Social Attitudes at various levels of education.

(iii) Tool to measure the Leadership Qualities at various levels of education.

2.3.1 TOOL TO MEASURE THE INTENSITY OF PARTICIPANTS OF PUPILS IN GAMES & SPORTS

The researcher had classified the students studying in

Schools, junior colleges and degree colleges into two groups i.e., (1) Participants in Games & Sports and (2) Non-Participants in Games & Sports.

The pupils who had never participated in Games & Sports at school, junior college and degree college levels were identified as non-participants.

The pupils who had participated in Games & Sports at

(1) school level

(2) school and junior college level

(3) school, junior college and degree college level

(4) junior college level

(5) junior college and degree college level

(6) degree college level only

were identified as participants.

The researcher approached four experts in the field of physical education to identify the levels of participation in Games & Sports. The weightage of marks as given by the four subject experts were taken into consideration by the researcher and the average weightage of marks computed which are shown in the Table 2.3.1.

TABLE 2.3.1

SHOWING THE AVERAGES OF WEIGHTAGES ASSIGNED BY THE EXPERTS IN ASSESSING THE PARTICIPATION OF GAMES & SPORTS AT VARIOUS LEVELS OF EDUCATION

Educational level	*Weightage of marks of participants at*			
	School/College level	*District level*	*State level*	*National level*
School	1.00(1.00)	3.50(4.00)	7.00(7.00)	10.25(10.00)
Junior College	1.75(2.00)	4.50(5.00)	8.75(9.00)	12.25(12.00)
Degree College	2.75(3.00)	5.50(6.00)	10.75(11.00)	15.75(16.00)

(While computing the data for working out the average weightages, the fraction i.e. less than 0.5 was reduced to lower round figure and more than 0.5 was rounded off to next round figures for the sake of easy calculations.)

The Table 2.3.1 reveals the averages of weightages of marks assigned by the four experts in the field of physical education.

The school students who has participated at school level were given 1 mark, district level-4 marks, state level-7 marks and at the national level-10 marks. The Inter students who had participated at junior college level were given 2 marks, district level 5 marks, state level 9 marks and national level 12 marks. And the degree level students who had participated at degree college level were given 3 marks, district level 6 marks, state level 11 marks, and national level 6 marks.

Thus the tool to measure the intensity of participation of pupils in Games & Sports was finalized according to the weightages of marks given by the experts in the field of physical education.

2.3.2 TOOL TO MEASURE THE SOCIAL ATTITUDES AT VARIOUS LEVELS OF EDUCATION

The formation of Social Attitudes was to be measured by this tool.

The researcher could not find any ready-made tool to measure the Social Attitudes of pupils. Hence, the researcher had made an attempt to construct a fresh tool to measure the Social Attitudes.

Methods Adopted in Construction And Standardization of Social Attitude Scale

Initially the investigator had identified the following dimensions pertinent to the Social Attitudes as suggested by various theoreticians and researchers in the fields of Sociology, Psychology and Education as detailed in the following table:

Dimensions	*Author's Name*
1	*2*
1. Citizenship	Rokeah, M.J.
2. Consideration for others	Kuppuswamy, B.
3. Social responsibility	-do-
4. Social reconstruction	-do-

cont.

1	2
5. Useful leisure	Young, K.
6. Time pursuit	-do-
7. Humanism and respect	-do-
8. Resourcefulness	Wheeler, W.M.
9. Respect for manual work	Williams, R. M.
10. Social Service	Homans, G. C.
11. Dignity of labour	-do-
12. Cooperation	Insko, C.A.
13. Behaviour	Allport
14. Behaviour as a spectator	-do-
15. Behaviour as a player in a sports situation	-do-
16. Brotherhood	Adler, A.
17. Physical growth	Christiansen, B.
18. Social adjustment	Alverdes
19. Social awareness	-do-
20. Personality	Gulford, J. P.
21. Psychological dispositions	-do-
22. Hibits	-do-
23. Self-control	Lott & Lott
24. Self-discipline	-do-
25. Harmonious Life	-do-
26. Toleration	-do-
27. Forbearance	-do-
28. Fortitude	-do-
29. Character	-do-
30. Open-mindedness	Bogardus
31. Self-confidence	-do-
32. Self-esteem	-do-

cont.

1	2
33. Creativity	Snygg and Comb
34. Confrontative	-do-
35. Appreciative	Sprott
36. Industrious	Cambell, D.T.
37. Love for knowledge	-do-
38. Cheerful nature	-do-
39. Honesty	-do-
40. Balance	-do-
41. Flexibility	Bhagwath Shailaja
42. Concentration	-do-
43. Uniformity	Toch, H.
44. Punctuality and regular	Kuppuswamy
45. Emotional control	-do-
46. Sense of accomplishment	-do-
47. Alertness	-do-
48. Loyalty for a balanced personality	Bowlby, J.
49. Imagination	McGurie, W.J.
50. Impartiality	McDavid & Harari

ESTABLISHING VALIDITY OF THE TOOL

The investigator had approached nine subject experts and considered their opinion on the dimensions listed.

These dimensions were scrupulously studied by the subject experts in the fields of education, sociology and psychology.

The investigator had personally met, two Professors of Psychology, two Professors of Sociology of Osmania University, one Professor of Education from Sagar University and other Professors of Education from Andhra University and Osmania Universities. The researcher had discussed the various modalities of the scale. The listed dimensions which were approved or disapproved by the experts are given hereunder:

Dimensions of Social Attitude	Judgements of Experts	
	Approved	Dis-approved
1	2	3
1. Citizenship	3	6
2. Consideration for others	9	0
3. Social responsibility	8	1
4. Social reconstruction	2	7
5. Useful leisure	3	6
6. Time pursuit	8	1
7. Humanism and respect	6	3
8. Resourcefulness	5	4
9. Respect for manual work	6	3
10. Social Service	6	3
11. Dignity of Labour	1	8
12. Cooperation	6	3
13. Behaviour	2	7
14. Behaviour as a spectator	1	8
15. Behaviour as a player in a sports situation	8	1
16. Brotherhood	6	3
17. Physical growth	7	2
18. Social adjustment	6	3
19. Social awareness	8	1
20. Personality	6	3
21. Psychological dispositions	2	7
22. Habits	8	1
23. Self-control	6	3
24. Self-discipline	9	0
25. Harmonious Life	8	1
26. Toleration	8	1

cont.

1		*2*	*3*
27.	Forbearance	6	3
28.	Fortitude	7	2
29.	Character	4	5
30.	Open-mindedness	8	1
31.	Self-confidence	8	1
32.	Self-esteem	1	8
33.	Creativity	2	7
34.	Confrontative	4	5
35.	Appreciative	2	7
36.	Industrious	8	1
37.	Love for knowledge	3	6
38.	Cheerful nature	6	3
39.	Honesty	7	2
40.	Balance	5	4
41.	Flexibility	3	6
42.	Concentration	1	8
43.	Uniformity	1	8
44.	Punctuality and regular	9	0
45.	Emotional control	9	0
46.	Sense of accomplishment	6	3
47.	Alertness	8	1
48.	Loyalty for a balanced personality	2	7
49.	Imagination	6	3
50.	Impartiality	8	1

The following dimensions were excluded by the researcher as the majority of experts did not respond positively towards them:

1. Citizenship
2. Social reconstruction
3. Useful leisure

4. Dignity of labour
5. Behaviour
6. Behaviour as a spectator
7. Psychological dispositions
8. Character
9. Self-esteem
10. Creativity
11. Confrontative
12. Appreciative
13. Love for knowledge
14. Flexibility
15. Concentration
16. Uniformity
17. Loyalty for a balanced person

Thus the researcher with the consultation of the subject experts (three Professors, one each from the fields of Psychology, Sociology and Education) had finalized the following 38 dimensions of Social Attitudes which were divided into the following three clusters accordingly:

Clusters of Social Attitude

1. Attitude to people - SA1
2. Attitude to work - SA2
3. General Life Attitudes - SA3

1. *Attitude to people - SA1*

The dimensions of Social Attitudes under Attitude to people —SA1 are lister hereunder:

1. Consideration for others
2. Social responsibility
3. Humanism and respect
4. Behaviour as a player in a sports situation
5. Social adjustment
6. Fortitude

7. Sympathetic and friendly attitude and avoid undue familiarity
8. Impartiality
9. Cooperation
10. Supportive to his members
11. Emotional control
12. Cheerful nature

2. *Attitude to work - SA2*

The dimensions of Social Attitudes under Attitude to work - SA2 re presented hereunder :

1. Time pursuit 63
2. Resourcefulness
3. Respect for manual work
4. Physical growth
5. Concentration
6. Sense of accomplishment
7. Alertness
8. Lover of work
9. Desire of name and fame
10. Self-confidence
11. Industrious
12. Honesty
13. Punctuality and regularity
14. Imagination

3. *General life attitudes - SA3*

The dimensions of Social Attitudes of General life attitudes - SA3 are presented hereunder :

1. Brotherhood
2. Harmonious life
3. Open mindedness
4. Balance

5. Courage of his convictions
6. Social awareness
7. Personality
8. Social service
9. Tolerance
10. Habits
11. Self-control
12. Self-discipline

The investigator prepared the statements for the 38 Social Attitude dimensions mentioned on a five point scale (Strongly Agree, Agree, Undecided, Disagree and Strongly Disagree). A seven point scale could have been more comprehensive and a three point scale too inadequate to measure the alternative precisely.

These statements were scientifically pruned by the subject experts from the fields of Sociology, Psychology and Education. A professor of English had gone through them in order to sharpen the language.

All these statements finally figured in the draft of the Social Attitude scale. It was translated into Telugu language by the experts in Telugu for the convenience of Telugu medium students.

To test the reliability of the draft scale a pilot study was conducted.

PILOT STUDY

To test the reliability of the draft Social Attitude scale the investigator had adopted a test re-test method.

ESTABLISHING THE TEST RE-TEST RELIABILITY

The investigator administered the test on 75 students (25 school students, 25 intermediate students and 25 degree students). Among these 75 students some of them were outstanding players in the sports field who were the national level players and a few had neither played any game nor seen even the play fields. The sample consisted of students of both the sexes of two community background-wise, i.e., rural and urban and of different ages. The test was conducted at Warangal and Hyderabad.

The same test was re-administered to the same group of pupils after a gap of one month.

The results pertaining to the test-1 and test-2 are presented in the Table 2.3.2.

TABLE 2.3.2

SHOWING THE CORRELATIONS (R-VALUES) OF THE TEST RETEST SCORES TO ESTABLISH THE RELIABILITY OF THE SOCIAL ATTITUDE SCALE

Institutional level	*No. of pupils (n)*	*r-Values of Test Restest scores*	*Level of Significance*
School	25	0.4284	< 0.05
Junior Colleges	25	0.5271	< 0.05
Degree Colleges	25	0.5166	< 0.05
Total at three levels of Education	75	0.4939	< 0.05

Table 2.3.2 shows the r-values of test and retest which were found to be signficant at 0.05 level.

Hence, it is clear that the Social Attitude scale which was constructed is scientifically approved.

The investigator has observed the following modifications of the scale while conducting the pilot study.

1. The difficult words and spelling mistakes in the scale (Telugu version) were simplified and corrected in order to make the test further easy to facilitate them to give their opinions.
2. Time taken in responding to the scale was kept in mind.

Thus the Social Attitude Scale with 38 statements was standardized and was used for the data collection. The scale of statements are presented hereunder in the form of three clusters :

Cluster-1: Attitude to People

1. When I have doubts about my own performance I prefer to opt out in favour of others.

2. While performing a bus journey suddenly my fellow passenger falls unconscious. Ignoring my work, I prefer to take him to a hospital.
3. I tend to help even my enemy in his hour of need.
4. Lara walked out of the cricket field declaring himself out even before the umpire could notice it. I admire Lara more for this act than the records he has created in the history of cricket.
5. Evenwhile I am sure that I am right, there is a possibility that I am wrong and the other is right.
6. I feel incensed/excited at every failure I encounter.
7. As a leader I express my sympathies to my team-mates whenever they need and deserve it.
8. When we are impartial we make some of our kith and kin our adversaries. Yet we should not mind it.
9. Even though I can score a goal from my position, I prefer to pass the ball to my fellow player who is unmarked and more sure of converting a goal.
10. I find myself helping my team-mates in their hour of need in a number of ways.
11. I admire people who are less emotive.
12. I admire a person who smiles even in his defeat.

Cluster-2: Attitude to Work

13. It is good if whenever one participants in any game or sport activity, he remains present till the completion of the game.
14. There are always multiple ways of tackling a problem.
15. Because of the scavenging he did, Gandhiji was called the scavenger of India. This title is greater than the title of Mahatma he got.
16. Leaders have often well built physique.
17. While making a pursuit I think of only the target and nothingelse.

18. Ever small successes give me satisfaction.
19. What is required in the games field is an alertness of what happens around rather than a sagic concentration of effort.
20. I have led the best part of my life in the work situations.
21. When one has achieved excellence it is natural that he should be recognized as such by the society.
22. I prefer to include in my team a good player even though he is critical of me.
23. Success ultimately courts a person who is capable of putting continuous hard work.
24. I prefer to hug poverty as honesty and proverty go together.
25. Like awards for standing first in games events, there must be an award for punctuality.
26. There is always scope for imagination even in activities like games and sports.

Cluster-3: General Life Attitudes

27. It is natural to trust play-mates rather than brothers.
28. Wise people prefer harmony in life rather than a life marked by achievements.
29. I am eager to learn even from my adversaries.
30. I admire the people who can keep their poise even in defeat.
31. I have often invited the wrath of my superiors for my strong convictions. I do not have any regrets for that.
32. Most of the human suffering is there because of the faulty social system that has evolved.
33. I agree with the dictum that a person who can lead outside can alone lead effectively in the games field.
34. Some meditate and worship god. Some serve others. I admire the latter.

35. Sometimes, I feel that my well considered opinion could be wrong and the other person could be right.
36. As there is a system in the nature, there must also be a regularity of habits.
37. I admire the people who can keep their calm when they are heckled for their righteousness.
38. I respect people who do not skip the traffic signals even when no one is there to regulate the traffic or even when there is no traffic at all.

The statements have been presented cluster-wise. However for efficacy the statements have been jumbled to give a wholistic picture and presented in the final form of the scheme.

2.3.3 TOOL TO MEASURE THE LEADERSHIP QUALITIES AT VARIOUS LEVELS OF EDUCATION

The development of Leadership Qualities was supposed to be measured by this scale.

As reported earlier in the case of Social Attitudes tool construction, the researcher could not find any ready-made tool to measure the Leadership Qualities of pupils of our required age group. Hence, the researcher had made an attempt to construct a fresh tool to measure the Leadership Qualities.

The investigator had inquired about the Leadership Qualities inventories at ICSSR, New Delhi, Psychological Foundations, Varanasi; NCERT, New Delhi and Times Research Foundation, Calcutta. As the ready-made tool in Leadership Qualities was not available, the researcher constructed the tool.

Methods Adopted in the Construction and Standardization of Leadership Qualities Scale

Initially the investigator had identified the following dimensions pertinent to the Leadership Qualities as suggested by the various theoreticians and researchers in the field of Sociology, Psychology and Education.

S.No.	Dimensionms	Author's Name
1	2	3
1.	A good leader should be a good follower himself	C. Thirunarayana & S. Hariharan
2.	He should be honest, truthful, sincere and pious	-do-
3.	He should have a degree of refinement	-do-
4.	He should have a well-groomed appearance	-do-
5.	He should have promotive and executive ability	-do-
6.	He should have a sense of humour	-do-
7.	He should have a sympathetic and friendly attitude and at the same time avoid undue familiarity	-do-
8.	He should have self-confidence and courage of his convictions	-do-
9.	He should have a capacity to lead the group democratically	-do-
10.	He should have a healthy, alert, vigorous and trained body abounding in vitality	-do-
11.	He should have the knowledge of psychology with adequate educational and professional background	B. Kuppu Swamy
12.	He should have the vision to see a little further ahead of his followers	Reuben B. Frost
13.	He should be supportive to his members	Stanley J. Marshall

cont.

1	2	3
14.	He should possess determination and perseverance	Barbara Day Lochart
15.	He should set the pace	Reuben B. Frost
16.	He should be sensitive to thoughts and feelings	Barbara Day Lockhart
17.	He must be flexible and adaptable enough	John Adair
18.	He must be able to communicate	R.B. Frost
19.	He should understand human nature	B.S.K.S. Chopra
20.	He should have faith and integrity	-do-
21.	He should be affectionate and maintain fraternity	-do-
22.	He must have resonant voice	-do-
23.	He must have intellectual penetration	-do-
24.	He must have soundness of feeling	-do-
25.	He must have technical mastery	-do-
26.	He must be open-minded	C.S.Dutt
27.	He must have creative ability	V. Lalini
28.	He must be confrontative	-do-
29.	He must have self-esteem	-do-
30.	He must have trait of ascendance	Allport
31.	He must have physical power	-do-
32.	He must have high mobility	-do-
33.	He must have zeal, tact, social participation and inscrutability	-do-

cont.

1	2	3
34.	He must be keenly susceptible to social stimulation	-do-
35.	He must be understandable and tactful	-do-
36.	He must have face to face mode of address, tonus, tenacity, reinformcement of energy, restraint, character	-do-
37.	He must be expansiveness to the field of action and high intelligence	-do-
38.	He must have erect and aggressive carriage	-do-
39.	He must have drive and determination	-do-
40.	He must have insight, sharp intellect, skill and acuity	-do-
41.	He must have moral sensitivity, justice, proper decision benevolent view point, moral outlook, selflessness, idealism	-do-
42.	He must have imagination, originality, love for truth foresight, curiosity, comprehensive interests and mental flexibility	Charles Bird
43.	He must have profundity and restraint self-control	Coffin
44.	He must have enthusiasm, inspiration, dynamic personality candidness, desire of name and fame, bravery, patience, concentration, the tendency to pursue to an end	Charles Bird

cont.

1	2	3
45.	He must be lover of work and have awareness of duties	Coffin
46.	He must have neuro-muscular co-ordination	-do-
47.	He must have imperturbability, balance, optimism, energy and decisiveness and also positive nature	-do-
48.	He must be model to others	Sprott
49.	He must mould the behaviour of his followers	Lapiere & Fransworth
50.	He must have environmental exposure	Pigor
51.	He must have reciprocal reinforcement	Britt
52.	He must be dominant and authoritative	Seeman & Morris
53.	He must have extrovert tendency	MacIver
54.	He must have social responsiveness, adaptability of social motivation and sociability	R. N. Sharma

The investigator had approached nine subject experts and asked their opinion on the dimensions listed.

These dimensions were studied by all the experts in the fields of Education, Sociology and Psychology.

The investigator had personally met the two Professors of Psychology, two Professors of Sociology of Osmania University, a Professor of Education from Sagar University and other Professors of Education from Andhra and Osmania Universities. The researcher had discussed the various modalities of the scale construction. Finally the dimensions listed in the preceding paras were simplified and were approved by the majority of subject experts as shown hereunder:

Dimensions of Leadership Qualities	Judgements of Experts	
	Approved	Dis-approved
1	2	3
1. Perseverance	9	0
2. Self-reliance	6	3
3. Tactful and understanding	5	4
4. Technical mastery	6	3
5. Creative ability	6	3
6. Intellectual penetration	9	0
7. Communicable	5	4
8. Trained body abounding in vatality	8	1
9. Administrative ability	7	2
10. See a little further ahead of his followers	7	2
11. Set the pace	8	1
12. Good Judgements	6	3
13. Inspiring fellow players to do their best	7	2
14. Reciprocal-reinforcement	8	1
15. Truthful	6	3
16. Adaptable	7	2
17. Sense of humour	5	4
18. Enthusiastic	7	2
19. Optimistic	8	1
20. Balance in defeat	9	0
21. Emotional stability	6	3
22. Faith	9	0
23. Integrity	5	4
24. Sensitive to others and feelings	6	3

cont.

1	2	3
25. Tough-mindedness	8	1
26. Dominant/Authoritative	6	3
27. Extrovert Tendency	6	3
28. Consistency	5	4
29. Sincere	9	0
30. Fair-mindedness	9	0
31. Moral outlook	5	4
32. Carefulness	6	3
33. Courtesy	8	1
34. Model to others	7	2
35. Environmental exposure	6	3
36. Dependable	5	4
37. Good follower himself	9	0
38. Capacity to lead the group democratically	7	2
39. Cooperation	7	2
40. Supportive to his members	8	1
41. Emotional control	6	3
42. Cheerful nature	6	3
43. Self-confidence	6	3
44. Industrious	8	1
45. Honesty	5	4
46. Punctuality and regular	7	2
47. Imagination	6	3
48. Social service	5	4
49. Tolerance	8	1
50. Habits	9	0
51. Self-control	9	0
52. Self-discipline	8	1

Thus the researcher with the consultation of the subject experts had finalised 52 dimensions of Leadership Qualities which were divided into the following three clusters on the advise of the experts.

Clusters of Leadership Qualities

1. Leadership Ability—LQ1
2. Leadership Temperamental—LQ2
3. Leadership Behavioural—LQ3

1. *Leadership Ability—LQ1*

The following dimensions of Leadership Qualities were considered under the Leadership Ability—LQ1 :

1. Perseverance
2. Self-reliance
3. Tactful and understanding
4. Technical mastery
5. Creative ability
6. Intellectual penetration
7. Communicable
8. Trained body abounding in vitality
9. Administrative ability
10. Sees a little further ahead of his followers
11. Sets the pace
12. Good Judgements
13. Inspiring fellow players to do their best
14. Reciprocal - reinforcement
15. Industrious
16. Imagination

2. Leadership Temperamental—LQ2

The following dimensions of Leadership Qualities were considered under the Leadership Temperamental—LQ2.

1. Truthful
2. Adaptable
3. Sense of humour
4. Enthusiastic
5. Optimistic
6. Balance in defeat
7. Emotional stability
8. Faith
9. Integrity
10. Sensitive to others@feelings
11. Tough-mindedness
12. Dominant/Authoritative
13. Emotional Control
14. Cheerful nature
15. Self-confidence
16. Honesty

3. ***Leadership Behavioural—LQ3***

The following dimensions of Leadership Qualities were considered under Leadership Behavioural—LQ3.

1. Extrovert Tendency
2. Consistency
3. Sincere
4. Fair-mindedness
5. Moral outlook
6. Carefulness
7. Courtesy
8. Model to others
9. Environmental exposure
10. Dependable

11. Good follower himself
12. Capacity to lead the group democratically
13. Cooperation
14. Supportive to his members
15. Punctuality and regularity
16. Social service
17. Tolerance
18. Habits
19. Self-control
20. Self-discipline

The investigator constructed the statements for the above mentioned 52 Leadership Qualities dimensions on five point scale (Strongly Agree, Agree, Undecided, Disagree and Strongly Disagree).

All these statements finally figured in the draft of the Leadership Qualities scale. It was translated into Telugu language by the experts in Telugu for the convenience of Telugu medium students.

To test the reliability of the draft scale a pilot study was conducted.

PILOT STUDY

To test the reliability of the constructed Leadership Qualities scale the investigator had adopted a test-re-test method.

ESTABLISHING THE TEST RE-TEST RELIABILITY

The investigator administered the test on 75 students (25 school students, 25 intermediate students and 25 degree students). Among these 75 students some of them were outstanding players in the sports field who were the national level players and a few had neither played any game nor seen even the play fields. The sample consisted of students of both the sexes with two community backgrounds, i.e., rural and urban and of different ages. The test was conducted at Warangal and Hyderabad.

The same test was re-administered to the same group of pupils after a gap of one month.

The results pertaining to the test-1 and test-2 are presented in the Table 2.3.3.

TABLE 2.3.3

SHOWING THE CORRELATIONS (r-VALUES) OF THE TEST RETEST SCORES TO ESTABLISH THE RELIABILITY OF THE LEADERSHIP QUALITIES SCALE

Institutional	*No. of pupils (n)*	*r-Values of Test Retest scores*	*Level of significance*
School	25	0.3603	< 0.05
Junior Colleges	25	0.5424	< 0.05
Degree Colleges	25	0.5549	< 0.05
Total at three levels of Education	75	0.5001	< 0.05

Table 2.3.3 shows the r-values of test and retest which were found to be significant at 0.05 level.

Hence, it is clear that the Leadership Qualities scale which was constructed is scientifically approved.

The investigator effected the following modifications of the scale after conducting the pilot study on the basis of the difficulties expressed by the Pilot study sample.

1. The verbal, spelling mistakes in the draft scale were simplified in order to make: further easy to the students to give their opinions. The only question in which the corrections were made is shown hereunder:

Even though made fun of some people tend to be more careful. I admire them. (Uncorrected form).

Even though made fun of some people insist on being more careful. I admire them. (Corrected form).

2. The ambiguous questions were rectified and further simplified. The only question in which the modification was made is shown hereunder:

Gazni Mohammed could be a model for emulation. (Unmodified form).

The entire sample could not be expected to know the Gazini Mohammed. So the modification.

When I decide to achieve, I never stop striving till I get the success. (Modified form).

3. Time taken in responding to the scale was kept in mind.

These statements were scientifically pruned by the subject exerts from the fields of Sociology, Psychology and Education. An English Professor went through it for the trimming of the language.

Thus the Leadership Qualities Scale with 52 statements was standardized and was used for the data collection. The scale of statements were presented hereunder in the form of three clusters:

Cluster-1: Leadership Ability

1. When I decide to achieve, I never stop striving till I get the success.
2. Rarely do I find an occasion to depend upon my friends.
3. I do not mind yielding some ground voluntarily of retreating temporarily with a view to wage an all out attack subsequently.
4. Persons who have mastery over all games can alone be effective captains.
5. As times move on we need to discard the old methods and create new ones: Only that way the society progresses.
6. I admire the western intellectuals who try to understand the mysteries of the universe through intellectual analysis.
7. I lend my ears to anyone who wants to speak to me.
8. I never suspended any work which I had undertaken in the middle because of my ill-health.
9. I feel happy whenever the junior in my team get higher positions.
10. While the fellow team-mates talk of winning a battle the leaders think of winning a war.

11. Unless and until one sets certain standards and records the leaders think of winning as a leader.
12. I do not hesitate to pronounce a well considered Judgements eventhough it helps my enemies and hurts my friends.
13. I cannot forget some of my captains who always motivated me to do my best in the play field.
14. I often offer critical appreciation of the performance of team-mate. I equally welcome from them critical appraisal of my own performance.
15. Success ultimately courts a person who is capable of putting continuous hard work.
16. There is always scope for imagination even in activities like Games & Sports.

Cluster-2: Leadership Temperamental

17. Truthfulness on our part often turns our friends into enemies. One should welcome it without a grumble.
18. I never found it inconvenient to move from my old class to a new class or from an old school to a new school.
19. I love the company of people who laugh and make others laugh.
20. Whenever I hit upon a novel idea, like a small child I enthusiastically share it with others.
21. Men often achieve what they strive for.
22. I admire the people who smile and remain undisturbed even in their defeat.
23. I intend to join the ranks for those people who remain undisturbed under greatest provocation.
24. I think I can achieve what I want to.
25. Integrity and material prosperity never go together.
26. Certain situations wherein I unwittingly hurt the feelings of my friends, haunt me regularly.
27. I find myself being tough even with the people for whom I have a weakness.

28. When persuasion fails to inspire conformity to the rule of law there is nothing wrong in being authoritarian.
29. I admire the people who are less emotive.
30. I admire a person who smiles even in his defeat.
31. I prefer to include in my team a good player eventhough he is critical of me.
32. I prefer to hug poverty as honesty and poverty to together.

Cluster-3: Leadership Behavioural

33. Whenever I get an opportunity I find myself participating enthusiastically in any activity however new the activity may be.
34. Why should one change one's opinions when nothing substantial providing a rationale for change has happened.
35. Eventhough it is not advantageous I hold on to my commitment to certain values/work which I consider to be good to the society.
36. I feel uncomfortable when my team members grow critical of our opponents.
37. For smooth running of the society one should uphold the social morals even by sacrificing self interest, if the self interest conflicts with the social morals.
38. Eventhough made fun of, some people insist on being more careful. I admire them.
39. Courtesy and good manners are ornaments that enrich a personality.
40. A leader is one who practices what he preaches.
41. Capabilities of a person as a captain are often related to the frequency and levels of exposure to Games & Sports situations.
42. My friends often go by my advice.
43. I adore the people who do what they say.

44. I admire the leaders who act according to the consensus of the followers.
45. Eventhough I can score a goal from my position. I prefer to pass the ball to my fellow player who is unmarked and more sure of scoring a goal.
46. I find myself helping my team-mates in their hour of need in a number of ways.
47. Like awards for standing first in a games event there must be awards for punctuality.
48. Some mediate and worship god. Some serve others. I admire the latter.
49. Sometimes I feel that my well considered opinion could be wrong and the others person could be right.
50. As there is a system in the nature there must also be a regularity of habits.
51. I admire the people who can keep their calm when heckled for their righteousness.
52. I respect people who do not skip the traffic signals even when no one is there to regulate the traffic or even when there is no traffic at all.

Thus the Leadership Qualities Scale with 52 statements was completed and standardized. Then it was used for the data collection.

2.4.0 DATA COLLECTION PROCEDURE

As explained earlier the sample of the study was the students who participated in Games & Sports and those who did not participate in Games & Sports at School, Junior College and Degree College Levels.

The researcher found it hard to trace the participants in Games & Sports especially at State level and National level. However, he could go round the places like Hyderabad, Karimnagar, Khammam, Adilabad and Warangal district Sports Centres for data collection.

The researcher had approached participants in Games & Sports on the play fields of the District Sports Stadia and the Non-participants at Schools, Junior Colleges and Degree Colleges.

The investigator included in the sample candidates competing in the Physical Education Common Entrance (PECET-95) Test conducted at Warangal, Rajamundry, Ananthapur and Tirupathi centres.

The researcher administered the Scales both Social Attitudes and Leadership Qualities on the subjects (690) as mentioned earlier.

The researcher had included in the sample pupils at School level, the just completed 10th class students, studying X class and a few IX class students.

The Inter 2nd year students and just completed inter students and Degree first year students were considered as inter level students.

The degree completed students, B.P.Ed. and B.Ed. students studying at Wargangal and Hyderabad were considered as Degree level sample for the data collection.

The scale consisting of both Social Attitudes and Leadership Qualities in a jumbled form (see appendix) with 76 statements (1-52 Leadership Qualities Statements; 39-76 Social Attitude Statement and 39-52 Common Questions) was used for data collection. The subjects were asked to give their opinions on five point scale i.e., Strongly Agree, Agree, Undecided, Dis-agree and Strongly Dis-agree.

2.5.0 Statistical Procedure Adopted

The present study sought to find out the relationship between various variables as shown in the following paras:

1. The study sought to find out the significance of difference of Social Attitudes formed at various levels of education between participants and non-participants in Games & Sports.
2. The study carried out to find out the significance of

difference of Leadership Qualities developed at various levels of education between participants and non-participants in Games & Sports.

3. The relationship between the measure of the Social Attitudes formed at various levels of education and the measure of the Leadership Qualities developed at various levels of education.

To test the above said relations the investigator computed the various **Co-efficient of correlations**, and tested the significance of differences if any, between the variables that were put forth in the study. **The means and standard deviations** of Social Attitudes and Leadership Qualities developed among participants and non-participants and the **t-test** were computed between the participants and non-participants at various levels of education.

The means and standard deviations of the scores on Social Attitude Scale between participants and non-participants in Games & Sports were computed under the following captions:

1. Education Level-wise
2. Sex-wise
3. Community Background-wise

The significance of difference on Social Attitudes scale between the participants and non-participants in Games & Sports was computed by adapting t-test.

The relationship between the formation of Social Attitudes and Age were computed by adapting the co-efficient of correlations.

The intensity of participation in Games & Sports and the Social Attitude formation too were computed with the coefficient of correlation.

Similarly, the means and standard deviations of Leadership Qualities development among Participants and Non-participants in Games & Sports were also computed under the following captions:

1. Education Level-wise
2. Sex-wise
3. Community Background-wise

The significance of difference on leadership scale between Participants and Non-participants in Games & Sports was computed by adapting t-test.

The relationship between the development of Leadership Qualities and Age was computed by coefficient of correlation.

The intensity of participation in Games & Sports and Leadership Qualities development too computed by the coefficient of correlation.

To find out the inter-relationship between these two variables i.e., Social Attitudes and Leadership Qualities the co-efficient of correlations were computed.

3

RESULTS AND DISCUSSIONS

3.0.0 INTRODUCTION

Previous chapters were devoted for the presentation of review of literature, for focusing the problem, for the discussion of significance of the study, for the formulation of objectives and hypotheses, for laying out the design of the study, for the construction of tools (Social Attitude Tool, Leadership Qualities Tool and Participation in Games & Sports Tool) and for the selection of the methods of sampling and procedure adopted for data collection and analysis.

The present chapter discusses the results relating to the levels of participation in Games & Sports and their association with the formation of Social Attitudes and the development of Leadership Qualities.

It has been specified that the main objectives of the research under were to find out the association between the following pairs of variables:

(i) Participation in Games & Sports and formation of social attitudes;

(ii) Participation in Games & Sports and development of leadership qualities; and

(iii) Interrelationship between the formation of social attitudes and the development of leadership qualities among students at Various Levels of Education.

3.1.0 PARTICIPATION IN GAMES & SPORTS AND FORMATION OF SOCIAL ATTITUDES

HYPOTHESIS-I

There will be a positive association between the participation of pupils in Games & Sports and Social Attitudes formed.

The measures of attitude formation were supposed to be contingent upon the Levels of Education Sex Differences, Community Background, Age Differences and intensity of participation in Games & Sports.

The results pertaining to the variables mentioned are presented in the following paras under captions, viz.

1. The Various Levels of Education and Attitude formation.
2. Sex and Attitude formation.
3. Community Background and Attitude formation.
4. Age and Attitude formation.
5. Levels of participation in Games & Sports and Attitude formation.

The results pertaining to caption-1 are presented hereunder.

1. Education Level and Attitude Formation

Education levels are conceived under three heads i.e.,

(a) School Level

(b) Inter Level

(c) Degree Level

(d) All Levels of Education

The participation in Games & Sports at three levels of education is considered cumulatively and its association with attitude formation is underscored.

(a) *School Level*

The results pertaining to the participation of pupils in Games & Sports at School Level and their scores on Social Attitude scale are presented in the Table 3.1.1.

The data pertaining to the Non-participants in Games & Sports too is presented along with that of the participants, as non-participation in Games & Sports and measures of participation in Games & Sports fall-in a continuum.

TABLE 3.1.1

SHOWING THE SIGNIFICANCE OF DIFFERENCE IN SOCIAL ATTITUDES AMONG PARTICIPANTS (PAG) AND NON PARTICIPANTS (NPAG) IN GAMES & SPORTS AT SCHOOL LEVEL

Variable	*PAG (n=125)*		*NPAG (n=125)*		*t-value*	*p-value*
	Mean	*SD*	*Mean*	*SD*		
SA1	48.31	5.86	46.06	4.57	3.38	.001*
SA2	55.89	6.42	53.36	5.36	3.39	.001*
SA3	47.50	5.83	45.77	4.47	2.63	.009*
SAT	151.71	16.26	145.20	11.86	3.61	.000*

** Significant at .05 level*

(Social Attitude are measured in terms of three categories i.e., SA1 = Attitude to people; SA2 = Attitude to work; and SA3 = General Life Attitudes).

Even the totals - SAT of these three segments are presented in the said table.

The results presented in the Table 3.1.1 show the scores on Social Attitude scale. The results yield a significant difference in Social Attitudes of participants in Games & Sports and non-participants in Games & Sports at School Level.

The p-values of all these segments of the Social Attitude variable are found to be significant at 0.05 level (The P-value shown against each segment in the table is lesser than the significant level i.e., 0.05 level).

Thus it can be concluded that the participation of pupils in Games & Sports at School Level develops the Social Attitudes in a significant measure.

(b) *Inter Level*

The results pertaining to the participation of pupils in Games & Sports at Inter Level and their scores on Social Attitude scale are presented in the Table 3.1.2

TABLE 3.1.2

SHOWING THE SIGNIFICANCE OF DIFFERENCE IN SOCIAL ATTITUDES AMONG PARTICIPANTS (PAG) AND NON-PARTICIPANTS (NPAG) IN GAMES & SPORTS AT INTER LEVEL

Variable	*PAG (n=110)*		*NPAG (n=110)*		*t-value*	*p-value*
	Mean	*SD*	*Mean*	*SD*		
SA1	47.60	4.76	44.90	4.84	4.15	.000*
SA2	54.38	5.50	52.36	4.73	2.92	.004*
SA3	46.18	5.47	44.69	4.81	2.15	.033*
SAT	148.16	13.82	141.96	11.83	3.57	.000*

** Significant at .05 level*

The results presented in the Table 3.1.2 reveal the scores on Social Attitude scale. The results show a significant different in Social Attitudes between the participants in Games & Sports and non-participants in Games & Sports at Inter Level.

The results reveal significant different in Social Attitudes in total as well as in segments between participants and non participants in Games & Sports. The p-values of all these segments of the Social Attitude variable are found to be significant at 0.05 level.

Thus it can be concluded that the participation of pupils in Games & Sports at Inter Level develops the Social Attitudes in a significant measure.

(c) *Degree Level*

The results pertaining to the participation in Games & Sports at Degree Level and their scores on Social Attitudes scale are presented in the Table 3.1.3.

The results presented in the Table 3.1.3 reveal the scores on Social Attitude scale. The results do not show any significant difference in Social Attitudes between the participants in Games & Sports and non-participants in Games & Sports at Degree Level.

TABLE 3.1.3
SHOWING THE SIGNIFICANCE OF DIFFERENCE IN SOCIAL ATTITUDES AMONG PARTICIPANTS (PAG) AND NON-PARTICIPANTS (NPAG) IN GAMES & SPORTS AT DEGREE LEVEL

Variable	*PAG (n=110)*		*NPAG (n=110)*		*t-value*	*p-value*
	Mean	*SD*	*Mean*	*SD*		
SA1	46.56	4.73	46.10	4.85	0.72	.474
SA2	52.56	5.50	51.96	6.05	0.77	.443
SA3	43.61	5.55	43.57	4.97	0.06	.949
SAT	142.74	13.22	141.63	13.42	0.62	.538

Level of Significance is .05 level

The p-values of all these segments of the Social Attitude variable are not found to be significant at 0.05 level (the p-values shown against each segment in the table is higher than the significant level).

Thus it can be concluded that the participation of pupils in Games & Sports at Degree Level does not develop Social Attitudes in a significant measure.

(d) ***All Levels of Education***

The results pertaining to the participation of pupils in Games & Sports at all Levels of Education and their scores on Social Attitude scale are presented in the Table 3.1.4.

TABLE 3.1.4
SHOWING THE SIGNIFICANCE OF DIFFERENCE IN SOCIAL ATTITUDES AMONG PARTICIPANTS (PAG) AND NON-PARTICIPANTS (NPAG) IN GAMES & SPORTS AT ALL LEVELS OF EDUCATION

Variable	*PAG (n=345)*		*NPAG (n=345)*		*t-value*	*p-value*
	Mean	*SD*	*Mean*	*SD*		
SA1	47.52	5.21	45.70	4.76	4.78	.000*
SA2	54.35	5.99	52.60	5.41	4.03	.000*
SA3	45.84	5.84	44.72	4.82	2.74	.006*
SAT	147.72	15.00	143.03	12.44	4.47	.000*

** Significant at .05 level*

The results presented in the Table 3.1.4 reveal the scores on Social Attitudes scale. The results show a significant difference between the participants in Games & Sports and non-participants in Games & Sports at All Levels of Education.

The results reveal significant difference in Social Attitudes in total as well as in three segments between participants and non participants in Games & Sports. The computed p-values of these segments of Social Attitude variable are found to be significant at 0.05 level.

Thus it can be concluded that the participation of pupils in Games & Sports at All Levels of Education generally develops the Social Attitudes in a significant measure.

2. Sex And Attitude Formation

Sex is conceived under two heads i.e., Male and Female. Under each head measurement was made separately for the two groups (i.e., participated and not participated groups) at three Levels of Education separately and cumulatively and their association with attitude formation is underscored.

(a) *School Level (Participation)*

The results pertaining to the male and female pupils who participate in Games & Sports at School Level and their scores on Social Attitudes scale are presented in the Table 3.1.1.1.

TABLE 3.1.1.1

SHOWING THE SIGNIFICANCE OF DIFFERENCE IN SOCIAL ATTITUDES AMONG MALE AND FEMALE PARTICIPANTS (PAG) IN GAMES & SPORTS AT SCHOOL LEVEL

Variable	*PAG (n=60)*		*NPAG (n=45)*		*t-value*	*p-value*
	Mean	*SD*	*Mean*	*SD*		
SA1	48.82	5.53	47.40	6.37	1.31	.194
SA2	56.25	6.21	55.26	6.80	0.82	.414
SA3	48.40	5.72	45.91	5.75	2.33	.022*
SAT	153.47	15.74	148.57	16.88	1.63	.106

* *Significant at .05 level*

The results presented in the Table 3.1.1.1 reveal the scores on Social Attitude scale. The results underline a significant difference in Social Attitudes between male and female participants in Games & Sports at School Level.

The p-values of these segments of Social Attitude variable except SA3 are not found to be significant at 0.05 level. The computed p-value of SA3 (General Life Attitudes) is found to be significant.

Thus it can be concluded that sex does not play a significant role at School Level in the formation of Social Attitudes of pupils with the exception of General Life Attitude (SA3) segment which shows a marginal development.

(b) *School Level (non-participation)*

The results pertaining to the male and female non-participation in Games & Sports at School Level and their scores on Social Attitude Scale are presented in the Table 3.1.1.2.

TABLE 3.1.1.2

SHOWING THE SIGNIFICANCE OF DIFFERENCE IN SOCIAL ATTITUDES AMONG MALE AND FEMALE NON-PARTICIPANTS (NPAG) IN GAMES & SPORTS AT SCHOOL LEVEL

Variable	*Male PAG (n=71)*		*Female NPAG (n=54)*		*t-value*	*p-value*
	Mean	*SD*	*Mean*	*SD*		
SA1	44.49	4.66	48.12	3.55	4.77	.000*
SA2	51.28	4.99	46.11	4.45	5.61	.000*
SA3	44.56	4.31	47.37	4.20	3.64	.000*
SAT	140.33	11.04	151.61	9.73	5.94	.000*

* *Significant at .05 level*

The results presented in the Table 3.1.1.2 reveal the scores on Social Attitude scale. The results show a significant difference in Social Attitude between male and female non-participants in Games & Sports at School Level.

The p-values of all these segments of Social Attitude variable are found to be significant at 0.05 level (the p-values shown against each segment in the table is lesser than the significant level).

Thus it can be concluded that the female non-participants in Games & Sports at School level are found to have better Social Attitudes when compared to the male non-participants.

(c) *Attitude Formation at School Level (Male & Female)*

The results pertaining to the male and female pupils at school level and their scores on Social Attitude scale are presented in the Table 3.1.1.3.

TABLE 3.1.1.3

SHOWING THE SIGNIFICANCE OF DIFFERENCE IN SOCIAL ATTITUDES AMONG MALE AND FEMALE PUPILS AT SCHOOL LEVEL

Variable	*Male (n=151)*		*Female (n=99)*		*t-value*	*p-value*
	Mean	*SD*	*Mean*	*SD*		
SA1	46.78	5.56	47.79	5.02	1.46	.146
SA2	53.91	6.17	55.72	5.62	2.35	.020*
SA3	46.59	5.44	46.70	4.99	0.16	.871
SAT	147.29	15.19	150.23	13.47	1.56	.120

** Significant at .05 level*

The results presented in the Table 3.1.1.3 reveal the scores on Social Attitude scale. The results do not yield a significant difference in Social Attitudes between male and female pupils at School Level.

The p-values of these segments of Social Attitude variable except SA2 (attitude to work) are not found to be significant at 0.05 level. The results do not yield any significant difference in Social Attitudes formed among the Male and Female pupils at School Level.

Thus it can be concluded that the differences social attitudes of male and female pupils at School Level are not significant.

(d) *Inter Level (Participation)*

The results pertaining to the male and female participants in Games & Sports at Inter Level and their scores on Social Attitude scale are presented in the Table 3.1.2.1.

The results presented in the Table 3.1.2.1 reveal the score on Social Attitude scale. The results show a significant difference between male and female participants in Games & Sports at Inter Level.

The p-values of all these segments of Social Attitude variable are found to be significant at .05 level (the p-values shown against each segment in the table are less than the significant level).

TABLE 3.1.2.1

SHOWING THE SIGNIFICANCE OF DIFFERENCE IN SOCIAL ATTITUDES AMONG MALE AND FEMALE PARTICIPANTS (PAG) IN GAMES & SPORTS AT INTER LEVEL

Variable	*Male PAG (n=85)*		*Female PAG (n=25)*		*t-value*	*p-value*
	Mean	*SD*	*Mean*	*SD*		
SA1	47.03	4.11	49.52	6.22	2.34	.021*
SA2	53.30	4.80	58.04	6.22	4.04	.000*
SA3	45.22	4.92	49.44	6.06	3.56	.001*
SAT	145.56	11.63	157.00	16.98	3.86	.000*

** Significant at .05 level*

Thus it can be concluded that the participation by females in Games & Sports at Inter Level develops the Social Attitudes in them in a significant measure than in males.

(e) *Inter Level (Non-participation)*

The results pertaining to the male and female pupils who do not participate in Games & Sports at Inter Level and their scores on Social Attitude scale are presented in the Table 3.1.2.2.

TABLE 3.1.2.2

SHOWING THE SIGNIFICANCE OF DIFFERENCE IN SOCIAL ATTITUDES AMONG MALE AND FEMALE NON-PARTICIPANTS (NPAG) IN GAMES & SPORTS AT INTER LEVEL

Variable	*Male NPAG (n=80)*		*Female NPAG (n=30)*		*t-value*	*p-value*
	Mean	*SD*	*Mean*	*SD*		
SA1	44.50	5.09	46.00	3.98	1.45	.149
SA2	51.18	4.98	52.83	4.00	0.64	.526
SA3	44.70	5.23	44.66	3.53	0.03	.974
SAT	141.38	12.77	143.50	8.87	0.83	.407

Level of Significance is .05 level

The results presented in the Table 3.1.2.2 reveal the scores on Social Attitude scale. The results do not yield any significant difference in Social Attitudes between male and female non-participants in Games & Sports at Inter Level.

The p-values of all these segments of Social Attitude variable are not found to be significant at 0.05 level (the p-values shown against each segment in the table are higher than the significant level).

Thus it can be concluded that the males and females who do not participate in Games & Sports do not show any significant difference in Social Attitude at Inter Level.

(f) *Attitude Formation at Inter Level (Male & Female)*

The results pertaining to the male and female pupils at Inter Level and their scores on Social Attitude scale are presented in the Table 3.1.2.3.

TABLE 3.1.2.3

SHOWING THE SIGNIFICANCE OF DIFFERENCE IN SOCIAL ATTITUDES AMONG MALE AND FEMALE PUPILS AT INTER LEVEL

Variable	*Male (n=165)*		*Female (n=55)*		*t-value*	*p-value*
	Mean	*SD*	*Mean*	*SD*		
SA1	45.80	4.77	47.60	5.37	2.34	.020*
SA2	52.76	4.91	55.20	5.71	3.05	.003*
SA3	44.96	5.07	46.83	5.36	2.33	.021*
SAT	143.53	12.34	149.63	14.71	3.02	.003*

** Significant at .05 level*

The results presented in the Table 3.1.2.3 reveal the scores on Social Attitude scale. The results show a significant difference in Social Attitudes between male and female pupils at Inter Level.

The p-values of these segments of Social Attitude variable are found to be significant at 0.05 level. The results reveal significant difference in Social Attitudes in total as well as in three segments among the Male and Female pupils at Inter Level. Thus the female pupils at Inter Level are found to be significantly higher Scorers than the male pupils on Social Attitude scale.

Now it can be concluded that the Social Attitudes get formed significantly more in the case of female pupils at Inter Level than in the case of males.

(g) ***Degree Level (Participation)***

The results pertaining to the male and female pupils participating in Games & Sports at Degree Level and their scores on Social Attitude scale are presented in the Table 3.1.3.1.

TABLE 3.1.3.1

SHOWING THE SIGNIFICANCE OF DIFFERENCE IN SOCIAL ATTITUDES AMONG MALE AND FEMALE PARTICIPANTS (PAG) IN GAMES & SPORTS AT DEGREE LEVEL

Variable	*Male PAG (n=98)*		*Female PAG (n=12)*		*t-value*	*p-value*
	Mean	*SD*	*Mean*	*SD*		
SA1	46.31	4.79	48.58	3.75	1.58	.118
SA2	52.28	5.62	54.83	3.90	1.52	.131
SA3	43.12	5.46	47.66	4.79	2.79	.007*
SAT	141.72	13.36	151.08	8.56	2.36	.020*

** Significant at .05 level*

The results presented in the Table 3.1.3.1 reveal the scores on Social Attitude scale. The results show a significant difference in Social Attitudes between male and female participants in Games & Sports at Degree Level.

The p-values of SA1 and SA2 are not found to be significant at 0.05 level. The p-values of SA3 and SAT are found to be significant at 0.05 level.

Thus it can be concluded that the females who participate in Games & Sports at Degree Level develop the Social Attitudes in a significantly greater measure than the male participants.

(h) ***Degree Level (Non-Participation)***

The results pertaining to the males and females who do not participate in Games & Sports at Degree Level and their scores on Social Attitude scale are presented in the Table 3.1.3.2.

The results presented in the Table 3.1.3.2 reveal the scores on Social Attitudes scale. The results do not yield any significant difference in Social Attitudes among males and females who do not participate in Games & Sports at Degree Level.

The p-values of all these segments of Social Attitude variable are not found to be significant (the p-values shown against each segment in the table are higher than the significant level i.e., 0.05 level).

TABLE 3.1.3.2
SHOWING THE SIGNIFICANCE OF DIFFERENCE IN SOCIAL ATTITUDES AMONG MALE AND FEMALE NON-PARTICIPANTS (NPAG) IN GAMES & SPORTS AT DEGREE LEVEL

Variable	Male NPAG (n=62)		Female NPAG (n=48)		t-value	p-value
	Mean	SD	Mean	SD		
SA1	46.24	5.40	45.91	4.06	0.35	.729
SA2	51.77	6.44	52.20	5.55	0.37	.711
SA3	43.90	5.21	43.14	4.65	0.79	.431
SAT	141.91	14.70	141.27	11.69	0.25	.803

Significant level is 0.05

Thus it can be concluded that the male and female pupils who do not partic pate in Games & Sports at Degree Level do not develop differences in Social Attitudes in a significant measure.

(l) *Attitude Formation at Degree Level (Male & Female)*

The results pertaining to the male and female pupils at degree level and their Social Attitude scores are presented in the Table 3.1.3.3.

TABLE 3.1.3.3
SHOWING THE SIGNIFICANCE OF DIFFERENCE IN SOCIAL ATTITUDES AMONG MALE AND FEMALE PUPILS AT DEGREE LEVEL

Variable	Male (n=160)		Female (n=60)		t-value	p-value
	Mean	SD	Mean	SD		
SA1	46.28	5.02	46.45	4.11	0.22	.823
SA2	52.08	5.94	52.73	5.34	0.74	.462
SA3	43.42	5.36	44.05	4.99	0.78	.434
SAT	141.80	13.85	143.23	11.76	0.71	.478

Significant level is .05

The results presented in the Table 3.1.3.3 reveal the scores on Social Attitude scale. The results do not show any significant difference in social attitudes between male and female pupils at Degree Level.

The p-values of these segments of Social Attitude variable are not found to be significant at 0.05 level. The results do not yield any significant difference in social attitudes formed among the Male and Female pupils at Degree Level.

Thus it can be concluded that there is no significant difference in Social Attitudes among male and female pupils at Degree Level.

(j) *All Levels of Education (Participation)*

The results pertaining to the males and females who participate in Games & Sports at All Levels of Education and their scores on Social Attitude scale are presented in the Table 3.1.4.1.

TABLE 3.1.4.1

SHOWING THE SIGNIFICANCE OF DIFFERENCE IN SOCIAL ATTITUDES AMONG MALE AND FEMALE PARTICIPANTS (PAG) IN GAMES & SPORTS AT ALL LEVELS OF EDUCATION

Variable	*Male PAG (n=263)*		*Female PAG (n=82)*		*t-value*	*p-value*
	Mean	*SD*	*Mean*	*SD*		
SA1	47.31	4.92	48.21	6.03	1.38	.169
SA2	53.82	4.79	56.04	6.36	2.97	.003*
SA3	45.40	5.77	47.24	5.87	2.50	.013*
SAT	146.53	14.42	151.51	16.25	2.64	.009*

** Significant at 0.5 level*

The results presented in the Table 3.1.4.1 reveal the scores on Social Attitude scale. The results show a significant difference in social attitudes between male and female participants in Games & Sports at All Levels of Education, the females scoring significantly higher scores than males.

The p-values of all these segments of Social Attitude variable except SA1 (Attitude to people) are found to be significant at 0.05 level.

Thus it can be concluded that the participation in Games & Sports at All Levels of Education by females develops in them Social Attitudes in a significantly higher measure than in males.

(k) *All Levels of Education (Non-Participation)*

The results pertaining to the males and females who do not participate in Games & Sports at All Levels of Education and their scores on Social Attitude scale are presented in the Table 3.1.4.2.

TABLE 3.1.4.2
SHOWING THE SIGNIFICANCE OF DIFFERENCE IN SOCIAL ATTITUDES AMONG MALE AND FEMALE NON-PARTICIPANTS (NPAG) IN GAMES & SPORTS AT ALL LEVELS OF EDUCATION

Variable	*Male NPAG (n=213)*		*Female NPAG (n=132)*		*t-value*	*p-value*
	Mean	*SD*	*Mean*	*SD*		
SA1	45.00	5.08	46.84	3.96	3.53	.000*
SA2	51.76	5.44	53.94	5.09	3.71	.000*
SA3	44.42	4.93	45.21	4.61	1.50	.136
SAT	141.19	12.79	146.00	11.28	3.55	.000*

** Significant at .05 level*

The results presented in the Table 3.1.4.2 reveal the scores on Social Attitude scale. The results show a significant difference in Social Attitudes of males and females who do not participate in Games & Sports at All Levels of Education.

The p-values of all these segments of Social Attitude variable except SA3 (General Life Attitude) are found to be significant at 0.05 level.

Thus it can be concluded that the females who do not participate in Games & Sports at All Levels of Education reveal higher measures of Social Attitudes in a significant measure than the non-participant males.

(l) *Attitude Formation at All Levels of Education (Male and Female)*

The results pertaining to the male and female pupils at all levels of education and their scores on Social Attitude scale are presented in the Table 3.1.4.3.

The results presented in the Table 3.1.4.3 reveal the scores on Social Attitude scale. The results show a significant difference in Social Attitudes between male and female pupils at All Levels of Education, the females scoring significantly higher than the males.

The p-values of all these segments of Social Attitude variable are found to be significant at 0.05 level. The results yield a significant difference in Social Attitudes formed among the male and female pupils at All Levels of Education.

TABLE 3.1.4.3
SHOWING THE SIGNIFICANCE OF DIFFERENCE IN SOCIAL ATTITUDES AMONG MALE AND FEMALE PUPILS AT ALL LEVELS OF EDUCATION

Variable	*Male (n=476)*		*Female (n=214)*		*t-value*	*p-value*
	Mean	*SD*	*Mean*	*SD*		
SA1	46.27	5.12	47.36	4.89	2.62	.009*
SA2	52.90	5.72	54.75	5.69	3.94	.000*
SA3	44.96	5.43	55.99	5.21	2.33	.020
SAT	144.14	13.96	148.11	13.64	3.48	.001*

** Significant at .05 level*

Thus it can be concluded that the formation of Social Attitudes among female pupils takes place in a significantly higher measure at All Levels of Education than among the male pupils.

3. Community Background And Attitude Formation

Community background was conceived under two heads i.e., (1) Rural and (2) Urban.

Under each head measurement was made separately for the two groups (i.e., participated and not participated groups) at three levels of education separately and cumulatively and their association with attitude formation is underscored in the following paras.

(a) *School Level (Participation)*

The results pertaining to the rural and urban participants in Games & Sports at School Level and their scores on Social Attitude scale are presented in the Table 3.1.1.4.

The results presented in the Table 3.1.1.4 reveal the scores on Social Attitude scale. The results do not show significant difference in Social Attitudes between rural and urban participants in Games & Sports at School Level.

TABLE 3.1.1.4
SHOWING THE SIGNIFICANCE OF DIFFERENCE IN SOCIAL ATTITUDES AMONG RURAL AND URBAN PARTICIPANTS (PAG) IN GAMES & SPORTS AT SCHOOL LEVEL

Variable	*Rural PAG (n=84)*		*Urban PAG (n=41)*		*t-value*	*p-value*
	Mean	*SD*	*Mean*	*SD*		
SA1	48.48	5.57	47.95	6.47	0.48	.633
SA2	56.44	5.94	54.78	5.26	1.36	.176
SA3	48.13	5.61	46.21	6.14	1.73	.086
SAT	153.05	15.29	148.95	17.98	1.33	.186

Level of Significance is 0.05 level

The p-values of all these segments of Social Attitude variable are not found to be significant at 0.05 level. The results do not yield any significant difference in the Social Attitudes formed among rural and urban participants in Games & Sports at School Level.

Thus it can be concluded that there is no significant difference in the Social Attitudes formed among rural and urban pupils who participate in the Games & Sports at School Level.

(b) *School Level (Non-Participation)*

The results pertaining to the rural and urban pupils who do not participate in Games & Sports at School Level and their scores on Social Attitude scale are presented in the Table 3.1.1.5.

TABLE 3.1.1.5
SHOWING THE SIGNIFICANCE OF DIFFERENCE IN SOCIAL ATTITUDES AMONG RURAL AND URBAN NON-PARTICIPANTS (NPAG) IN GAMES & SPORTS AT SCHOOL LEVEL

Variable	*Rural NPAG (n=94)*		*Urban NPAG (n=31)*		*t-value*	*p-value*
	Mean	*SD*	*Mean*	*SD*		
SA1	45.98	4.58	46.29	4.63	0.32	.752
SA2	52.17	5.66	53.96	4.14	0.72	.472
SA3	45.86	4.53	45.51	4.35	0.37	.711
SAT	145.02	12.38	145.77	10.30	0.31	.761

Level of Significance is 0.05 level

The results presented in the Table 3.1.1.5 reveal the scores on Social Attitude scale. The results do not yield any significant difference in Social Attitudes between rural and urban pupils who do not participate in Games & Sports at School Level.

The p-values of all these segments of Social Attitude variable are not found to be significant at 0.05 level. The results do not yield any significant difference in the Social Attitudes formed among rural and urban non-participants in Games & Sports at School Level.

Thus it can be concluded that the rural and urban pupils who do not participate in Games & Sports at School Level do not yield any differences in Social Attitudes in a significant measure.

(c) *Attitude Formation at School Level (Rural & Urban)*

The results pertaining to the rural and urban pupils at School Level and their scores on Social Attitude scale are presented in the Table 3.1.1.6.

TABLE 3.1.1.6

SHOWING THE SIGNIFICANCE OF DIFFERENCE IN SOCIAL ATTITUDES AMONG RURAL AND URBAN PUPILS AT SCHOOL LEVEL

Variable	*Rural (n=178)*		*Urban (n=72)*		*t-value*	*p-value*
	Mean	*SD*	*Mean*	*SD*		
SA1	47.16	5.21	47.23	5.77	0.09	.928
SA2	54.71	6.00	54.43	6.09	0.34	.737
SA3	46.93	5.18	45.91	5.42	1.38	.167
SAT	148.81	14.36	147.58	15.15	0.60	.546

Level of Significance is .05 level

The results presented in the Table 3.1.1.6 reveal the scores on Social Attitude scale. The results do not show any significant difference in Social Attitudes between rural and urban pupils at School Level.

The p-values of all these segments of Social Attitude variable are not found to be significant at 0.05 level. The results do not yield any significant difference in Social Attitudes formed among the rural pupils at School Level.

Thus it can be concluded that the Social Attitudes formed

among rural and urban pupils at School Level do not differ in a significant measure.

(d) ***Inter Level (Participation)***

The results pertaining to the rural and urban participants in Games & Sports at Inter Level and their scores on Social Attitude scale are presented in Table 3.1.2.4.

TABLE 3.1.2.4

SHOWING THE SIGNIFICANCE OF DIFFERENCE IN SOCIAL ATTITUDES AMONG RURAL AND URBAN PARTICIPANTS (PAG) IN GAMES & SPORTS AT INTER LEVEL

Variable	*Rural PAG (n=76)*		*Urban PAG (n=34)*		*t-value*	*p-value*
	Mean	*SD*	*Mean*	*SD*		
SA1	46.81	4.27	49.35	5.36	2.65	.009
SA2	54.09	5.18	55.02	6.18	0.82	.412
SA3	45.81	5.26	47.00	5.19	1.05	.296
SAT	146.72	12.79	151.38	15.59	1.65	.103

Level of Significance is .05 level

The results presented in the Table 3.1.2.4 reveal the scores on Social Attitude Scale. The results do not show any significant difference in social attitudes between rural and urban participants in Games & Sports at Inter Level.

The p-values of all these segments of Social Attitude variable except SA1 (Attitude to People) are not found to be significant at 0.05 level. The results do not yield any significant difference in Social Attitudes formed among rural and urban participants in Games & Sports in Inter Level. However, The scores of SA1 show a significant difference at 0.05 level.

Thus it can be concluded that the rural and urban pupils who participate in Games & Sports at Inter Level do not score on the Social Attitudes scale in a significant measure. However, it is found that the urban participants record higher levels of scores in SA1 (Attitude to People) than the rural participants.

(e) ***Inter Level (Non-Participation)***

The results pertaining to the rural and urban pupils who do not participate in Games & Sports at Inter Level and their scores on Social Attitude scale are presented in the Table 3.1.2.5.

TABLE 3.1.2.5

SHOWING THE SIGNIFICANCE OF DIFFERENCE IN SOCIAL ATTITUDES AMONG RURAL AND URBAN NON-PARTICIPANTS (NPAG) IN GAMES & SPORTS AT INTER LEVEL

Variable	*Rural NPAG (n=75)*		*Urban NPAG (n=35)*		*t-value*	*p-value*
	Mean	*SD*	*Mean*	*SD*		
SA1	44.53	4.94	45.71	4.59	1.19	.236
SA2	52.46	4.68	52.14	4.90	0.33	.740
SA3	44.54	4.97	45.00	4.51	0.46	.648
SAT	141.54	11.94	142.85	11.70	0.54	.591

Level of Significance is .05 level

The results presented in the Table 3.1.2.5 reveal the scores on Social Attitude scale. The results do not show any significant difference in Social Attitudes between rural and urban pupils who do not participate in Games & Sports at Inter Level.

The p-values of all these segments of Social Attitude variable are not found to be significant.

Thus it can be concluded that the rural and urban pupils who do not participate at Inter Level do not display differences in Social Attitudes in a significant measure.

(f) *Attitude Formation at Inter Level (Rural & Urban)*

The results pertaining to the rural and urban pupils at Inter Level and their scores on Social Attitude scale are presented in the Table 3.1.2.6.

TABLE 3.1.2.6

SHOWING THE SIGNIFICANCE OF DIFFERENCE IN SOCIAL ATTITUDES AMONG RURAL AND URBAN PUPILS AT INTER LEVEL

Variable	*Rural (n=151)*		*Urban (n=69)*		*t-value*	*p-value*
	Mean	*SD*	*Mean*	*SD*		
SA1	45.68	4.74	47.50	5.28	2.55	.011
SA2	53.28	4.99	53.56	5.71	0.37	.712
SA3	45.18	5.14	45.98	5.30	1.06	.290
SAT	144.15	12.61	147.05	14.32	1.52	.130

Level of Significance is .05 level

The results presented in the Table 3.1.2.6 reveal the scores on Social Attitude scale. The results do not yield any significant difference in Social Attitudes between rural and urban pupils at Inter Level.

The p-values of all these segments of Social Attitude variable except SA1 (Attitude to People) are not found to be significant. The results do not yield any significant difference in Social Attitudes formed among the rural and urban pupils at Inter Level. The differences in scores of rural and urban pupils on SA1 (Attitude to People) segment are found to be significant at 0.05 level.

Thus it can be concluded that the Social Attitudes formed among rural and urban pupils do not show any differences in a significant measure at Inter Level. The difference in Attitude to People (SA1) between the rural and urban pupils, however, is found to be significant—the urban pupils scoring significantly higher than the rural pupils.

(g) ***Degree Level (Participation)***

The results pertaining to the rural and urban pupils who participate in Games & Sports at Degree Level and their scores on Social Attitude scale are presented in the Table 3.1.3.4.

TABLE 3.1.3.4

SHOWING THE SIGNIFICANCE OF DIFFERENCE IN SOCIAL ATTITUDES AMONG RURAL AND URBAN PARTICIPANTS (PAG) IN GAMES & SPORTS AT DEGREE LEVEL

Variable	*Rural PAG (n=62)*		*Urban PAG (n=48)*		*t-value*	*p-value*
	Mean	*SD*	*Mean*	*SD*		
SA1	46.25	4.72	46.95	4.76	0.77	.444
SA2	52.17	5.49	53.06	5.53	0.84	.405
SA3	43.59	5.29	43.64	5.94	0.05	.964
SAT	142.03	13.05	143.66	13.53	0.64	.523

Level of Significance is .05 level

The results presented in the Table 3.1.3.4 show the scores on Social Attitudes scale. The results do not show any significant difference in Social Attitudes between rural and urban participants in Games & Sports at Degree Level.

The p-values of all these segments of Social Attitude variable are not found to be significant. The results do not yield any significant difference in the Social Attitudes formed among rural and urban participants in Games & Sports at Degree Level.

Thus it can be concluded that the rural and urban pupils who participate in Games & Sports at Degree Level do not display any differences in Social Attitudes in a significant measure.

(h) *Degree Level (Non-Participation)*

The results pertaining to the rural and urban pupils who do not participate in Games & Sports at Degree Level and their scores on Social Attitude scale are presented in the Table 3.1.3.5.

TABLE 3.1.3.5

SHOWING THE SIGNIFICANCE OF DIFFERENCE IN SOCIAL ATTITUDES AMONG RURAL AND URBAN NON-PARTICIPANTS (NPAG) IN GAMES & SPORTS AT DEGREE LEVEL

Variable	*Rural NPAG (n=61)*		*Urban NPAG (n=49)*		*t-value*	*p-value*
	Mean	*SD*	*Mean*	*SD*		
SA1	45.59	4.98	46.73	4.65	1.23	.220
SA2	51.49	6.00	52.55	6.12	0.91	.364
SA3	43.19	4.77	44.04	5.21	0.88	.379
SAT	140.27	13.50	143.32	13.25	1.19	.238

Level of Significance is .05 level

The results presented in Table 3.1.3.5 reveal the scores on Social Attitude scale. The results do not show any significant difference in Social Attitudes between rural and urban non-participants in Games & Sports at Degree Level.

The p-values of all the segments of Social Attitude variable are not found to be significant.

Thus it can be concluded that the rural and urban pupils who do not participate in Games & Sports at Degree Level do not show any differences in the formation of Social Attitudes in a significant measure.

(i) *Attitude Formation at Degree Level (Rural & Urban)*

The results pertaining to the rural and urban pupils at Degree

Level and their scores on Social Attitude scale are presented in the Table 3.1.3.6.

TABLE 3.1.3.6
SHOWING THE SIGNIFICANCE OF DIFFERENCE IN SOCIAL ATTITUDES AMONG RURAL AND URBAN PUPILS AT DEGREE LEVEL

Variable	*Rural (n=123)*		*Urban (n=97)*		*t-value*	*p-value*
	Mean	*SD*	*Mean*	*SD*		
SA1	45.92	4.84	46.84	4.68	1.42	.158
SA2	51.83	5.74	52.80	5.81	1.23	.219
SA3	43.39	5.02	43.84	5.56	0.62	.533
SAT	141.16	13.25	143.49	13.32	1.29	.197

Level of Significance is .05 level

The results presented in the Table 3.1.3.6 reveal the scores on Social Attitude scale. The results do not show any significant difference in Social Attitudes between rural and urban pupils at Degree Level.

The p-values of all these segments of Social Attitude variable are not found to be significant.

Thus it can be concluded that the differences in Social Attitudes among rural and urban pupils at Degree Level are not found to be statistically significant.

(j) *All Levels of Education (Participation)*

The results pertaining to the rural and urban participants in Games & Sports at All Levels of Education and their scores are presented in the Table 3.1.4.4.

TABLE 3.1.4.4
SHOWING THE SIGNIFICANCE OF DIFFERENCE IN SOCIAL ATTITUDES AMONG RURAL AND URBAN PARTICIPANTS (PAG) IN GAMES & SPORTS AT ALL LEVELS OF EDUCATION

Variable	*Rural PAG (n=222)*		*Urban PAG (n=123)*		*t-value*	*p-value*
	Mean	*SD*	*Mean*	*SD*		
SA1	47.29	4.99	47.95	5.58	1.12	.262
SA2	54.44	5.80	54.17	6.34	0.40	.693
SA3	46.07	5.68	45.43	6.13	0.98	.330
SAT	147.81	14.51	147.56	15.91	0.15	.882

Level of Significance is .05 level

The results presented in the Table 3.1.4.4 reveal the scores on Social Attitude scale. The results do not yield any significant difference in Social Attitudes between rural and urban participants in Games & Sports at All Levels of Education.

The p-values of all these segments of Social Attitude variable are not found to be significant.

Thus it can be concluded that the rural and urban pupils who do not participate in Games & Sports at All Levels of Education do not betray any differences in Social Attitudes.

(k) *All Levels of Education (Non-Participation)*

The results pertaining to the rural and urban pupils who do not participate in Games & Sports at All Levels of Education and their scores on Social Attitude scale are presented in the Table 3.1.4.5.

TABLE 3.1.4.5

SHOWING THE SIGNIFICANCE OF DIFFERENCE IN SOCIAL ATTITUDES AMONG RURAL AND URBAN NON-PARTICIPANTS (NPAG) IN GAMES & SPORTS AT ALL LEVELS OF EDUCATION

Variable	*Rural NPAG (n=230)*		*Urban NPAG (n=115)*		*t-value*	*p-value*
	Mean	*SD*	*Mean*	*SD*		
SA1	45.40	4.82	46.30	4.61	1.65	.100
SA2	52.49	5.47	52.80	5.29	0.51	.613
SA3	44.72	4.84	44.73	4.78	0.01	.994
SAT	142.63	12.66	143.84	12.00	0.85	.394

Level of Significance is .05 level

The results presented in the Table 3.1.4.5 reveal the scores on Social Attitude scale. The results do not show any significant difference in Social Attitudes between rural and urban pupils who do not participate in Games & Sports at All Levels of Education.

The p-values of all these segments of Social Attitude variable are not found to be significant.

Thus it can be concluded that the rural and urban pupils who do not participate in Games & Sports at All Level of Education do not display differences in Social Attitudes in a significant measure.

(I) *Attitude Formation at All Levels of Education (Rural & Urban)*

The results pertaining to the rural and urban pupils at All Levels of Education and their scores on Social Attitude scale are presented in the Table 3.1.4.6.

TABLE 3.1.4.6

SHOWING THE SIGNIFICANCE OF DIFFERENCE IN SOCIAL ATTITUDES AMONG RURAL AND URBAN PUPILS AT ALL LEVELS OF EDUCATION

Variable	*Rural (n=452)*		*Urban (n=238)*		*t-value*	*p-value*
	Mean	*SD*	*Mean*	*SD*		
SA1	46.33	4.99	47.15	5.19	2.02	.043
SA2	53.45	5.72	53.51	5.88	0.14	.891
SA3	45.38	5.31	45.09	5.52	0.68	.495
SAT	145.17	13.83	145.76	14.25	0.53	.598

Level of Significance is .05 level

The results presented in the Table 3.1.4.6 reveal the scores on Social Attitude scale. The results do not show any significant difference in Social Attitudes between rural and urban pupils at All Levels of Education cumulatively.

The p-values of all these segments of Social Attitude variable, except Attitude to People (SA1) are not found to be significant statistically. The Attitude to People (SA1) segment shows significant difference between the rural and urban pupils at All Levels of Education. The urban pupils have scored significantly higher than the rural pupils in this aspect.

Thus it can be concluded that rural and urban pupils at All Levels of Education do not display differences in the Social Attitudes in a significant measure.

4. Age And Attitude Formation

The average age of the group of pupils (n = 345) that has participated in Games & Sports was found to be 19.84 years and for the group of pupils (n = 345) that has not participated in Games & Sports it was 18.62 years.

The average age for the entire population (n = 690) was 19.23 years.

(a) *Age and Attitude Formation (Participated Group)*

The results pertaining to the age of pupils who have participated in the Games & Sports and their scores on Social Attitude scale are presented in the Table 3.1.4.7.

TABLE 3.1.4.7

SHOWING THE CORRELATION BETWEEN THE AGE AND SCORES ON SOCIAL ATTITUDE SCALE OF PARTICIPATED GROUP (N = 345) AT ALL LEVELS OF EDUCATION

Variable	*Age*	*Significant level*
SA1 - Attitude to people	.1566	.01
SA2 - Attitude to work	.2325	.001
SA3 - General Life Attitudes	.2413	.001
SAT - Social Attitudes Total	.2414	.001

The results pertaining to the Table 3.1.4.7 reveal the correlation between the age and Social Attitude scale. The results show positive relationship between the Age and Attitude Formation of all the participants in Games & Sports.

The computed r-values of all these segments of Social Attitude variable shown in the table are found to be significant at 0.001 level excepting the first segment i.e., Attitude to People (SA1) which is also significant but at 0.01 level.

Thus it can be concluded that Social Attitudes develop with age in a significant measure in the case of pupils who participate in Games & Sports at All Levels of Education.

(b) *Age and Attitude Formation (Not Participated Group)*

The results pertaining to the Age and Social Attitude scale of group of pupils that had not participated in the Games & Sports at All Levels of Education are presented in the Table 3.1.4.8.

TABLE 3.1.4.8

SHOWING THE CORRELATION BETWEEN THE AGE AND SCORES ON SOCIAL ATTITUDE SCALE OF NON-PARTICIPATED GROUP (N = 345) AT ALL LEVELS OF EDUCATION

Variable	*Age*	*Significant level*
SA1 - Attitude to people	.0334	NS
SA2 - Attitude to work	.1501	.01
SA3 - General Life Attitudes	.2065	.001
SAT - Social Attitudes Total	.1580	.01

NS = Not significant

The results pertaining to the Table 3.1.4.8 reveal the correlations between the Age and scores on Social Attitude scale. The results show positive relationship between the Age and Social Attitudes formed of all the non-participants in Games & Sports at All Levels of Education.

The computed r-values of all these segments of Social Attitude variable except Attitude to People (SA1) shown in the table are found to be significant 0.01 level and 0.001 level respectively. The first segment i.e., Attitude to People (SA1) is not found to be significant.

Thus it can be concluded that even in the case of non-participant pupils in Games & Sports at All Levels of Education the social attitudes develop with age in a significant measure.

(c) ***Age and Attitude Formation (Entire Group)***

The results pertaining to the Age and scores on the Social Attitude scale of the entire group (n = 690) are presented in the Table 3.1.4.9.

TABLE 3.1.4.9

SHOWING THE CORRELATION BETWEEN THE AGE AND SCORES ON SOCIAL ATTITUDE SCALE OF ENTIRE GROUP (N = 690) AT ALL LEVELS OF EDUCATION

Variable	*Age*	*Significant level*
SA1 - Attitude to people	.0741	NS
SA2 - Attitude to work	.1702	.001
SA3 - General Life Attitudes	.2081	.001
SAT - Social Attitudes Total	.1774	.001

NS = Insignificant

The results pertaining to the Table 3.1.4.9 reveal the correlations between the age and scores on Social Attitude scale. The results show positive relationship between the Age and Attitude Formation of the entire group in Games & Sports.

The computed r-values of all these segments of Social Attitude variable shown in the table are found to be significant 0.001 level excepting the first segment i.e., Attitude to People (SA1) which is not found to be significant.

Thus it can be concluded that the entire group of pupils at All Levels of Education develops the Social Attitudes with age in a significant measure.

5. Levels of Participation and Attitude Formation (Participated Group)

The results pertaining to the Levels of Participation in Games & Sports and their scores on Social Attitude scale of the group the has participated are presented in the Table 3.1.4.10.

TABLE 3.1.4.10

SHOWING THE CORRELATION BETWEEN THE LEVEL OF PARTICIPATED GROUP (N = 345) AND THEIR SCORES ON SOCIAL ATTITUDE SCALE AT ALL LEVELS OF EDUCATION

Variable	*Participation level*	*Significant level*
SA1 - Attitude to people	.0172	NS
SA2 - Attitude to work	.0762	NS
SA3 - General Life Attitudes	.0759	NS
SAT - Social Attitudes Total	.0540	NS

NS = No significant

The results pertaining to the Table 3.1.4.10 reveal the correlations between the Levels of Participation of participated group and their scores on Social Attitude scale. The results do not yield any relationship between the Levels of Participation and Attitude Formation of the participated group.

The computed r-values of all these segments of Social Attitude variable shown in the table are found to be significant.

Thus it can be concluded that the Levels of Participation of pupils in Games & Sports at All Levels of Education do not have any association with the Social Attitudes formed.

3.1.5 DISCUSSIONS OF THE RESULTS

In the foregoing pages the results pertaining to the Social Attitude formation in relation to Levels of Education, Sex, Community Background, Age and intensity of participation in Games & Sports have been furnished. In the following paras the discussion covering the said results is presented under 3.1.5.1 to 3.1.5.5. The relevant results too are furnished in abstract forms.

3.1.5.1 EDUCATIONAL LEVEL AND ATTITUDE FORMATION

Abstracts of the resulted presented in the Tables 3.1.1 to 3.1.4 showing the association between education levels and attitude formation were presented in the Table 3.1.5.1.

TABLE 3.1.5.1

SHOWING THE P-VALUES OF PARTICIPANTS IN GAMES & SPORTS (PAG) AND NON-PARTICIPANTS IN GAMES & SPORTS (NPAG) AND THEIR FORMATION OF SOCIAL ATTITUDES WITH REFERENCE TO EDUCATIONAL LEVELS

Education Level	*School*	*Inter*	*Degree*	*All level of Education*
PAG & NPAG	.000*	.000*	.538 (NS)	.000*

** = Significant at 0.05 level*
NS = Not Significant

The result furnished in the Table 3.1.5.1 cover the significance of difference in Social Attitudes formed between the Participants in Games & Sports and Non-participants in Games & Sports at School, Inter Degree and At All Levels of Education.

It is found that the differences in Social Attitudes formed at School, Inter and at All Levels of Education are significant at 0.05 level. It is only at the degree level the differences in the Social Attitude formed are not found to be significant.

It can be concluded that the Social Attitudes get formed significantly during the School and Intermediate level and not so much at the degree level. The over all differences in Social Attitudes when taken into consideration cumulatively throughout the period of education concluding with the degree level are found to be significant; the participants in Games & Sports scoring higher on the scale of Social Attitudes than the Non-participants in the Games & Sports. Thus it can be safely concluded that by and large the Social Attitudes get formed when the pupils participate in Games & Sports.

The review of related researches presented under the caption does not throw any light on this aspect as no researches measuring the association between the participants in Games & Sports at various levels of education and Social Attitude formation are recorded.

Thus it can be concluded that the research under report is a pioneering work undertaken which underscores a significant relationship between the participation in Games & Sports at various levels of education and Social Attitude formation.

3.1.5.2 SEX AND ATTITUDE FORMATION

Under sex caption three categories were identified, they are:

1. Male and Female participants in Games & Sports.
2. Male and Female non-participants in Games & Sports.
3. Male and Female Total Population.

Abstract of the results presented in the Tables 3.1.1.1 to 3.1.4.3 showing the association between Sex and Social Attitude formation were presented in the Table 3.1.5.2.

TABLE 3.1.5.2

SHOWING THE P-VALUES OF PARTICIPANTS IN GAMES & SPORTS (PAG) AND NON-PARTICIPANTS IN GAMES & SPORTS (NPAG) AND THEIR FORMATION OF SOCIAL ATTITUDES WITH REFERENCE TO SEX OF THE PUPILS

Sex	*School*	*Inter*	*Degree*	*All level of Education*
Male & Female PAG	.106(NS)	.000*	.020*	.009*
Male & Female NPAG	.000*	.407(NS)	.803(NS)	.000*
Male & Female Total	.120(NS)	.003*	.478(NS)	.001*

** = Significant at 0.05 level*
NS = Not Significant

The results furnished in the Table 3.1.5.2 show the significance of difference in Social Attitudes formed between Male and Female participants in Games & Sports and non-participants in Games & Sports separately at School, Inter, Degree and at All Levels of Education.

The results clearly reveal that among participants in Games & Sports, the male participants at Inter, Degree and at All Levels of Education have shown greater development of Social Attitudes formation when compared to female participants in Games & Sports. But it is only at their early years of study i.e., at School Level the Social Attitude formation is not much as per the results.

Similarly in the case of non-participants in Games & Sports the formation of Social Attitude is far better at an early age i.e., at School Level but as these non-participants go higher up in studies, the development of Social Attitudes decreases.

Finally, it is concluded that among the non-participants in Games & Sports, the Social Attitudes form rapidly and the same level of growth is not recorded at higher levels of education.

3.1.5.3. COMMUNITY BACKGROUND AND ATTITUDE FORMATION

Like sex, the Community Background is also studied under three headings, viz.,

1. Rural and Urban among participants in Games & Sports.
2. Rural and Urban among non-participants in Games & Sports.
3. Rural and Urban, Total Population.

Abstract of the results presented in the Tables 3.1.1.3 to 3.1.4.6 showing the association between Community Background and Social Attitude formation are presented in the Table 3.1.5.3.

TABLE 3.1.5.3

SHOWING THE P-VALUES OF PARTICIPANTS IN GAMES & SPORTS (PAG) AND NON-PARTICIPANTS IN GAMES & SPORTS (NPAG) AND THEIR FORMATION OF SOCIAL ATTITUDES WITH REFERENCE TO COMMUNITY BACKGROUND OF THE PUPILS

Community Background	*School*	*Inter*	*Degree*	*All level of Education*
Rural & Urban PAG	.186(NS)	.103(NS)	.523(NS)	.882(NS)
Rural & Urban NPAG	.761(NS)	.591(NS)	.238(NS)	.394(NS)
Rural & Urban Total	.546(NS)	.130(NS)	.197(NS)	.598(NS)

NS = Not Significant

The results presented in the Table 3.1.5.3 clearly indicate that the community background variable has got no impact of its own on Social Attitude formation at any level of education on participants and non-participants in Games & Sports.

Thus it can be concluded that the community background of pupils does not influence development in the formation of Social Attitudes.

3.1.5.4 AGE AND ATTITUDE FORMATION

One of the objectives of the research was to find out the association between Age and Social Attitude formation. Such an association was sought to be found covering the cases of the participants in Games & Sports and non-participants in Games & Sports.

As abstract of the results presented in the Tables 3.1.4.7 to 3.1.4.9 is presented in the following Tables 3.1.5.4.

TABLE 3.1.5.4

SHOWING THE ABSTRACT OF THE RESULTS PRESENTED IN THE TABLES 3.1.4.7 TO 3.1.4.9 AND THE ASSOCIATION BETWEEN AGE AND SOCIAL ATTITUDE FORMATION

Variable	*AGE*		
	Participants in Games & Sports	*Non-Participants in Games & Sports*	*Total Population*
SA1 - Attitude to People	.1566*	.0334***	.0741(NS)
SA2 - Attitude to Work	.2325**	.1501*	.1702**
SA3 - General Life Attitude	.2413**	.2065**	.2081**
SAT - Social Attitudes Total	.2414**	.1580*	.1774**

** = Significant at 0.01 level* *** = Significant at 0.001 level*
**** = Significant at 0.05 level* *NS = Not Significant*

The abstract of the results presented in the Table 3.1.5.4 reveal that the Social Attitudes get formed with age. All the three segments of the Social Attitudes record an increase significant with the age. The increase is significant in the cases of both participants and non-participants in Games & Sports. Thus, without any reference to the participation in Games & Sports the Social Attitudes increase significantly with age.

Even when the total population including the participants and non-participants in Games & Sports is taken into consideration the results display a similar trend.

The review of the researches presented under the caption 1.1.0 does not show any researches conducted in this area. This underscores the fact that the research under report is a pioneering one in this area.

Now it is finally concluded that the Social Attitudes of the pupil studying in Schools and Colleges get formed with Age without any reference to their participation in Games & Sports.

3.1.5.5 LEVELS OF PARTICIPATION IN GAMES & SPORTS AND SOCIAL ATTITUDE FORMATION

Through the present research it was intended to find out the association, if any, between the levels of participation of pupils in Games & Sports and Social Attitude formation at various levels of Education.

The results presented in the Table 3.1.4.10 are again presented in the Table 3.1.5.5.

TABLE 3.1.5.5

SHOWING THE RELATIONSHIP BETWEEN THE LEVEL OF PARTICIPATION OF PARTICIPATED GROUP (N = 345) AT ALL LEVELS OF EDUCATION AND THEIR SCORES ON SOCIAL ATTITUDE SCALES

Variable	*Participation level*	*Significant level*
SA1 - Attitude to people	.0172	NS
SA2 - Attitude to work	.0762	NS
SA3 - General Life Attitudes	.0759	NS
SAT - Social Attitudes Total	.0540	NS

NS = Insignificant

The results do not underline any association between the levels of participation in Games & Sports and the Social Attitude formation.

Out of the three segments of the Social Attitude the first segment i.e., Attitude to People-SA1 alone appear to have significant association with levels of participation and other segments i.e., Attitude to Work-SA2 and General Life Attitude-SA3 do not underscore significant association with the levels of participation in Games & Sports. Even the Social Attitude Total-SAT does not seem to have any significant association with levels of participation.

Thus it can be concluded that by and large the levels of participation of pupils in Games & Sports do not have any association with Social Attitude formation.

The review of researches present under the caption 1.1.0 does not through any light on this aspect.

3.2.0 PARTICIPATION IN GAMES & SPORTS AND DEVELOPMENT OF LEADERSHIP QUALITIES

HYPOTHESIS-II

There will be a positive association between the participation of pupils in Games & Sports and Leadership Qualities development.

The measures of leadership development were supposed to be contingent upon the levels of participation in Games & Sports, Sex Differences, Community Background and Age Differences.

The results pertaining to the variables mentioned above are presented in the following paras under captions, viz.,

1. Various levels of education and Leadership Development.
2. Sex and Leadership Development.
3. Community Background and Leadership Development.
4. Age and Leadership Development.
5. Levels of Participation in Games & Sports and Leadership Development.

The results pertaining to Caption-1 are presented hereunder :

1. Education Level And Leadership Development

Education levels are conceived under four heads i.e.,

(a) School Level
(b) Inter Level
(c) Degree Level
(d) All Levels of Education

(The participation in Games & Sports at three levels of education is considered cumulatively and its association with Leadership Development is underscored).

(a) *School Level*

The results pertaining to the participation of pupils in Games

& Sports at School Level and their scores on Leadership scale are presented in the Table 3.2.1.

The data pertaining to the Non-participants in Games & Sports too is presented along with that of the participants, as non-participation in Games & Sports and measures of participation in Games & Sports fall-in a continuum.

TABLE 3.2.1

SHOWING THE SIGNIFICANCE OF DIFFERENCE IN LEADERSHIP QUALITIES AMONG PARTICIPANTS (PAG) AND NON-PARTICIPANTS (NPAG) IN GAMES & SPORTS AT SCHOOL LEVEL

Variable	*PAG (n=125)*		*NPAG (n=125)*		*t-value*	*p-value*
	Mean	*SD*	*Mean*	*SD*		
LQ1	63.13	6.91	59.80	5.54	4.21	.000*
LQ2	58.26	8.08	56.10	5.76	2.43	.016*
LQ3	81.16	8.99	78.11	6.35	3.09	.002*
LQT	202.56	21.38	194.01	14.70	3.68	.000*

** = Significant at 0.05 level*

Leadership Qualities are measured in terms of three categories (i.e., LQ1 = Leadership Ability; LQ2 = Leadership Temperamental and LQ3 = Leadership Behavioural).

The total - LQT of these three segments are presented in the said table.

The results presented in the Table 3.2.1 reveal the scores on Leadership Qualities scale. The results show a significant difference in Leadership Qualities between the participants and non-participants in Games & Sports at School Level.

The p-values of all these segments of Leadership Qualities variable presented in the table are found to be significant at 0.05 level (the p-value shown against each segment in the table is lesser than the significant level).

Thus it can be concluded that the participation of pupils in Games & Sports at school level develops the leadership qualities in a significant measure.

(b) *Inter Level*

The results pertaining to the participation of pupils in Games

& Sports at Inter Level and their scores on Leadership scale are presented in the Table 3.2.2.

TABLE 3.2.2

SHOWING THE SIGNIFICANCE OF DIFFERENCE IN LEADERSHIP QUALITIES AMONG PARTICIPANTS (PAG) AND NON-PARTICIPANTS (NPAG) IN GAMES & SPORTS AT INTER LEVEL

Variable	PAG (n=110)		NPAG (n=110)		t-value	p-value
	Mean	SD	Mean	SD		
LQ1	62.02	6.01	58.79	5.30	4.23	.000*
LQ2	58.05	6.33	56.55	5.77	1.84	.068
LQ3	79.81	7.48	76.74	6.52	3.25	.001*
LQT	199.90	16.60	192.09	13.74	3.80	.000*

* = Significant at 0.05 level

The results presented in the Table 3.2.2 reveal the scores on Leadership scale. The results show a significant difference in Leadership Qualities between the participants and non-participants in Games & Sports at Inter Level.

The p-values of these segments of Leadership Qualities variable except LQ2 (Leadership Temperamental) presented in the table are found to be significant at 0.05 level (the p-value shown against each segment in the table is lesser than the significant level).

Thus it can be concluded that the participation of pupils in Games & Sports at Inter Level develops the leadership qualities in a significant measure.

(c) *Degree Level*

The result pertaining to the participation of pupils in Games & Sports at Degree Level and their scores on Leadership scale are presented in the Table 3.2.3.

The results presented in the Table 3.2.3 reveal the scores on Leadership scale. The results do not yield any significant difference in Leadership Qualities among the participants and non-participants in Games & Sports at Degree Level. However, the p-value of LQ1 (Leadership Ability) is found to be significant at 0.05 level.

TABLE 3.2.3

SHOWING THE SIGNIFICANCE OF DIFFERENCE IN LEADERSHIP QUALITIES AMONG PARTICIPANTS (PAG) AND NON-PARTICIPANTS (NPAG) IN GAMES & SPORTS AT DEGREE LEVEL

Variable	*PAG (n=110)*		*NPAG (n=110)*		*t-value*	*p-value*
	Mean	*SD*	*Mean*	*SD*		
LQ1	61.10	4.96	59.10	5.90	2.71	.007*
LQ2	56.82	5.67	57.08	5.94	0.32	.746
LQ3	77.44	8.60	76.90	8.17	0.47	.636
LQT	195.37	16.36	193.10	17.05	1.01	.314

** = Significant at 0.05 level*

Thus it can be concluded that the participation of pupils in Games & Sports at Degree Level does not develop the leadership qualities in a significant measure. However, the LQ1 (Leader Ability) segment shows a marginal development.

(d) *All Levels of Education*

The results pertaining to the participation of pupils in Games & Sports at All Levels of Education and their scores on Leadership scale are presented in the Table 3.2.4.

TABLE 3.2.4

SHOWING THE SIGNIFICANCE OF DIFFERENCE IN LEADERSHIP QUALITIES AMONG PARTICIPANTS (PAG) AND NON-PARTICIPANTS (NPAG) IN GAMES & SPORTS AT ALL LEVELS OF EDUCATION

Variable	*PAG (n=345)*		*NPAG (n=345)*		*t-value*	*p-value*
	Mean	*SD*	*Mean*	*SD*		
LQ1	62.13	6.09	56.25	5.58	6.46	.000*
LQ2	57.73	6.84	56.55	5.82	2.44	.015*
LQ3	79.54	8.53	77.29	7.04	3.79	.000*
LQT	199.42	18.59	193.11	15.18	4.88	.000*

** = Significant at 0.05 level*

The results presented in the Table 3.2.4 reveal the scores on Leadership scale. The results show a significant difference in Leadership Qualities between the participants and non-participants in Games & Sports at All Levels of Education.

The p-values of all these segments of Leadership Qualities variable are presented in the table are found to be significant at 0.05 level (the p-value shown against each segment in the table is lesser than the significant level).

Thus it can be concluded that the participation of pupils in Games & Sports at All Levels of Education develops the Leadership Qualities in a significant measure.

2. Sex and Leadership Development

Sex was conceived under two heads i.e., male and female. Under each head measurement was made separately for the two groups (i.e., participated and not participated) at three levels of education, separately and cumulatively, and their association with scores on Leadership scale is underscored.

(a) ***School Level (Participation)***

The results pertaining to the participation by males and females in Games & Sports at School Level and their scores on Leadership scale are presented in the Table 3.2.1.1.

TABLE 3.2.1.1

SHOWING THE SIGNIFICANCE OF DIFFERENCE IN LEADERSHIP QUALITIES AMONG MALE AND FEMALE PARTICIPANTS (PAG) IN GAMES & SPORTS AT SCHOOL LEVEL

Variable	*Male PAG (n=80)*		*Female PAG (n=45)*		*t-value*	*p-value*
	Mean	*SD*	*Mean*	*SD*		
LQ1	63.78	7.00	61.97	6.67	1.41	.161
LQ2	58.86	7.52	57.20	8.98	1.10	.272
LQ3	81.68	9.04	82.22	8.94	0.87	.384
LQT	204.33	21.09	199.40	21.75	1.24	.217

Level of Significance = 0.05

The results presented in the Table 3.2.1.1 reveal the scores on Leadership scale. The results do not yield any significant difference in Leadership Qualities between the male and female participants in Games & Sports at School Level.

The p-values of all these segments of Leadership Qualities variable presented in the table are not found to be significant at

0.05 level (the p-value shown against each segment in the table in higher than the significant level).

Thus it can be concluded that the male and female pupils who participate in Games & Sports at School Level do not have significant difference in Leadership Qualities.

(b) *School Level (Non-Participation)*

The results pertaining to the males and females who do not participate in Games & Sports at School Level and their scores on Leadership scale are presented in the Table 3.2.1.2.

TABLE 3.2.1.2
SHOWING THE SIGNIFICANCE OF DIFFERENCE IN LEADERSHIP QUALITIES AMONG MALE AND FEMALE NON-PARTICIPANTS (NPAG) IN GAMES & SPORTS AT SCHOOL LEVEL

Variable	*Male NPAG (n=71)*		*Female NPAG (n=54)*		*t-value*	*p-value*
	Mean	*SD*	*Mean*	*SD*		
LQ1	57.49	4.71	62.83	5.09	6.06	.000*
LQ2	53.64	5.36	59.33	4.57	6.25	.000*
LQ3	75.76	6.16	81.20	5.19	5.22	.000*
LQT	186.90	13.01	203.37	11.18	7.44	.000*

** = Significant at 0.05 level*

The results presented in the Table 3.2.1.2 reveal the scores on Leadership scale. The results show a significant difference in Leadership Qualities between the males and females who do not participate in Games & Sports at School Level.

The p-values of all these segments of Leadership Qualities variable presented in the table are found to be significant at 0.05 level (the p-value shown against each segment in the table is lesser than the significant level).

Thus it can be concluded that the female pupils who do not participate in Games & Sports at School Level have better Leadership Qualities than the males who do not participate in Games & Sports.

(c) *School Level (Male and Female)*

The results pertaining to the male and female pupils at School Level and their scores on Leadership scale are presented in the Table 3.2.1.3.

TABLE 3.2.1.3

SHOWING THE SIGNIFICANCE OF DIFFERENCE IN LEADERSHIP QUALITIES AMONG MALE AND FEMALE PUPILS AT SCHOOL LEVEL

Variable	*Male (n=151)*		*Female (n=99)*		*t-value*	*p-value*
	Mean	*SD*	*Mean*	*SD*		
LQ1	60.82	6.79	62.44	5.85	1.94	.053
LQ2	56.41	7.07	58.36	6.97	2.15	.033*
LQ3	78.90	8.34	80.75	7.12	1.82	.070
LQT	196.13	19.73	201.56	16.85	2.25	.025*

** = Significant at 0.05 level*

The results presented in the Table 3.2.1.3 reveal the scores on Leadership scale. The results show a significant cifference in Leadership Qualities between the male and female pup ls at School Level.

The p-values of all these segments of Leadership Qualities variable except LQ3 (Leadership Behavioural) presented in the table are found to be significant at 0.05 level.

Thus it can be concluded that the Leadership Qualities of female pupils at School Level develop in a significantly higher measure than in males.

(d) *Inter Level (Participation)*

The results pertaining to the participation in Games & Sports by male and female pupils at Inter Level and their scores on Leadership scale are presented in the Table 3.2.2.1.

TABLE 3.2.2.1

SHOWING THE SIGNIFICANCE OF DIFFERENCE IN LEADERSHIP QUALITIES AMONG MALE AND FEMALE PARTICIPANTS (PAG) IN GAMES & SPORTS AT INTER LEVEL

Variable	*Male PAG (n=85)*		*Female PAG (n=25)*		*t-value*	*p-value*
	Mean	*SD*	*Mean*	*SD*		
LQ1	61.15	5.57	65.00	6.58	2.91	.004*
LQ2	56.94	5.97	61.84	6.13	3.58	.001*
LQ3	78.67	7.11	83.72	7.52	3.08	.003*
LQT	196.76	15.08	210.56	17.39	3.88	.000*

** = Significant at 0.05 level*

The results presented in the Table 3.2.2.1 reveal the scores on Leadership scale. The results show a significant difference in Leadership Qualities between the male and female participants in Games & Sports at Inter Level.

The p-values of all these segments of Leadership Qualities variable presented in the table are found to be significant at 0.05 level (the p-values shown against segment in the table is lesser than the significant level).

Thus it can be concluded that the females who participate in Games & Sports at Inter Level develop the Leadership qualities in a significantly higher measure than the males who participate in Games & Sports.

(e) *Inter Level (Non-Participation)*

The results pertaining to the male and female pupils who have not participated in Games & Sports at Inter Level and their scores on Leadership scales are presented in the Table 3.2.2.2.

TABLE 3.2.2.2

SHOWING THE SIGNIFICANCE OF DIFFERENCE IN LEADERSHIP QUALITIES AMONG MALE AND FEMALE NON-PARTICIPANTS (NPAG) IN GAMES & SPORTS AT INTER LEVEL

Variable	*Male NPAG (n=80)*		*Female NPAG (n=30)*		*t-value*	*p-value*
	Mean	*SD*	*Mean*	*SD*		
LQ1	58.80	5.40	58.76	5.11	0.03	.977
LQ2	56.23	6.06	54.40	4.92	0.94	.350
LQ3	76.13	6.59	78.36	6.15	1.61	.111
LQT	191.17	14.31	194.53	11.97	1.14	.256

Level of significance is 0.05

The results presented in the Table 3.2.2.2 reveal the scores on Leadership scale. The results do not show any significant difference in Leadership Qualities between the male and female pupils who have not participated in Games & Sports at Inter Level.

The p-values of all these segments of Leadership Qualities variable presented in the table are not found to be significant (the p-value shown against each segment in the table is higher than the significant level).

Thus is can be concluded that the male and female pupils who do not participate in Games & Sports at Inter Level do not display differences in the leadership qualities in a significant measure.

(f) *Inter Level (Male and Female)*

The results pertaining to the male and female pupils at Inter Level and their scores on Leadership scale are presented in the Table 3.2.2.3.

TABLE 3.2.2.3

SHOWING THE SIGNIFICANCE OF DIFFERENCE IN LEADERSHIP QUALITIES AMONG MALE AND FEMALE PUPILS AT INTER LEVEL

Variable	*Male (n=165)*		*Female (n=55)*		*t-value*	*p-value*
	Mean	*SD*	*Mean*	*SD*		
LQ1	60.01	5.60	61.60	6.56	1.74	.083
LQ2	56.60	6.01	59.41	5.89	3.02	.003*
LQ3	77.44	6.96	80.80	7.26	3.06	.002*
LQT	194.05	14.93	201.81	16.62	3.24	.001*

** = Significant at 0.05 level*

The results presented in the Table 3.2.2.3 reveal the scores on Leadership scale. The results show a significant difference in Leadership Qualities between the male and female pupils at Inter Level.

The p-values of all these segments of Leadership Qualities variable except LQ1 (Leadership Ability) presented in the table are found to be significant at 0.05 level.

Thus it can be concluded that the Leadership Qualities of female pupils at Inter Level are found to be in a significantly higher measure than that of males.

(g) *Degree Level (Participation)*

The results pertaining to the male and female pupils who have participated in Games & Sports at Degree Level and their scores on Leadership scale are presented in the Table 3.2.3.1.

TABLE 3.2.3.1
SHOWING THE SIGNIFICANCE OF DIFFERENCE IN LEADERSHIP QUALITIES AMONG MALE AND FEMALE PARTICIPANTS (PAG) IN GAMES & SPORTS AT DEGREE LEVEL

Variable	Male PAG (n=98)		Female PAG (n=12)		t-value	p-value
	Mean	SD	Mean	SD		
LQ1	60.81	4.91	63.41	4.92	1.73	.087
LQ2	56.70	5.74	57.83	5.20	0.65	.518
LQ3	76.90	8.73	81.83	6.10	1.89	.061
LQT	194.42	16.52	203.08	13.20	1.75	.084

Significant level is 0.05

The results presented in the Table 3.2.3.1 reveal the scores on Leadership scale. The results do not yield any significant difference in Leadership Qualities between the male and female participants in Games & Sports at Degree Level.

The p-value of all the segments of Leadership Qualities variable presented in the table are not found to be significant (the p-value shown each segment in the table is higher than the significant level).

Thus it can be concluded that the male and female pupils who participate in Games & Sports at Degree Level do not display differences in the Leadership Qualities in a significant measure.

(h) *Degree Level (Non-Participation)*

The results pertaining to the male and female pupils who have not participated in Games & Sports at Degree level and their scores on Leadership scale are presented in the Table 3.2.3.2.

TABLE 3.2.3.2
SHOWING THE SIGNIFICANCE OF DIFFERENCE IN LEADERSHIP QUALITIES AMONG MALE AND FEMALE NON-PARTICIPANTS (NPAG) IN GAMES & SPORTS AT DEGREE LEVEL

Variable	Male NPAG (n=62)		Female NPAG (n=48)		t-value	p-value
	Mean	SD	Mean	SD		
LQ1	59.40	5.92	58.72	5.92	0.59	.555
LQ2	57.95	6.38	55.95	5.16	1.76	.081
LQ3	77.67	8.29	75.91	7.98	1.12	.264
LQT	195.03	17.96	190.60	15.63	1.36	.178

Significant level is 0.05

The results presented in the Table 3.2.3.2 reveal the scores on Leadership scale. The results do not show any significant difference in Leadership Qualities between the male and female pupils who have not participated in Games & Sports at Degree level.

The p-value of all the segments of Leadership Qualities variable presented in the table are not found to be significant (the p-value shown against each segment in the table is higher than the significant level).

Thus it can be concluded that the male and female pupils who do not participate in Games & Sports at Degree Level do not display differences in Leadership Qualities in a significant measure.

(i) *Degree Level (Male and Female)*

The results pertaining to the male and female pupils at Degree Level and their scores on Leadership scale are presented in the Table 3.2.3.3.

TABLE 3.2.3.3

SHOWING THE SIGNIFICANCE OF DIFFERENCE IN LEADERSHIP QUALITIES AMONG MALE AND FEMALE PUPILS AT DEGREE LEVEL

Variable	*Male (n=160)*		*Female (n=60)*		*t-value*	*p-value*
	Mean	*SD*	*Mean*	*SD*		
LQ1	60.26	5.35	59.66	6.00	0.72	.473
LQ2	57.18	6.01	56.33	5.18	0.97	.332
LQ3	77.20	8.55	77.10	7.96	0.08	.933
LQT	194.66	17.04	193.10	15.88	0.62	.538

Significant level is 0.05

The results presented in the Table 3.2.3.3 reveal the scores on Leadership Qualities scale. The results do not yield any significant difference in Leadership Qualities between the male and female pupils at Degree Level.

The p-values of all these segments of Leadership Qualities variable presented in the table are not found to be significant at 0.05 level.

Thus it can be concluded that the Leadership Qualities of male and female pupils at Degree Level do not differ in a significant measure.

(j) *All Levels of Education (Participation)*

The results pertaining to the male and female pupils who have participated in Games & Sports at All Levels of Education and their scores on Leadership scale are presented in the Table 3.2.4.1.

TABLE 3.2.4.1
SHOWING THE SIGNIFICANCE OF DIFFERENCE IN LEADERSHIP QUALITIES AMONG MALE AND FEMALE PARTICIPANTS (PAG) IN GAMES & SPORTS AT ALL LEVELS OF EDUCATION

Variable	*Male PAG (n=263)*		*Female PAG (n=82)*		*t-value*	*p-value*
	Mean	*SD*	*Mean*	*SD*		
LQ1	61.82	5.95	63.10	6.49	1.66	.097
LQ2	57.43	6.45	58.70	7.94	1.47	.143
LQ3	78.93	8.54	81.52	8.22	2.42	.016*
LQT	198.19	18.04	203.34	19.88	2.20	.029*

** = Significant at 0.05 level*

The results presented in the Table 3.2.4.1 reveal the scores on Leadership scale. The cumulative results show a significant difference in Leadership Qualities between the male and female participants in Games & Sports at All Levels of Education.

The p-values of all these segments of Leadership Qualities variable presented in the table are found to be significant at 0.05 level except LQ1 (Leadership Ability) and LQ2 (Leadership Temperamental) which are not found to be significant.

Thus it can be concluded that the female pupils who have participated in Games & Sports at Degree Level display significantly higher Leadership Qualities than the males.

(k) *All Levels of Education (Non-Participation)*

The results pertaining to the male and female pupils who do not participate in Games & Sports at All Levels of Education and their scores on Leadership scale are presented in the Table 3.2.4.2.

The results presented in the Table 3.2.4.2 reveal the scores on Leadership scale. The results show a significant difference in Leadership Qualities between the male and female pupils who do not participate in Games & Sports at All Levels of Education.

TABLE 3.2.4.2

SHOWING THE SIGNIFICANCE OF DIFFERENCE IN LEADERSHIP QUALITIES AMONG MALE AND FEMALE NON-PARTICIPANTS (NPAG) IN, GAMES & SPORTS AT ALL LEVELS OF EDUCATION

Variable	Male NPAG (n=213)		Female NPAG (n=132)		t-value	p-value
	Mean	SD	Mean	SD		
LQ1	58.53	5.37	60.41	5.74	3.07	.002
LQ2	55.87	6.15	57.66	5.06	2.81	.005
LQ3	76.46	7.01	78.63	6.90	2.82	.005*
LQT	190.87	15.34	196.71	14.25	3.53	.000*

* = Significant at 0.05 level

The p-values of all these segments of Leadership Qualities variable presented in the table are found to be significant at 0.05 level (the p-value shown against each segment in the table is lesser than the significant level).

Thus it can be concluded that the female pupils who do not participate in Games & Sports at All Levels of Education cumulatively display significant difference in Leadership Qualities and their scores are found to be significantly higher on the Leadership scale than that of the males.

(I) ***All Levels of Education (Male and Female)***

The results pertaining to the male and female pupils at All Levels of Education and their scores on Leadership scale are presented in the Table 3.2.4.3.

TABLE 3.2.4.3

SHOWING THE SIGNIFICANCE OF DIFFERENCE IN LEADERSHIP QUALITIES AMONG MALE AND FEMALE PUPILS AT ALL LEVELS OF EDUCATION

Variable	Male (n=476)		Female (n=214)		t-value	p-value
	Mean	SD	Mean	SD		
LQ1	60.35	5.92	61.44	6.16	2.21	.027*
LQ2	56.73	6.36	58.06	6.32	2.54	.011*
LQ3	77.82	7.98	79.74	7.55	2.97	.003*
LQT	194.92	17.26	199.25	16.90	3.07	.002*

* = Significant at 0.05 level

The results presented in the Table 3.2.4.3 reveal the scores on Leadership scale. The results show a significant difference in Leadership Qualities between the male and female pupils at All Levels of Education.

The p-values of all the segments of Leadership Qualities variable presented in the table are found to be significant at 0.05 level.

Thus it can be concluded that the Leadership Qualities of female pupils at All Levels of Education are found to be significantly higher than that of the pupils.

3. Community Background and Leadership Development

Community Background is conceived under two heads, (i) Rural and (ii) Urban.

The scores of rural and urban segments on Leadership Scale have been compared educational level-wise. The results are presented in the following paras:

(a) *School Level (Participation)*

The results pertaining to the Rural and Urban pupils who participate in Games & Sports at School Level and their scores on Leadership scale are presented in the Table 3.2.1.4.

TABLE 3.2.1.4

SHOWING THE SIGNIFICANCE OF DIFFERENCE IN LEADERSHIP QUALITIES AMONG RURAL AND URBAN PARTICIPANTS (PAG) IN GAMES & SPORTS AT SCHOOL LEVEL

Variable	*Rural PAG (n=84)*		*Urban PAG (n=41)*		*t-value*	*p-value*
	Mean	*SD*	*Mean*	*SD*		
LQ1	63.76	6.89	61.85	6.85	1.46	.140
LQ2	58.48	7.46	57.80	9.31	0.44	.650
LQ3	81.66	9.07	80.12	8.85	0.90	.370
LQT	203.91	21.01	199.78	22.11	1.02	.312

Significant level is 0.05

The results presented in the Table 3.2.1.4 reveal the scores on Leadership scale. The results do not yield any significant difference in Leadership Qualities between rural and urban participants in Games & Sports at School Level.

The p-values of all these segments of Leadership Qualities variable presented in the table are not found to be significant (the p-value shown against each segment in the table is higher than the significant level).

Thus it can be concluded that the rural and urban pupils who participate in Games & Sports at School Level do not display significant differences in the Leadership Qualities.

(b) *School Level (Non-Participation)*

The results pertaining to the Rural and Urban pupils who do not participate in Games & Sports at School Level and their scores on Leadership scale are presented in the Table 3.2.1.5.

The results presented in the Table 3.2.1.5 reveal the scores on Leadership scale. The results do not yield any significant difference in Leadership Qualities between rural and urban non-participants in Games & Sports at School Level.

TABLE 3.2.1.5

SHOWING THE SIGNIFICANCE OF DIFFERENCE IN LEADERSHIP QUALITIES AMONG RURAL AND URBAN NON-PARTICIPANTS (NPAG) IN GAMES & SPORTS AT SCHOOL LEVEL

Variable	*Rural NPAG (n=94)*		*Urban NPAG (n=31)*		*t-value*	*p-value*
	Mean	*SD*	*Mean*	*SD*		
LQ1	59.30	5.63	61.29	5.05	1.74	.084
LQ2	55.82	5.81	56.93	5.59	0.93	.356
LQ3	77.96	6.58	78.54	5.67	0.44	.661
LQT	193.10	15.00	186.77	13.59	1.21	.230

Significant level is 0.05

The p-values of all these segments of Leadership Qualities variable presented in the table are not found to be significant (the p-value shown against each segment in the table is higher than the significant level).

Thus it can be concluded that the rural and urban pupils who do not participate in Games & Sports at School Level do not display any significant differences in the Leadership Qualities.

(c) *School Level (Rural and Urban)*

The results pertaining to the Rural and Urban pupils at School Level and their scores on Leadership scale are presented in the Table 3.2.1.6.

TABLE 3.2.1.6
SHOWING THE SIGNIFICANCE OF DIFFERENCE IN LEADERSHIP QUALITIES AMONG RURAL AND URBAN PUPILS AT SCHOOL LEVEL

Variable	*Rural (n=178)*		*Urban (n=72)*		*t-value*	*p-value*
	Mean	*SD*	*Mean*	*SD*		
LQ1	61.41	6.62	61.61	6.10	0.22	.825
LQ2	57.08	6.76	57.43	7.89	0.35	.727
LQ3	79.71	8.05	79.44	7.64	0.24	.808
LQT	198.20	18.83	198.48	18.86	0.11	.916

Significant level is 0.05

The results presented in the Table 3.2.1.6 reveal the scores on Leadership scale. The results do not yield any significant difference in Leadership Qualities between rural and urban pupils at School Level.

The p-values of all the segments of Leadership Qualities variable presented in the table are not found to be significant at (the p-value shown against each segment in the table is higher than the significant level).

Thus it can be concluded that the Leadership Qualities of rural and urban pupils at School Level do not differ in a significant measure.

(d) *Inter Level (Participation)*

The results pertaining to the rural and urban pupils who participate in Games & Sports at Inter Level and their scores on Leadership scale are presented in the Table 3.2.2.4.

The results presented in the Table 3.2.2.4 reveal the scores on Leadership scale. The results do not yield any significant difference in Leadership Qualities between rural and urban participants in Games & Sports at Inter Level.

The p-values of all the segments of Leadership Qualities

variable except LQ2 (Leadership Temperamental) presented in the table are not found to be significant (the p-value shown against each segment in the table is higher than the significant level). The p-value of LQ2 (Leadership Temperamental) is found to be significant.

TABLE 3.2.2.4

SHOWING THE SIGNIFICANCE OF DIFFERENCE IN LEADERSHIP, QUALITIES AMONG RURAL AND URBAN PARTICIPANTS (PAG) IN GAMES & SPORTS AT INTER LEVEL

Variable	*Rural PAG (n=76)*		*Urban PAG (n=34)*		*t-value*	*p-value*
	Mean	*SD*	*Mean*	*SD*		
LQ1	61.71	6.31	62.73	5.28	0.82	.411
LQ2	56.93	6.40	60.55	5.46	2.86	.005
LQ3	79.44	7.64	80.64	7.15	0.78	.440
LQT	198.09	17.66	203.94	13.31	1.72	.088

Significant level is 0.05

Thus it can be concluded that the rural and urban pupils who participate in Games & Sports at Inter Level generally do not develop differences in the leadership qualities in a significant measure.

(e) *Inter Level (Non-Participation)*

The results pertainng to the Rural and Urban pupils who do not-participate in Games & Sports at Inter Level and their scores on Leadership scale are presented in the Table 3.2.2.5.

TABLE 3.2.2.5

SHOWING THE SIGNIFICANCE OF DIFFERENCE IN LEADERSHIP QUALITIES AMONG RURAL AND URBAN NON-PARTICIPANTS (NPAG) IN GAMES & SPORTS AT INTER LEVEL

Variable	*Rural NPAG (n=75)*		*Urban NPAG (n=35)*		*t-value*	*p-value*
	Mean	*SD*	*Mean*	*SD*		
LQ1	58.21	5.19	60.02	5.41	1.69	.095
LQ2	56.09	5.88	57.54	5.49	1.23	.222
LQ3	76.45	6.56	77.37	6.49	0.69	.494
LQT	190.76	13.72	194.94	13.54	1.50	.138

Significant level is 0.05

The results presented in the Table 3.2.2.5 reveal the scores on Leadership scale. The results do not yield any significant difference in Leadership Qualities between rural and urban people was do not participate in Games & Sports at Inter Level.

The p-values of all these segments of Leadership Qualities variable presented in the table are not found to be significant (the p-value shown against each segment in the table is higher than the significant level).

Thus it can be concluded that the rural and urban pupils who do not participate in Games & Sports at Inter Level do not display differences in Leadership Qualities in a significant measure.

(f) *Inter Level (Rural and Urban)*

The results pertaining to the Rural and Urban pupils at Inter Level and their scores on Leadership scale are presented in the Table 3.2.2.6.

TABLE 3.2.2.6

SHOWING THE SIGNIFICANCE OF DIFFERENCE IN LEADERSHIP QUALITIES AMONG RURAL AND URBAN PUPILS AT INTER LEVEL

Variable	*Rural (n=151)*		*Urban (n=69)*		*t-value*	*p-value*
	Mean	*SD*	*Mean*	*SD*		
LQ1	59.97	6.02	61.36	5.48	1.63	.105
LQ2	56.51	6.14	59.02	5.64	2.88	.004*
LQ3	77.96	7.26	78.98	6.92	0.98	.326
LQT	194.45	16.19	199.37	14.08	2.18	.031*

**= Significant at 0.05 level*

The results presented in the Table 3.2.2.6 reveal the scores on Leadership scale. The results show a significant difference in Leadership Qualities between rural and urban pupils at Inter Level.

The p-values of all the segments of Leadership Qualities variable presented in the table are found to be significant at 0.05 level except LQ1 (Leadership Ability) and LQ3 (Leadership Behavioural).

Thus it can be concluded that the differences in Leadership

Qualities among rural and urban pupils at Inter Level are generally found to be significant. The urban pupils are found to be scoring significantly higher on Leadership scale than the rural students.

(g) *Degree Level (Participation)*

The results pertaining to the Rural and Urban pupils who participate in Games & Sports at Degree Level and their scores on Leadership scale are presented in the Table 3.2.3.4.

The results presented in the Table 3.2.3.4 reveal the scores on Leadership scale. The results do not yield any significant difference in Leadership Qualities between rural and urban pupils who participate in Games & Sports at Degree Level.

The p-values of all the segments of Leadership Qualities variable presented in the table are not found to be significant (the p-value shown against each segment in the table is higher than the significant level).

TABLE 3.2.3.4

SHOWING THE SIGNIFICANCE OF DIFFERENCE IN LEADERSHIP QUALITIES AMONG RURAL AND URBAN PARTICIPANTS (PAG) IN GAMES & SPORTS AT DEGREE LEVEL

Variable	*Rural PAG (n=62)*		*Urban PAG (n=48)*		*t-value*	*p-value*
	Mean	*SD*	*Mean*	*SD*		
LQ1	61.09	5.41	61.10	4.37	0.01	.994
LQ2	56.64	6.16	57.06	5.02	0.38	.704
LQ3	77.29	7.64	77.64	9.78	0.21	.831
LQT	195.03	16.66	195.81	16.13	0.25	.805

Significant level is 0.05

Thus it can be concluded that the rural and urban pupils who participate in Games & Sports at Degree Level do not show any difference in the Leadership Qualities.

(h) *Degree Level (Non-Participation)*

The results pertaining to the Rural and Urban pupils who do not participate in Games & Sports at Degree Level and their scores on Leadership scale are presented in the Table 3.2.3.5.

TABLE 3.2.3.5

SHOWING THE SIGNIFICANCE OF DIFFERENCE IN LEADERSHIP QUALITIES AMONG RURAL AND URBAN NON-PARTICIPANTS (NPAG) IN GAMES & SPORTS AT DEGREE LEVEL

Variable	Rural NPAG (n=61)		Urban NPAG (n=49)		t-value	p-value
	Mean	SD	Mean	SD		
LQ1	58.80	6.17	59.48	5.59	0.60	.547
LQ2	57.08	6.40	57.08	5.37	0.00	.100
LQ3	76.09	8.57	77.91	7.60	1.16	.247
LQT	191.98	18.79	194.48	14.66	0.76	.446

Significant level is 0.05

The results presented in the Table 3.2.3.5 reveal the scores on Leadership scale. The results do not yield any significant difference in Leadership Qualities between rural and urban pupils who do not participate in Games & Sports at Degree Level.

The p-values of all the segments of Leadership Qualities variable presented in the table are not found to be significant (the p-value shown against each segment in the table is higher than the significant level).

Thus it can be concluded that the rural and urban pupils who do not participate in Games & Sports at Degree Level do not display any significant differences in the Leadership Qualities.

(i) *Degree Level (Rural and Urban)*

The results pertaining to the Rural and Urban pupils at Degree Level and their scores on Leadership scale are presented in the Table 3.2.3.6.

TABLE 3.2.3.6

SHOWING THE SIGNIFICANCE OF DIFFERENCE IN LEADERSHIP QUALITIES AMONG RURAL AND URBAN PUPILS AT DEGREE LEVEL

Variable	Rural (n=123)		Urban (n=97)		t-value	p-value
	Mean	SD	Mean	SD		
LQ1	59.95	5.89	60.28	5.06	0.44	.662
LQ2	56.86	6.26	57.07	5.18	0.27	.790
LQ3	76.69	8.11	77.78	8.70	0.95	.342
LQT	193.52	17.74	195.14	15.34	0.71	.475

Significant level is 0.05

The results presented in the Table 3.2.3.6 reveal the scores on Leadership scale. The results do not show any significant difference in Leadership Qualities between rural and urban pupils at Degree Level.

The p-values of all the segments of Leadership Qualities variable presented in the table are not found to be significant (the p-value of each selected segment are found to be higher than the significant level).

Thus it can be concluded that the Leadership Qualities of rural and urban pupils at Degree Level do not show any difference in the Leadership Qualities.

(j) *All Levels of Education (Participation)*

The results pertaining to the Rural and Urban pupils who participate in Games & Sports at All Levels of Education and their cumulative scores on Leadership scale are presented in the Table 3.2.4.4.

TABLE 3.2.4.4

SHOWING THE SIGNIFICANCE OF DIFFERENCE IN LEADERSHIP QUALITIES AMONG RURAL AND URBAN PARTICIPANTS (PAG) IN GAMES & SPORTS AT ALL LEVELS OF EDUCATION

Variable	*Rural PAG (n=222)*		*Urban PAG (n=123)*		*t-value*	*p-value*
	Mean	*SD*	*Mean*	*SD*		
LQ1	62.31	6.39	61.80	5.54	0.74	.457
LQ2	57.44	6.78	58.27	6.95	1.09	.279
LQ3	79.68	8.36	79.30	8.84	0.40	.690
LQT	199.44	19.02	199.38	17.87	0.03	.977

Significant level is 0.05

The results presented in the Table 3.2.4.4 reveal the scores on Leadership scale. The results do not yield any significant difference in Leadership Qualities between rural and urban pupils who participate in Games & Sports at All Levels of Education.

The p-values of all the segments of Leadership Qualities variable presented in the table are not found to be significant (the p-value shown against each segment in the table is higher than the significant level).

Thus it can be concluded that the rural and urban pupils who participate in Games & Sports at All Levels of Education do not display significant differences in the Leadership Qualities.

(k) ***All Levels of Education (Non-Participation)***

The results pertaining to the Rural and Urban pupils who do not participate in Games & Sports at All Levels of Education and their cumulative scores on Leadership scale are presented in the Table 3.2.4.5.

TABLE 3.2.4.5

SHOWING THE SIGNIFICANCE OF DIFFERENCE IN LEADERSHIP QUALITIES AMONG RURAL AND URBAN NON-PARTICIPANTS (NPAG) IN GAMES & SPORTS AT ALL LEVELS OF EDUCATION

Variable	*Rural NPAG (n=230)*		*Urban NPAG (n=115)*		*t-value*	*p-value*
	Mean	*SD*	*Mean*	*SD*		
LQ1	58.81	5.63	60.13	5.40	2.08	.038
LQ2	56.24	5.99	57.18	5.43	1.41	.160
LQ3	76.97	7.17	77.92	6.75	1.17	.241
LQT	192.04	15.68	195.24	13.95	1.85	.065

Significant level is 0.05

The results presented in the Table 3.2.4.5 reveal the scores on Leadership scale. The results do not yield any significant difference in Leadership Qualities Total (LQT), Leadership Temperamental (LQ2) and Leadership Behavioural (LQ3) between the rural and urban pupils who do not participate in Games & Sports at All Levels of Education. The results show a significant difference in Leadership Ability (LQ1).

The p-values of all the segments of Leadership Qualities variable presented in the table are not found to be significant except the Leadership Ability (LQ1) which shows the significance at 0.05 level.

Thus it can be concluded that the rural and urban pupils who do not generally participate in Games & Sports at All Levels of Education do not display significant differences in the Leadership Qualities. But the Leadership Abilities (LQ1) of urban pupils who do not participate in Games & Sports are found to be significantly higher.

(I) *All Levels of Education (Rural and Urban)*

The results pertaining to the Rural and Urban pupils at All Levels of Education and their scores on Leadership scale are presented in the Table 3.2.4.6.

The results presented in the Table 3.2.4.6 reveal the scores on Leadership scale. The results do not yield any significant difference in Leadership Qualities between rural and urban pupils at All Levels of Education.

The p-values of all the segments of Leadership Qualities variable are not found to be significant.

TABLE 3.2.4.6

SHOWING THE SIGNIFICANCE OF DIFFERENCE IN LEADERSHIP QUALITIES AMONG RURAL AND URBAN PUPILS AT ALL LEVELS OF EDUCATION

Variable	*Rural (n=452)*		*Urban (n=238)*		*t-value*	*p-value*
	Mean	*SD*	*Mean*	*SD*		
LQ1	60.53	6.26	61.00	5.52	0.96	.335
LQ2	56.83	6.41	57.74	6.24	1.79	.074
LQ3	78.30	7.89	78.63	7.91	0.52	.606
LQT	195.67	17.77	197.38	16.20	1.23	.217

Significant level is 0.05

Thus it can be concluded that the Leadership Qualities of rural and urban pupils at All Levels of Education do not display differences in a significant measure.

4. Age and Leadership Development

The average age of the group of pupils (n = 345) that had participated in Games & Sports was found to be 19.84 years and the group of pupils (n = 345) that had not participated in Games & Sports was 18.62.

The average age for the entire population (n = 690) was 19.23 years.

(a) *Age and Leadership Development (Participant Group)*

The results pertaining to the Age and scores on Leadership

scale of group that has participated in Games & Sports are presented in the Table 3.2.4.7.

The results pertaining in the Table 3.2.4.7 reveal the correlation between the age and scores on Leadership scale. The results show a positive relationship between the Age and Leadership Qualities developed of all the participants in Games & Sports.

The computed r-values between the segments of Leadership Qualities variable shown in the table are found to be significant at 0.001 level. However, the relationship between Age and Leadership Ability (LQ1) is found to be significant at 0.01 level.

TABLE 3.2.4.7

SHOWING THE CORRELATION BETWEEN THE AGE AND SCORES ON LEADERSHIP SCALE OF PARTICIPATED GROUP (N = 345) AT ALL LEVELS OF EDUCATION

Variable	*Age*	*Significant level*
LQ1 - Leadership Ability	.1593	.01
LQ2 - Leadership Temperamental	.1109	NS
LQ3 - Leadership Behavioural	.2201	.001
LQT - Leadership Qualities Total	.1940	.001

Thus it can be concluded that the Leadership Qualities of pupils who participated in Games & Sports at All Levels of Education develop with their age in a significant measure.

(b) ***Age and Leadership Qualities (Non-Participant Group)***

The results pertaining to the Age and scores on Leadership scale of the group that has not participated in Games & Sports are presented in the Table 3.2.4.8.

TABLE 3.2.4.8

SHOWING THE CORRELATION BETWEEN THE AGE AND SCORES ON LEADERSHIP SCALE OF NOT PARTICIPATED GROUP (N = 345) AT ALL LEVELS OF EDUCATION

Variable	*Age*	*Significant level*
LQ1 - Leadership Ability	.0808	NS
LQ2 - Leadership Temperamental	.0248	NS
LQ3 - Leadership Behavioural	.1189	NS
LQT - Leadership Qualities Total	.0754	NS

The results pertaining to the Table 3.2.4.8 reveal the correlations between the Age and Leadership. The results do not show any association between the Age and Leadership scores of the group of pupils who do not participate in Games & Sports at All Levels of Education.

The computed r-values of all the segments of Leadership Qualities variable shown in the table are not found to be significant statistically.

Thus it can be concluded that the group of pupils who do not participate in Games & Sports at All Levels of Education does not develop the Leadership Qualities inspite of the Age factor in a significant measure.

(c) *Age and Leadership Development (Entire Group)*

The results pertaining to the Age and scores on Leadership scale of the entire group (n = 690) are presented in the Table 3.2.4.9.

TABLE 3.2.4.9

SHOWING THE CORRELATION BETWEEN THE AGE AND SCORES ON LEADERSHIP SCALE OF THE ENTIRE GROUP (N = 690) AT ALL LEVELS OF EDUCATION

Variable	*Age*	*Significant level*
LQ1 - Leadership Ability	.0850	NS
LQ2 - Leadership Temperamental	.0403	NS
LQ3 - Leadership Behavioural	.1541	.001
LQT - Leadership Qualities Total	.1151	.01

The results presented in the Table 3.2.4.9 reveal the correlations between Age and Leadership. The results show a positive association between Age and Leadership Behavioural (LQ3), and Leadership Qualities Total (LQT). The results do not show any relationship in Leadership Ability (LQ1) and Leadership Temperamental (LQ2) between the Age and scores on Leadership scale of entire group in Games & Sports at All Levels of Education.

The computed r-values between Age and Leadership Ability (LQ1) and Leadership Temperamental (LQ2) are not found to be significant. The r-values between Age and Leadership Behavioural (LQ3) are found to be significant at .001 level. The correlation between Age and Leadership Qualities Total (LQT) is found to be significant at .01 level.

Thus it can be concluded that the Leadership Qualities of the entire group of pupils at All Levels of Education develop with the Age in a significant measure.

5. Level of Participation in Games & Sports and Leadership Development (Participant Group)

The results pertaining to the levels of participation and the scores on Leadership scale of the group that has participation in Games & Sports are presented in the Table 3.2.4.10.

TABLE 3.2.4.10

SHOWING THE CORRELATION BETWEEN THE LEVELS OF PARTICIPATION OF PARTICIPATED GROUP (N = 345) AT ALL LEVELS OF EDUCATION AND THEIR SCORES ON LEADERSHIP QUALITIES DEVELOPMENT

Variable	*Participation level*	*Significant level*
LQ1 - Leadership Ability	.0159	NS
LQ2 - Leadership Temperamental	.0533	NS
LQ3 - Leadership Behavioural	.0276	NS
LQT - Leadership Qualities Total	.0018	NS

NS = Not Significant

The results presented in the Table 3.2.4.10 reveal the correlation between Levels of Participation in Games & Sports and scores on Leadership scale. The results do not show any relationship between the Levels of Participation and Leadership of the group that has participated in Games & Sports.

The computed r-values between the Age and all the segments of Leadership Qualities variable shown in the table are not found to be significant statistically.

Thus it can be concluded that the Levels of Participation of the group of pupils which has participated in Games & Sports at All Levels of Education does not develop the leadership qualities in a significant measure.

3.2.5 DISCUSSION OF THE RESULTS

One of the major objectives of the research was to find out, if participants in Games & Sports at Various Levels of Education develop Leadership Qualities or not. Even it sought to find out if the sex factor has any association with the Leadership development. Likewise the association between the Community Background and Leadership Qualities developed. Age and Leadership Qualities developed and the Levels of Partcipation in Games & Sports and Leadership Qualities developed were to be researched into.

The relevant results are presented under captions 3.2.5.1 to 3.2.5.5.

The discussion of the said results is presented variable wise in the following paras.

3.2.5.1 EDUCATIONAL LEVEL AND LEADERSHIP DEVELOPMENT

A positive association was hypothesized between participation of Games & Sports at Various Levels of Education and Leadership Qualities developed.

An abstract of the results presented in the Tables 3.2.1 to 3.2.4 is presented in the Table 3.2.5.1.

TABLE 3.2.5.1

SHOWING THE P-VALUES OF PARTICIPANTS IN GAMES & SPORTS (PAG) AND NON-PARTICIPANTS IN GAMES & SPORTS (NPAG) AND THEIR DEVELOPMENT OF LEADERSHIP QUALITIES WITH REFERENCE TO EDUCATIONAL LEVELS

Education Level	*School*	*Inter*	*Degree*	*All level* of *Education*
PAG & NPAG	.000*	.000*	.314	.000*

** = Significant at 0.05 level*

The results furnished in the Table 3.2.5.1 cover the significance of difference in Leadership Qualities developed between the Participants in Games & Sports and Non-participants in Games & Sports at School, Inter, Degree and At all Levels of Education.

It is established that barring at Degree level the differences in Leadership Qualities developed between Participants and Non-participants in Games & Sports at School and Inter Levels were found to be significant. The scores on Leadership Qualities scale were found to be significantly higher in the case of Participants than Non-Participants in Games & Sports at All Levels of Education.

Thus it can be concluded that the Leadership Qualities get developed because of Participation in Games & Sports in a significant way.

A perusal of the review of researches presented under caption 1.1.0 does not throw any light on this aspect.

Thus it can be concluded that the research under report is a pioneering effort underlining the need to lay greater premium on Games & Sports Activities which are sure to develop Leadership Qualities among the students.

3.2.5.2 SEX AND LEADERSHIP DEVELOPMENT

Under sex caption three categories were identified, they are :

1. Male and Female participants in Games & Sports. 2. Male and Female non-participants in Games & Sports. 3. Male and Female Total Population.

An abstract of the results presented in the Tables 3.2.1.1 to 3.2.4.3 showing the association between Sex and Leadership Development were presented in the Table 3.2.5.2.

TABLE 3.2.5.2

SHOWING THE P-VALUES OF PARTICIPANTS IN GAMES & SPORTS (PAG) AND NON-PARTICIPANTS IN GAMES & SPORTS (NPAG) AND THEIR DEVELOPMENT OF LEADERSHIP QUALITIES WITH REFERENCE TO SEX OF THE PUPILS

Sex	*School*	*Inter*	*Degree*	*All level of Education*
Male & Female PAG	.210	.000*	.084*	.029*
Male & Female NPAG	.000*	.256	.178	.000*
Male & Female Total	.025	.001*	.538	.002*

** = Significant at 0.05 level*

The results furnished in the Table 3.2.5.2 reveals that while the differences in the Leadership Qualities developed among the boys and girls who participate in Games & Sports are not significant at School and Degree Level, they are found to be significant at Inter Level and at All Levels of Education. One significant feature is that the differences which may be significant or not it is the girls who have invariably scored higher on the Leadership Qualities Scale than the boys.

Likewise, while the differences in the Leadership Qualities developed among non-participant boys and girls at Inter and Degree Levels are not found to be significant, they are found to be significant at the School Level and at All Levels of Education.

Even in this case, the most striking feature is that the girls outshined boys in Leadership Qualities development throughout their period of education.

When the total sample of boys and girls is taken into consideration by clubbing the Leadership Qualities scores of Participants and Non-participants in Games & Sports, it is found that the girls score significantly higher than the boys at School, Inter and at All Levels of Education. Only at Degree Level the differences are not found to be significantly. Even in this case it is found that the scores of girls on Leadership Qualities scale are higher than that of boys.

Thus, it is established that the girls command Leadership Qualities in a greater measure than the boys. May be better Leadership Abilities are inherent in the female sex.

A review of related literature throws some light amply supporting the findings of this research.

Thus it gets conclusively established that while the Participation in Games & Sports develops the Leadership Qualities in a greater measure, girls display relatively better Leadership Qualities than their counterparts both in the case of Participation and Non-Participation in Games & Sports.

3.2.5.3 COMMUNITY BACKGROUND AND LEADERSHIP QUALITIES DEVELOPMENT

Like sex, the Community Background is also studied under three headings, viz.,

1. Rural and Urban among participants in Games & Sports.

2. Rural and Urban among non-participants in Games & Sports.
3. Rural and Urban, Total Population.

Abstract of the results presented in the Tables 3.2.1.4 to 3.2.4.6 showing the association between Community Background and Leadership Qualities development are presented in the Table 3.2.5.3.

A perusal of the results presented in the Table 3.2.5.3 reveals that barring at the intermediate level when the total sample is taken into consideration the differences between the rural and urban pupils at Various Levels of Education are not found to be significant. They are not found to be significant both in the case of Participants and Non-Participants in Games & Sports.

TABLE 3.2.5.3

SHOWING THE P-VALUES OF PARTICIPANTS IN GAMES & SPORTS (PAG) AND NON-PARTICIPANTS IN GAMES & SPORTS (NPAG) AND THEIR DEVELOPMENT OF LEADERSHIP QUALITIES WITH REFERENCE TO COMMUNITY BACKGROUND OF THE PUPILS

Community Background	*School*	*Inter*	*Degree*	*All level of Education*
Rural & Urban PAG	.310	.088	.805	.977
Rural & Urban NPAG	.230	.138	.446	.065
Rural & Urban Total	.916	.031*	.475	.217

** = Significant at 0.05 Level*

Thus it can be generally concluded that Community Background has nothing to do with Leadership Qualities development.

3.2.5.4 AGE AND LEADERSHIP QUALITIES DEVELOPMENT

One of the objectives of the research was to find out the association between Age and Leadership Qualities development. Such an association was sought to be found covering the cases of the participants in Games & Sports and non-participants in Games & Sports.

As abstract of the results presented in the Tables 3.2.4.7 to 3.2.4.9 is presented in the following Table 3.2.5.4.

TABLE 3.2.5.4
SHOWING THE ABSTRACT OF THE RESULTS PRESENTED IN THE TABLES 3.2.4.7 TO 3.2.4.9 AND THE ASSOCIATION BETWEEN AGE AND LEADERSHIP QUALITIES DEVELOPMENT

Variable	*AGE*		
	Participants in Games & Sports	*Non-Participants in Games & Sports*	*Total Population*
LQ1 - Leadership Ability	.1593*	.0808NS	.0850NS
LQ2 - Leadership Temperamental	.1109NS	.0248***	.0403***
LQ3 - Leadership Behavioural	.2201**	.1189NS	.1541**
LQT - Leadership Qualities Total	.1940**	.0754NS	.1151*

** = Significant at 0.01 level* *** = Significant at 0.001 level*
**** = Significant at 0.05 level* *NS = Not Significant*

The results presented in the Table 3.5.2.4 reveal the results which appear to be categorical in the sense that by and large there is a positive correlation between Age and Leadership Qualities developed particularly in the case of Participants in Games & Sports. The correlations between Age of Participants in Games & Sports and LQ1, LQ3 and LQT were found to be significant while they are not found to be significant in the case of Non-participants in Games & Sports. The only exception was LQ2 in the case of Non-participants in Games & Sports.

Even when the entire population was taken into consideration the correlations were found be significant with regard to LQ2, LQ3 and LQT. It simply signifies that while the correlation between Age and Leadership Qualities development was found to be significant in a generally way, the Age was closely associated with the Leadership Qualities development with regard to the Participation in Games & Sports.

It can be hypothesized that the kind of significant association was found between Age and Leadership Qualities development with regard to total population was mainly because of the presence of the sample which had Participated in the Games & Sports.

Thus it can be concluded that while there is positive association between Age and Leadership Qualities development it is highly significant in case of the sample that has participated in the Games & Sports.

Finally, it gets established that the Participation in Games & Sports is instrumental in developing Leadership Qualities.

3.2.5.5 LEVELS OF PARTICIPATION IN GAMES & SPORTS AND LEADERSHIP QUALITIES DEVELOPMENT

Through the present research it was intended to find out the association, if any, between the levels of participation of pupils in Games & Sports and Leadership Qualities development at various levels of Education.

The results presented in the Table 3.2.4.10 are again presented in the Table 3.2.5.5.

The intensity of the participation in Games & Sports is construed to be Participation in Games & Sports at higher levels i.e. the National level, State level, Inter-varsity level etc.

TABLE 3.2.5.5

SHOWING THE CORRELATION BETWEEN THE LEVELS OF PARTICIPATION OF PARTICIPATED GROUP (N = 345) AT ALL LEVELS OF EDUCATION AND THEIR SCORES ON LEADERSHIP QUALITIES DEVELOPMENT

Variable	*Participation Level*	*Significant level*
LQ1 - Leadership Ability	.0159	NS
LQ2 - Leadership Temperamental	.0533	NS
LQ3 - Leadership Behavioural	.0276	NS
LQT - Leadership Qualities Total	.0018	NS

NS = Not Significant

It was hypothesized that the intensity of Participation in Games & Sports would have a positive bearing on the development of Leadership Qualities in a significant way.

The results presented in the Table 3.2.5.5 do not seem to support the hypothesis. The association between the intensity of Participation in Games & Sports and Leadership Qualities development is not found to be significant i.e., the intensity of Participation in Games & Sports does not add to the Leadership Qualities development in a significant measure.

At the first sight it appears to be a contradiction in terms. While it has been established that the Participation in Games and Sports develops the Leadership Qualities in a significant way, the intensity of Participation in Games & Sports does not add to the development of Leadership Qualities. What could be reason? Only a thorough research in this regard could provide an answer.

Meanwhile a tentative hypothesis could be formulated in this regard. The lack of significant association between intensity of Participation in Games & Sports and Leadership Qualities development could be mainly because of the concentrated effort an individual directs in a situation of intensive participation. The entire attention of the participation is probably directed to the development of expertise in a narrow sense which excludes the development of concomitant attributes like Leadership Qualities development and Social Attitude formation. However, this needs to be confirmed by a subsequent research.

III. RELATIONSHIP BETWEEN SOCIAL ATTITUDES FORMATION AND LEADERSHIP QUALITIES DEVELOPMENT

HYPOTHESIS

There will be inter-relationship between the developments of Social Attitudes and Leadership Qualities among pupils at Various Levels of Education.

3.3.0 INTRODUCTION

The inter-relationship between the formation of Social Attitudes and the development of Leadership Qualities among pupils at various levels of education are presented under the following captions:

1. School Level
2. Inter Level
3. Degree Level
4. All Levels of Education

1. *School Level*

The results pertaining to the relationship between Social

Attitudes and the development of Leadership Qualities at School Level are presented in the Table 3.3.1.

TABLE 3.3.1
SHOWING THE RELATIONSHIP BETWEEN FORMATION OF SOCIAL ATTITUDES AND SCORES ON LEADERSHIP SCALE OF PUPILS (N = 250) AT SCHOOL LEVEL

Variable	*SA1*	*SA2*	*SA3*	*SAT*
LQ1	.5878**	.6568**	.5275**	.6782**
LQ2	.6971**	.6770**	.5993**	.7527**
LQ3	.7165*	.7547*	.7351**	.8409**
LQT	.7669*	.7992*	.7171**	.8414**

*** = Significant at .001 level*

The social attitudes are measured in terms of three categories (i.e., SA1 = Attitude to People; SA2 = Attitude to work; and SA3 = General life attitudes).

Even the total - SAT of these three segments are presented in the said table.

Leadership Qualities are measured in terms of three categories (i.e., LQ1 = Leadership Ability; LQ2 = Leadership Temperamental; LQ3 = Leadership Behavioural).

Even the totals - LQT of these three segments are presented in the said table.

The results presented in the Table 3.3.1 reveal the correlations between Social Attitudes and Leadership Qualities. The results show positive association between the social attitudes and Leadership Qualities among pupils at School Level.

The r-values of all the selected variables shown against each other are found to be significant at 0.001 level.

Thus it can be concluded that there is inter-relationship between Social Attitudes and Leadership Qualities among pupils at School Level.

2. *Inter Level*

The results pertaining to the relationship between Social Attitudes and the development of Leadership Qualities at Inter Level are presented in the Table 3.3.2.

TABLE 3.3.2

SHOWING THE RELATIONSHIP BETWEEN FORMATION OF SOCIAL ATTITUDES AND SCORES ON LEADERSHIP SCALE OF PUPILS (N = 220) AT INTER LEVEL

Variable	*SA1*	*SA2*	*SA3*	*SAT*
LQ1	.4491**	.4987**	.3767**	.5147**
LQ2	.6219**	.5280**	.4735**	.6295**
LQ3	.6500*	.6119*	.6556**	.7449**
LQT	.7065*	.6713*	.6243**	.7775**

*** = Significant at .001 level*

The results presented in the Table 3.3.2 reveal the correlations between Social Attitudes and scores on Leadership scale. The results show a positive association between the social attitudes and Leadership Qualities among pupils at Inter Level.

The r-values of all the selected variables shown in the table are found to be significant at 0.001 level.

Thus it can be concluded that there is inter-relationship between Social Attitudes and Leadership Qualities among pupils at Inter Level.

3. *Degree Level*

The results pertaining to the relationship between Social Attitudes and the scores on Leadership scale at Degree Level are presented in the Table 3.3.3.

TABLE 3.3.3

SHOWING THE RELATIONSHIP BETWEEN FORMATION OF SOCIAL ATTITUDES AND SCORES ON LEADERSHIP SCALE OF PUPILS (N = 220) AT DEGREE LEVEL

Variable	*SA1*	*SA2*	*SA3*	*SAT*
LQ1	.4640**	.6439**	.4536**	.6260**
LQ2	.6029**	.5994**	.4823**	.6679**
LQ3	.6242*	.6576*	.6664**	.7737**
LQT	.6757*	.7507*	.6515**	.8268**

*** = Significant at .001 level*

The results presented in the Table 3.3.3 show the correlations between Social Attitudes and Leadership Qualities. The results show a positive association between the Social Attitudes and Leadership Qualities among pupils at Degree Level.

The r-values of all the variables are shown in the table are found to be significant at 0.001 level.

Thus it can be concluded that there is inter-relationship between Social Attitudes and Leadership Qualities among pupils at Degree Level.

(a) *All Levels of Education*

The results pertaining to the relationship between Social Attitudes and the scores on Leadership scale at All Levels of Education are presented in the Table 3.3.4a.

The results presented in the Table 3.3.4a show the correlations between Social Attitudes and Leadership Qualities. The results show a positive association between the Social Attitudes and Leadership Qualities among pupils at All Levels of Education.

TABLE 3.3.4a

SHOWING THE RELATIONSHIP BETWEEN THE FORMATION OF SOCIAL ATTITUDES AND SCORES ON LEADERSHIP SCALE OF PUPILS (N = 690) AT ALL LEVELS OF EDUCATION

Variable	*SA1*	*SA2*	*SA3*	*SAT*
LQ1	.5144**	.6108**	.4641**	.6181**
LQ2	.1660**	.6043**	.5142**	.6825**
LQ3	.6667*	.6887*	.6925**	.7936**
LQT	.7233*	.7516*	.6688**	.8310**

*** = Significant at .001 level*

The r-values of all the variables shown in the table are found to be significant at 0.001 level.

Thus it can be concluded that there is a positive association between Social Attitudes and Leadership Qualities among pupils at All Levels of Education.

(b) *All Levels of Education (Participant Group)*

The results pertaining to the relationship between Social

Attitudes and the scores on Leadership scale at All Levels of Education (participant group) are presented in the Table 3.3.4b.

TABLE 3.3.4b

SHOWING THE RELATIONSHIP BETWEEN FORMATION OF SOCIAL ATTITUDES AND SCORES ON LEADERSHIP SCALE OF PUPILS (N = 345) AT ALL LEVELS OF EDUCATION (PARTICIPANT GROUP)

Variable	*SA1*	*SA2*	*SA3*	*SAT*
LQ1	.5430**	.6507**	.5358**	.6577**
LQ2	.6913**	.6278**	.5997**	.7250**
LQ3	.6860*	.7041**	.7495**	.8120**
LQT	.7473*	.7675**	.7403**	.8550**

*** = Significant at .001 level*

The results presented in the Table 3.3.4b reveal the correlations between Social Attitudes and Leadership Qualities. The results show a positive association between the Social Attitudes and Leadership Qualities among pupils at All Levels of Education (participant group).

The r-values of all the variables shown in the table are found to be significant at 0.001 level.

Thus it can be concluded that there is a Inter-relationship between Social Attitudes and Leadership Qualities among pupils at All Levels of Education (participated group).

(c) *All Levels of Education (Not Participant Group)*

The results pertaining to the relationships between Social Attitudes and the Leadership Qualities at All Levels of Education (non-participant group) are presented in the Table 3.3.4c.

The results presented in the Table 3.3.4c show the correlations between Social Attitudes and Leadership Qualities. The results show a positive association between the Social Attitudes and Leadership Qualities among pupils at All Levels of Education even in the case of the group that has not participated in Games & Sports.

The r-values of all the variables shown in the table are found to be significant at 0.001 level.

TABLE 3.3.4C

SHOWING THE RELATIONSHIP BETWEEN FORMATION OF SOCIAL ATTITUDES AND SCORES ON LEADERSHIP SCALE OF PUPILS (N = 345) AT ALL LEVELS OF EDUCATION (NON-PARTICIPANT GROUP)

Variable	*SA1*	*SA2*	*SA3*	*SAT*
LQ1	.4346**	.5355**	.3491**	.5345**
LQ2	.5806**	.5637**	.3810**	.6150**
LQ3	.6238*	.6535*	.5986**	.7549**
LQT	.6718*	.7163*	.5522**	.7826**

*** = Significant at .001 level*

Thus it can be concluded that even in the case of the group that has not participated in Games & Sports there is inter-relationship between Social Attitudes and Leadership Qualities developed among pupils at All Levels of Education.

3.3.5 DISCUSSIONS OF THE RESULTS

HYPOTHESIS-3

There will be Inter-relationship between the developments of Social Attitudes and Leadership Qualities among pupils at Various Levels of Education.

An abstract of the results presented in the Tables 3.3.1 to 3.3.4 is presented in the Table 3.3.5.1.

TABLE 3.3.5.1

SHOWING THE INTER-RELATIONSHIP BETWEEN THE VARIABLES I.E., SOCIAL ATTITUDES AND LEADERSHIP QUALITIES AT DIFFERENT LEVELS OF EDUCATION

Levels of Education	*r-Values of Social Attitudes & Leadership Qualities*
School	.8714**
Inter	.7775**
Degree	.8268**
All Levels of Education	.8310**

*** = Significant at .001 level*

The results presented in the Table 3.3.5.1 underscore a

consistently significant association between the two variables i.e., Social Attitudes and Leadership Qualities. The association is found to be significant at School Level, Inter Level, Degree Level and All Levels of Education.

It signifies that the Social Attitudes and Leadership Qualities develop simultaneously among students at Various Levels of Education.

Thus, a positive association between Social Attitudes and Leadership Qualities can be underscored.

3.4.0 COMPREHENSIVE DISCUSSION

The research under report intended to find out the association between Participation in Games & Sports and the development of concomitant attributes like Social Attitudes and Leadership Qualities among students at Various Levels of Education.

The results have highlighted a significant association between Participation in Games & Sports and development of leadership Qualities and formation of Social Attitudes. Even though these attributes develop with Age, the development of these attributes is significant in the case of those who Participate in Games & Sports.

The most significant finding of this research is the pre-eminents of the female sex in the development of Leadership Qualities and formation of Social Attitudes. These findings are corroborated by the findings of other researches. This spectacular result explodes the myth of masculine superiority in providing leadership. Generally an illusion was hugged all through that males are born leaders and females, followers. But the present findings dismantle such assumptions and demonstrates categorically the superior potential Leadership Abilities of women.

The Community Background does not seem to have any association with either the Leadership Qualities development or the Social Attitude formation and surprisingly one more significant finding of the research is lack of any significant association between the intensity of Participation in Games & Sports and Leadership Qualities development and Social Attitude formation. However, a deeper probe into this aspect is in order.

Finally, a strong association has been discerned between Social Attitudes and Leadership Qualities among students at Various Levels of Education.

Thus a greater provision of Games & Sports and better participation of the students in them are likely to develop both the Leadership Qualities and Social Attitudes.

Finally, the need for the women to get their due share in the Leadership roles in any sphere of human activity is to be highlighted. Infact, they appear to be are inherently better equipped than males for any Leadership role. The absence of women Leadership reflects the inability of the society to exploit the feminine leadership potentialities.

To that extent the human societies have pauperized themselves in a predominantly male Chaunistic Milieu.

4

SUMMARY, CONCLUSIONS AND SUGGESTIONS

4.0.0 INTRODUCTION

Education to be complete must have many dimensions relating to the multiple activities of the human being: the physical, the mental, the psychic, the emotional, the social and the spiritual. Usually, these phases of education succeed each other in a chronological order following the growth of the individual. This however, does not mean that one should replace another but that all must continue, supplementing each other, till the end of life.

Physical education is an essential part of an ideal educational system. For even a highest and completest education of the mind is not enough without the education of the body. But this aspects of education has been overlooked in many developing countries of the world including India. During the early years of this century, Sri Aurobindo pointed out the need for rigorous physical education.

Sri Aurobindo said that, we must organize physical education all over the country and train up the rising generation not only in the moral strength and courage for which Swedeshism has given us the materials, but in physical strength and courage and the habit of rising immediately and boldly to the height of even the greatest emergency.

Perfection, the true aim of all culture, if our seeking is for a total perfection of the being, the physical part of it cannot be left aside, for the body is the material basis, the body is the instrument which we have to use.

It is true that (in the past) the body has been regarded by spiritual seekers rather as an obstacle, as something to be overcome and discarded than as an instrument of spiritual perfection and a field of the spiritual change.

In fact, whatever type of body a man may have, he must accept as a starting point and bring out, by a concentrated effort and an appropriate training, the possibilities it contains and make it into a fit instrument for as perfect a life as possible.

Physical education takes care of the most vital aspect of human life which is the very basis of human existence and strength. It is the basis of a healthy, happy and harmonious life. It helps in the development of a well-balanced, well-integrated and vitally alive human personality. It inculcates the habits of self-discipline, self-control, toleration and forbearance, fortitude and spirit of sportsmanship that enable a person to withstand life's setbacks and shocks and brave all risks ad hazards with a smiling face and quiet graceful demeanour.

The concept of Physical Education has been broadened, as it should contribute not only to physical fitness but also to physical efficiency, mental alertness and the development of certain qualities like perseverance, team spirit, leadership, obedience to rules, moderation in victory and balance in defeat.

Leadership is a social phenomenon that exists every where throughout the world. Leadership arises only where there is a group with norms striving to reach a goal. Sprott (1960), said that 'Any one, who acts as model to others is often called a leader'. Every person who leads a group of people is called a leader. Leadership behaviour is in demand in various fields of life situations—social, political, cultural, educational, Sports & Games fields etc. Groups and organization of all sorts are liable to survive and succeed only under effective leadership. Good leadership is a prime necessity for the promotion and enhancement of physical education in educational institutions. An institution may possess all the other facilities but if there is no adequate leadership and supervision, it will be a ship without a captain, a factor without a manager, a temple without a priest, and a rest house without a care-taker. Leadership is therefore the mainspring for the proper conduct of the co-ordinated programmes of physical education in schools and colleges.

Similarly the development of desirable Social Attitudes or reshaping or undesirable attitudes is a gigantic task. It needs the co-operation of all the forces of environment. Parents, members of the society, teachers, schools and colleges and government authorities, all need to join hands in this task of desirable attitude formation in the young generation. Physical growth and development of the child plays a significant role in the development of social attitudes. Poor physical health, low vitality and undeveloped somatic structure is responsible for poor emotional and social adjustment and poor social adjustment inevitably exercises an important effect on the formation of attitudes in many different directions.

The main aim of education is to modify the behaviour of the child according to the needs and expectancy of the society. Behaviour is composed of so many attributes. One of these important attributes is attitude. One's behaviour, to a great extent depends upon one's attitude towards the things—idea, person, or object, in this environment. The entire personality and development of the child is influenced by the nature of this attitudes. Learning of a subject and acquisition of habits, interests and other psychophysical dispositions are all effected by his attitudes. According to Travers, 'An attitude is a readiness to respond in such a way that behaviour is given a certain direction'. Whittaker said, 'An attitude is a predisposition or readiness to respond in a pre-determined manner to relevant stimuli'.

According to Allport's definition an attitude has at least five aspects: (1) It is a mental and neural state, (2) of readiness to respond, (3) organized, (4) through experience, (5) exerting a directive and or influence on behaviour.

It is obvious that all students are not exposed to physical programmes in our educational institutions in equal measures.

But a few pupils are exposed to physical education programmes at school level alone, some at junior college level, and others at degree college level, while others are exposed throughout. Among these participants in physical education programmes some of them get the honour for national level participation, inter-varsity level participation, state level participation, Inter Schools and Junior College level participation and district level participation. So the participants in Games & Sports are exposed in different measures and at different stages of their education. Hence it is assumed that these differences in exposure would result in differences in Social Attitudes and Leadership Qualities developed.

4.1.0 SUMMARY

The present investigation was undertaken to find out the impact of Physical Education in developing Social Attitudes and Leadership Qualities among Participants and Non-Participants in Games & Sports at various levels of education.

The results have been furnished in the preceding chapter. This chapter presents the summaries of the previous three chapters in a nut shell. The conclusions and suggestions too are presented in this Chapter.

4.1.1 SUMMARY OF CHAPTER-I

In the First Chapter, the Reviews of the Research was presented, the Problem was focused, Significance of the study was discussed, Objectives were stated, Hypotheses were Formulated, operational definitions of the terms used were presented and the limitations of the study were specified.

4.1.1.1 REVIEWS OF PREVIOUS RESEARCHES

The review of research literature normally provides a backdrop to the research. It identifies the thrust areas needing immediate research attention. It even classifies researches done in each thrust area in its dimension-wise.

But the pioneering researches in the areas, where sufficient number of researches have not be conducted, find it difficult to classify and present the relevant researches to provide the needed backdrop.

The research under report is one such pioneeing work and so the researcher could not find out sufficient number of researches covering the sub-dimensions of the research.

So an attempt is made to cover only the main dimensions i.e., the Social Attitudes and Leadership Qualities. The researches reported in various research journals and in the books covering conceptual theory are reported in the following paras chronologically highlighting the sub-areas whenever possible.

Social Attitudes: Review of Researches

The researches covering Social Attitudes are classified under the following headings:

1. Identification of Variables/Dimensions.
2. Formation of Social Attitudes.
3. Social Attitudes in relation to other variables.

Identification of Variables/Dimensions

Probably no branch of social psychology has received more attention than this problem of social attitudes since 1920. It is looked upon as the central problem in social psychology. The net product of the socialization process is the formation of the attitudes among individuals. These attitudes are reflected by the words and deeds of an individual. In his interaction with other persons and groups, in his dealing with the cultural products, in all these we see the influence of the Social Attitudes. It is by forming the appropriate Social Attitudes that one become a Hindu or Muslim or a Christian: a Congressman or a Socialist, or a Communist: a Capitalist or a labour leader. Nobody is born one way or the other. He becomes one by the formation of the appropriate social attitudes. In the last 60 years, considerable work has been done regarding the formation, the change and the measurement of Social Attitudes. Studies have been made about the way in which groups of people, incline towards the church, the social, the political party, the economic programmes, war and such other institutions.

Attitude (Dictionary Meaning)

Attitude towards the community and other members of the community—H. Wallerstein.

Meaning of the term "Attitude"

Attitude represents an individual's feeling towards something for or against (in modern psychological literature).

Explaining the term "Social Attitude"

Social attitude plays an important part in directing man's social behaviour. Man's behaviour is influenced by his beliefs, assumptions and decisions. All these are affected by the individual attitude towards different persons and objects. They are the motivating forces. Hence, it is only natural for the individual's social behaviour to be influenced by these attitudes.

Definition of Attitude

Allport (1935): 'An attitude is a mental and neural set or readiness, exerting a directive dynamic influence upon the individual' response to all objects and situations with which it is related.

Formation of Attitudes

Social Attitudes are formed in relation to social stimulus situation. These attitudes may be formed towards persons or groups of persons or towards the products of human interaction. These products of human interaction may be material like the technological devices or they may be non-material like the values or norms of a group.

Attitudes are learned or acquired dispositions. How Social Attitudes are formed has been a question for investigation to the psychologists. Based on the opinion of Allport and Stanger had suggested that attitudes have formed under one of the following four conditions:

1. *The integration of experiences*: The accumulation and integration of a number of related experiences about an object gives birth to an attitude towards that object.

Attitude of Hindus towards Muslims or Vice Versa has been formed in this way.

2. *The differentiation of experiences*: When the new experiences are acquired, they are differentiated or segregated from the already acquired experiences. This segregation or differentiation may tend to make certain attitudes more specific.
3. *Taruma or dramatic experience*: Attitudes are formed with greater speed and intensity on account of the suddenly unusual, shocking and painful experiences. A shopkeeper whose shop has been burnt by the striking students may develop intensely negative attitudes towards all students.
4. *The adoption of the available attitudes*: A large number of attitudes are acquired in a ready made fashion by simply following suggestions or examples of friends, teachers, parents or adopting the mores and traditions of the community or society. Negative attitude of the children of Tamilnadu towards Hindi has been formed through the process of adoption, rather than as result of first had experience.

Attitudes are formed in the context of the individual's wants, information, group affiliation and responsibility development.

Social Attitudes in relation to other Variables

A child's attitudes towards authority figures is obviously an important element of socialization and determines much of his behaviour in school. Early experiences involving the child and his parents are responsible for the beginnings of this attitudes. A rebellious attitude towards authority figures (teacher, principal, leader and others) may spring from a conflict with someone in authority, usually a parent or parent substitute. Itkin (1955) in a study involving 400 students and their parents, found a very significant relationship (one per cent level) between both male and female students' attitudes towards the father figure and the father's acceptance-rejection of the child. This relationship was not the result of dominance of laxity of the parent but simply the kind of feeling between father and child. Another important element in the early development of a child's attitude towards adults is the satisfaction or dissatisfaction derived from the child's dependency upon parents, particularly the mother figure. Spitz and Ribble (1944) have contributed significantly to this subject. Their findings seem to be well expressed by Roudinesco (1952) in the remark that 'any separation from the family, and especially from the mother, is for a young child a painful and distressing experience which is not tolerable before he has acquired the concepts of time and space. Such an experience in children under three years of age usually brings a change in their relationship with adults'. Separation over a period of time accompanied by deprivation of needs is likely to produce an incapacity to achieve close and intimate human relationships. Koch (1955) in her study of 384 children five and six years of age, found that the child's attitude towards the teacher was strongly influenced by the following elements of the mother-child relationship.

1. Satisfying experiences with mother.
2. Mother's experiences and what she expected of the child.
3. Mother's attitude towards other child in the family.

Prabhat, Gurnam Singh (1973) made a comparative study of the Social Attitudes of the Physically Handicapped and normal children studying in secondary schools in Punjab.

He made the comparative study with the following objectives :

To verify whether Physically Handicapped and normal children show any differences in their Social Attitudes.

To study the direction of Social Attitudes of normal children.

To study the direction of Social Attitudes of Physically Handicapped children.

To determine the differences, if any, between the Social Attitudes of different types of Physically Handicapped children, specially visually impaired, crippled and speech defective ones.

To study the sources of Social Attitudes.

The researcher had picked-up 309 pairs of children studying in 8th, 9th and 10th classes in secondary schools of Punjab including two equal matched groups of Physically Handicapped and normal children covering an equal number from each class of the sample.

The findings of the study were as follows:

Both Physically Handicapped and normal children have positive attitudes in all the five areas i.e., Religion, Peers, School, Country and Family.

Physically Handicapped and normal children do not differ with respect to their attitudes towards religion.

The visually impaired children have a less positive attitude towards family as compared to the normal group of children.

The sources of attitudes of Physically Handicapped and normal children are the same.

Dhillon, G. K. (1979) : Conducted a comparative study of the personality characteristics, adjustments and motivation level of Non-participant and Participant children of secondary schools in physical activities.

The major objectives of the research were:

To study the differences on personality dimensions, school adjustment, achievement motivation and academic achievement between Participants and Non-participants in sports at district level.

The study was conducted on 800 students of secondary schools of Punjab.

The major findings of the study were as follows:

Participants are high on extraversion and neuroticism in comparison to Non-participants.

In all the spheres of school adjustment, academic matters, with school-mates, school-administration, teacher, self and over all school adjustment, participants are higher than non-participants.

Participants have more achievement motivation than Non-participants.

Among the Participants, Non-participants and the total

sample, overall school adjustment scores and academic achievement scores of female are higher than that of males.

Banga, U.S. (1982) : Studied the Impact of Teacher Training Programme in Physical Education on Physical Fitness, Personality, Adjustment and Motivity of Student Teachers.

The objectives of the study were:

To measure the changes in physical fitness, personality characteristics, adjustment and motivity in student teachers caused as a result of undergoing a one year training in Physical Education.

To identify the areas in the training programme in which improvement is needed.

The following findings were observed:

The training programme is a useful and a modifying experience for trainees and improves their personalities and physical fitness.

The impact is significant and positive for boys. The girls do not gain much in personality, adjustment, physical fitness and motivity.

The programme of training needs to be modified and enriched.

Male dominance in it has to be balanced and such elements which act negatively have to be eliminated and substituted with components which have positive effects.

Leadership Qualities: Review of Researches

The researches covering Leadership Qualities are classified under the following headings:

1. Leadershi—Identification of Variables
2. Development of Leadership
3. Theories of Leadership
4. Types of Leadership

Leadership—Identification of Variables

'The speed of the boss is the speed of the team'—Ralph Walso Emerson

Ralph Walso Emerson (1942) perceptively remarked: 'An institution is the lengthened shadow of one man'. History tells us that whenever a leader has achieved extraordinary success, he has gathered his team first—he has inspired them, set course, provided the momentum and steered them in profitable directions.

A leader is a person who directs, commands or heads a group, an organization or a nation. The word 'leader' has originated from 'Lord' which in the old Nordic language meant the course or path of a ship at area. The leader was the captain, who, in olden times, was usually the steersman and navigator as well.

Leadership—Dictionary Meaning

The exercise of authority in a social group; the quality or qualities upon which such exercise of authority depends, varying with the nature of the social group, and the circumstances in which leadership is displayed or established (Penguin Psychological Dictionary).

Explanation of the term

The word 'Leadership' is most talked about and the least understood phenomena in the world. By 'leadership' a majority of people bring to their mind a number of leaders who have had direct or indirect impact upon them and upon their world. While talking on leadership almost invariably the attributes and the methods of the famous leaders were discussed. These leaders may include individuals limelighting themselves in any area—moral, amoral or immoral; benefactors or malefactors of humanity; persons who regard human beings or reject them outrightly.

Various thinkers have defined the world leadership in a functional as well as behavioural manner. Terry (1960) writes that 'leadership is the activity of influencing people to strive willingly for group objectives'. Tannenbaunm et. al. (1961) define it as 'interpersonal influence exercised in a situation and directed through the communication process, towards the attainment of a specialized goal or goals'. Stogdill (1950) takes leadership as 'the process of influencing activities of an organized group in its efforts towards setting goal achievement'. These definitions are more concerned with the actions which are required by the group in various conditions if they are to achieve their goals. Leadership is the performance of those acts which help the group to achieve its preferred outcomes. The preferred outcomes naturally differ from situation to situation. There is an innumerable variety of situations calling for leadership but all these situations do comprise certain relations, in which leadership is exerted. Leadership and isolation are incompatible. While sitting by himself, a leader may feel loneliness but it is only through relationships and effective communication that he can exercise his leadership.

The statement by Cartwright and Zander (1968) needs mention here. To consider leadership consisting of 'such actions by group members as those which aid in setting group goals, moving the group towards its goals, improving the quality of the interactions among the members, building the cohesiveness of the group, and making resources available to the group. In principle, leadership may be performed by one or many members of the group.'

Definitions of Leadership

Sprott 'Any one, who acts as model to other is often called a leader'.

Kimball Young 'What is popularly called leadership is the more accurately to be discussed in terms of dominance'.

Cattell 'Leader is the person who creates the most effective change in group performance'.

The researcher has defined the term 'leadership' in the following lines:

'A person who is a good follower of himself is called a leader'.

Leadership Development

Leadership Development is a broad concept that includes but goes beyond teaching skills and enchancing career mobility.

While individuals must create opportunities to develop themselves, institutions must help them to do so by effectively managing human resources, by establishing a climate that encourages participation and innovation and by actively promoting leadership development.

Origin and development of Leadership

Various factors are responsible for the origin and development of leadership. Various social thinkers and sociologists have put forward their views in this regard. Some of them consider the origin of leadership as a matter of divine origin while others feel that it is the result of certain social phenomenon. The theories in regard to the origin and development of leadership as given by different sociologists and psychologists are enumerated below.

Origin and development of Leadership as given by psychoanalysists

Psycho-analysists have held out the view that for the origin of leadership, desire, sex feeling, failures, greedings, desire to acquired prestige, repression, family experiences and such other qualities are necessary. This school of the social thinkers is of the view that it is these psychological traits that contribute to the origin and development of leadership. They lay greater stress on 'feeling sex' and put forward the view that leader tries to sublime this desire by assuming the role of a leader. Several studies were carried on the basis of the theory, and the results arrived at by many psychologists corroborate that family quarrels, sex, depression, guilt feeling, power seeking, inferiority complex are responsible for leadership. These studies were carried by Lasswill (1965).

The does not mean that only unhealthy psychological traits are responsible for the origin and development of leadership.

Theories of Leadership

Various theories have been advanced on Leadership Behaviour. These theories can be classified into the following broad headings:

1. Interaction theory
2. Classical theory

3. Times theory
4. Psychoanalytic theory

Types of Leadership

Leadership is an ambiguous concept. Its exact meaning depends on the types of relationship that is established between the leader and the followers. Tricket has suggested classification in terms of (a) traditional, (b) situational and (c) behavioural approaches.

Stogdill (1948) reviewed 124 studies of the characteristics of leaders and found that an average person occupying the position of leadership had some qualities which exceeded an average member of his group to some degree. The qualities, characteristics and skills required in a leader are determined to a large extent by the demand to the situation in which he is to function. Intellectual fortitude and personal integrity are positively related to leadership in adult groups whereas there tends to be very little relationship to leadership with age, height or appearance. It seems clear that leadership cannot be discussed adequately apart from the situation in which it operates.

Halpin (1955) made a comparative study of the leader behaviour and leadership ideology of educational administrators and aircraft commanders. The results of this study revealed that both sample leaders were found to have low relationship between their belief in how they should behave and their behaviour as described by their group members. This study shows that the LBDQ can be successfully used in any situation to study leadership behaviour.

Moser (1959) undertook with regard to stages of leadership, in which he involved 12 superintendents and 24 principals of 12 school districts. The subjects answered the interview questions which were designed to stimulate their own leadership ability and that of others. In this study, Moster identified three styles of leadership: (i) the nomothetic dimension characterized by goal accomplishment in terms of the institution, (ii) the ideographic dimension characterized by behaviour of the individual self; (iii) the transactional dimensions characterized by elements of both nomothetic and idiographic. Among the findings, it was the principals emphasized idiographic behaviour in dealing with teachers, and nomothetic behaviour in their relations with the superintendents. Superintendents who professed nomothetic behaviour, indicated the highest level of personal satisfaction and were given the highest ratings by the principals. This study points out the different styles of leadership.

Mann (1959) found that inner personality is indeed a condition of leadership. Thus, people with high intelligence who are well adjusted personally and who tend towards extroversion are more likely than others to become leaders; also, to be popular in the group and to contribute positively to the group activity.

Lewis (1959) conducted a study to discover how 300 selected high school principals in 11 western states functioned in their offices. This study gives clear indication that a majority of the principals responding felt that they would be performing superior services if they spent a much larger percentage of their time and effort in such functions as evaluation and reorganization of curriculum, supervision of instruction, selecting competent staff members, managing the school building, including the testing programme and establishing good staff relationships.

Kumar, P. (1964) attempted a Personality Study of Student Leadership. The enquiry aimed at studying certain personality variables associated with student leadership. It was hypothesized that certain personality variables would be found significantly needed for the enactment of a leadership role in the situation under study; and that the perceptions of the two groups the leader and non-leader, would show an agreement as to the ideal and the perceived leadership qualities. It was also hypothesized that certain personal factors would show a significant relationship with the leadership.

The study was conducted on a sample of 50 student leaders and 50 non-leaders, Sinha's Self-analysis Form. Eysenck's Short Questionnaire, the Ascendance Submission Study, the Revised Adjustment Inventory Test for Rigidity and Ambiguity Tolerance and the Allport, Vernon Value Scale were used for collecting data. Chi-square, critical ration and correlation techniques were used for anlaying the data.

The findings were:

Age, caste and length of stay in the university were found significantly related to student leadership.

The leaders tended to be more anxious and more dominating than the non-leaders.

Extroversion, neuroticism, adjustment, rigidity and ambiguity-tolerance failed to give any relationship.

Leaders were higher on social and economic values, and lower on theoretical and religious values. Aesthetic and political values failed to discriminate significantly between the leaders and the non-leaders.

Leadership was ideally imaged as responsible, hard-working, social, honest and helping. But the actually perceived leadership image deviated greatly from the ideal. It was perceived as ambitious, emotional, social, dominating and tactful.

The inter-group analysis of the ideal and perceived leadership images failed to give a positively significant relationship. There was agreement that the student leaders did not possess qualities ideally required for the fulfilment of a leadership role in the given situation.

Deshpande S. (1983) attempted an Analytical Study of Leadership Qualities in Junior College Students in Vidarbha Region.

The main purpose of the study was to identify leadership qualities among junior college students in the Vidarbha region of Maharashtra State.

The sample consisted of 1046 boys and girls of class XI and XIII from 22 junior colleges in eight district of Vidarbha. The tools used for the study were : (i) questionnaire for the students, (ii) interview schedule for the teachers, and (iii) sociometric scale of selecting the leaders. Statistical techniques were used for (i) ranking leadership qualities percentage-wise, (ii) for calculating the coefficient of correlation, and (iii) for preparing diagrams and graphs.

The following were some of the major findings of the study:

Twenty-four leadership qualities were identified in the junior college students.

There was no relationship between parents education and student leadership qualities.

There was no relationship between parents' political or social status and student leadership qualities.

There was no significant relationship between parents' economic status and student leadership qualities.

There was no significant relationship between parents' occupation and students leadership qualities.

The student leaders mentioned reading and games as their hobbies.

The student leaders had good and cheerful nature, honesty, good conduct, punctual cooperativeness, industriousness and good study habits, in the opinion of the lecturers.

The student leaders possessed self-confidence, discipline, cooperativeness, love for knowledge and industry.

The student leaders liked doing social work, social service and other social activities in the course of their college career.

Researchable Areas

Various research studies show that leadership remains comparatively an ignored area in educational research in India. Researchers have done very little to unfold the mysteries of leadership and to know the various variables related to it.

Leadership may be researched in the context of the following thrust areas:

(a) Leadership and its various dimensions—Do the emerging situations demand revised dimensions of leadership behaviour?

(b) Leadership and organizational health.

(c) Leadership and staff morale.

(d) Leadership and its various styles.

(e) Training of leaders at various levels.

(f) Leadership and its correlates like age, sex, areas of adjustment, teaching experience and administrative experience.

(g) Leaderships and its various models.

(h) Moral leadership.

(i) Leadership among teachers, students and non-teaching employees.

(j) Leadership and institutional planning.

(k) Role performance of leaders at various levels.

(l) Leadership behaviour and systems approach.

4.1.1.2 THE PROBLEM

The present research was designed to study the impact of Physical Education (Participation in Games & Sports) in the formation of Social Attitude and development of Leadership Qualities. It further studied, the inter-relationship between these two variables.

4.1.1.3 STATEMENT OF THE PROBLEM

The study has been undertaken to find out the answer to the following posers:

1. Is there any association between physical education programmes offered (Participation in Games & Sports) and the formation of Social Attitudes?
2. Is there any association between physical education programmes offered (Participation in Games & Sports) and development of Leadership Qualities?
3. Is there any inter-relationship between the formation of Social Attitudes and the development of Leadership Qualities?

4.1.1.4 SIGNIFICANCE OF THE STUDY

Social Attitudes and the Leadership Qualities are the attributes that are basic to the development of any society, particularly when the society is a developing one.

The most striking feature of the present Indian Scenario is the crisis of Leadership. During the freedom struggle the movement which was a sustained one and fought on high moral grounds, had thrown out world class leadership—a leadership which any country in any era could be proud of. Each leader was excelling the other in personal integrity, self negation, commitment to the society—nay, humanity as such. Leaders like Mahatma Gandhi and Jawaharlal Nehru, Swami Vivekananda and Aurabindo, Raja Rammohan Roy and Rabindranath Tagore etc. etc., guided the destinies of the nation. They were the models for emulations for the younger generation.

But alas! presently there appears to be none who could be regarded as a father figure, or a model for emulation or a friendly philosopher who can extricate one from the morass and guide in the right direction.

Thus the crisis in Leadership highlights the need for the systematic grooming and training of the leaders particularly in the absence of a movement.

Likewise, people seem to become exceedingly selfish, self-centered, asocial and sometimes anti-social getting isolated from the social moorings. A need is there to sensitise the future citizens towards the social needs and integrating them deep with the society so that an individual feels that he is a part of the society; wherein his future is predicted on the development of the society.

How to develop the Leadership Qualities and Social Attitudes?

One possible way of building the Leadership Qualities and Social Attitudes in men and women is by providing situation where Leadership attributes and Social Attitudes get formed and developed. It is possible that a situation of Games & Sports provides the needs and milieu for the development of the said attributes.

But it is hypothetical that a situation of a Games & Sports develops in the participants the attributes of Leadership Qualities and Social Attitudes. It is to be established to what extent the Leadership Qualities and Social Attitudes get formed and developed through Games & Sports activities. If any research highlights the connection between Games & Sports and Leadership Qualities and Social Attitudes, we need to include in our school agenda the Games & Sports Activities which inter-alia develop the Leadership Qualities and Social Attitudes. The research findings can demand a pride of place for the Games & Sports in such a situation.

Thus the findings of the research, if they go on the expected lines can transform the educational system by altering the existing scheme of priorities by putting a premium on Games & Sports Activities.

4.1.1.5 OBJECTIVES OF THE STUDY

Now the present study seeks to work with the following objectives:

1. To find out the association between the levels of participation of pupils in Games & Sports and Social Attitudes formed at various levels of education i.e., school, junior college and degree level.
2. To find out the association between the levels of participation of pupils in Games & Sports and leadership qualities formed at various levels of education i.e., school, junior college and degree level.
3. To find out the inter-relationship between the developments of social attitudes and leadership qualities at various levels of education.

4.1.1.6 HYPOTHESES

1. There will be a positive association between the participation in Games & Sports, and Social Attitudes formed.
2. There will be a positive association between the participation in Games & Sports, and Leadership Qualities formed.
3. There will be a inter-relationship between the developments of social attitudes and leadership qualities formed among pupils at various levels of education.

4.1.1.7 OPERATIONAL DEFINITIONS

The definitions of the terms used are given in the following paras:

1. Participants in Games & Sports (PAG)

The students who had participated in the Games & Sports

at school level, junior college level and degree level are named as participants in Games & Sports.

2. Non-Participants in Games & Sports (NPAG)

The students who had not participated in the Games & Sports at school level, junior college level and degree level are named as Non-participants in Games & Sports.

3. Social Attitudes

'An Attitude is one's behaviour towards the community or society and other members of the community or society'. (given by the researcher).

4. Leadership Qualities

'A person who is a good follower of himself is called a leader'. (given by the researcher).

4.1.1.8 LIMITATIONS OF THE STUDY

This study was undertaken in schools, colleges, play fields of district sport centres of various towns i.e., Warangal, Hyderabad, Adilabad, Khammam and Karimnagar.

The sample had been drawn from the participants in Games & Sports and non-participants in Games & Sports from the different levels of education i.e., school, junior college and degree college in the districts, Warangal, Hyderabad, Khammam, Tirupati, Ananthapur, Rajahmundry, Karimnagar and Adilabad.

For the sake of convenience of the data collection, the Physical Education Common Entrance Test (PECET)-92 conducted at different centres of State like, Warangal, Rajahmundry, Ananthapur, Tirupathi was considered for the study as the researcher faces a hard time to trace the participants in Games & Sports especially at Inter Level. The Inter completed students appearing for the PE-CET for admission into Under Graduate Diploma (UGD) course in Physical Education and the Degree completed students appearing for the B. PEd. Entrance Test at PE-CET-95 were selected were as participants in Games & Sports.

The non-participants in Games & Sports at School, Junior College and Degree College level from the educational institutions of Warangal, Hyderabad, Karimnagar and Khammam were considered for present study.

4.1.2 SUMMARY RELATED TO CHAPTER-II

The methodology adopted for the study is presented in the Chapter-II.

In this chapter the design of the study is shown, sample of the study discussed, tools used presented, data collection procedure given and the statistical techniques used specified.

4.1.2.1 DESIGN OF THE STUDY

A schematic representation of the design of the investigation carried out is given in the Figure 4.1.2.1.

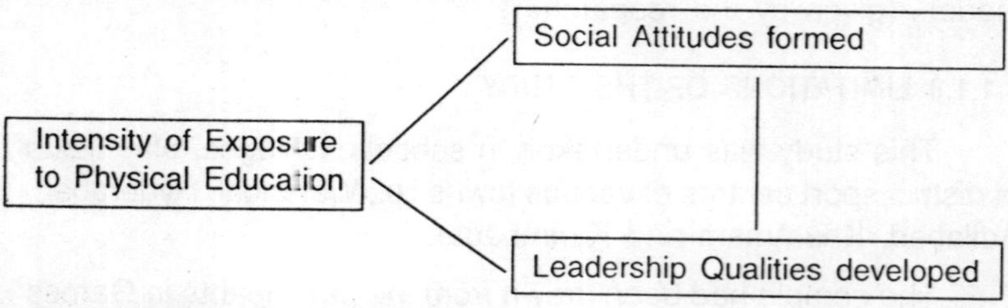

4.1.2.2 SAMPLE OF THE STUDY

A sample of 690 pupils, participants in Games & Sports and non-participants in Games & Sports studying in schools, junior colleges and degree colleges was selected for the study.

TABLE 4.1.2.2

SHOWING THE SAMPLE EDUCATIONAL LEVEL-WISE OF PARTICIPANTS AND NON-PARTICIPANTS IN GAMES & SPORTS AT DIFFERENT LEVELS OF EDUCATION

Institutional level	*Participants in Games & Sports*	*Non-Participants in Games & Sports*	*Total Population*
School	125	125	250
Junior Colleges	110	110	220
Degree Colleges	110	110	220
Total at three levels of Education	345	345	690

The sample considered for the study was Education Level-wise, Community Background-wise, Age-wise among participants in Games & Sports and Non-Participants in Games & Sports.

Table 4.1.2.2 reveals that in all the total sample consisted of 690 pupils. Out of which 345 pupils were participants in Games & Sports and 345 pupils non-participants in Games & Sports, studying at three levels of education i.e., School, Junior College and Degree College.

4.1.2.3 TOOLS USED

Since the research involved the assessment of both Social Attitudes and Leadership Qualities among students at various levels of education, the following tree tools were required to measure the impact of the physical education in the development of Social Attitude and Leadership Qualities.

(i) Tool to measure the intensity of participation of pupils in Games & Sports.

(ii) Tool to measure Social Attitudes at various levels of Education.

(iii) Tool to measure Leadership Qualities at various levels of Education.

The investigator had constructed and standardized these three tools as he could not get the ready-made tools required to measure these two variables.

Particularly the tools designed to measure the Social Attitudes and Leadership Qualities have been standardized with utmost care going through the processes of standardising the tools scientifically. The delicate nuances of Scientific research have been scrupulously observed.

4.1.2.3A TOOL TO MEASURE THE INTENSITY OF PARTICIPATION OF PUPILS IN GAMES & SPORTS

The researcher had classified the students studying in schools, junior colleges and degree colleges into two groups i.e., (1) Participants in Games & Sports and (2) Non-Participants in Games & Sports.

The pupils who have never participated in Games & Sports at school, junior college and degree college levels were identified as non-participants.

The pupils who have participated in Games & Sports at (1) school level, (2) school and junior college level, (3) school, junior college and degree college level, (4) junior college level, (5) junior college and degree college level and (6) degree college level only were identified as participants.

The researcher has approached four experts in the field of physical education to identify the levels of participation in Games & Sports. The weightage of marks given by the four subject experts (the scores sheets are shown in the appendix) were taken into consideration by the researcher and the average weightage of marks computed. The same are shown in the Table 4.1.2.3.

TABLE 4.1.2.3

SHOWING THE WEIGHTAGE OF MARKS IN ASSESSING THE PARTICIPATION OF GAMES & SPORTS AT VARIOUS LEVELS OF EDUCATION

Educational level	*Weightage of marks of participants at*			
	School/College level	*District level*	*State level*	*National level*
School	1.00(1.00)	3.50(4.00)	7.00(7.00)	10.25(10.00)
Junior College	1.75(2.00)	4.50(5.00)	8.75(9.00)	12.25(12.00)
Degree College	2.75(3.00)	5.50(6.00)	10.75(11.00)	15.75(16.00)

While computing the data for the average marks, the fractional number less than 0.5 was reduced to lower round figure and more than 0.5 was rounded off to higher round figures for the sake of easy calculations.

The Table 4.1.2.3 reveals the average weightages of marks assigned by the four experts in the field of physical education. The school students who has participated at school level were given 1 mark, district level-4 marks, state level-7 marks and at the national level-10 marks. The Inter students who have participated at junior college level were given 2 marks, district level 5 marks, state level 9 marks and national level 12 marks. And the degree level students who had participated at degree college level were given 3 marks, district level 6 marks, state level 11 marks, and national level 16 marks.

Thus the tool to measure the intensity of participation of pupils in Games & Sports was finalized according to the weightages of marks given by the experts in the field of physical education.

4.1.2.3B TOOL TO MEASURE SOCIAL ATTITUDES AND LEADERSHIP QUALITIES

The Participation of pupils in Games & Sports at various levels of education and the formation of Social Attitudes and the development Leadership Qualities is supposed to be measured by these said tools.

The researcher could not find any read made scales of Social Attitude and Leadership Qualities hence, he made an attempt to construct the fresh tools to measure these two variables.

Initially the investigator identified 50 Social Attitudes dimensions and 54 Leadership Qualities dimensions suggested by various theoreticians and researchers from the fields of Psychology, Sociology and Education.

These dimensions were subjected to scrutiny by the nine experts in the concerned subjects and they suggested the following dimensions for these two variables viz., Social Attitudes and Leadership Qualities.

DIMENSIONS OF LEADERSHIP QUALITIES & SOCIAL ATTITUDES

01. Perseverance
02. Self-reliance
03. Tactful and understanding
04. Technical mastery
05. Creative ability
06. Intellectual penetration
07. Communicable
08. Trained body abounding in vitality
09. Administrative ability
10. See a little further ahead of his followers
11. Set the pace

12. Good judgment
13. Inspiring fellow players to do their best
14. Reciprocal—reinforcement
15. Truthful
16. Adaptable
17. Sense of humor
18. Enthusiastic
19. Optimistic
20. Balance in defeat
21. Emotional stability
22. Faith
23. Integrity
24. Sensitive to others and feelings
25. Tough-mindedness
26. Dominant/Authoritative
27. Extrovert Tendency
28. Consistency
29. Sincere
30. Fair-mindedness
31. Moral-outlook
32. Carefulness
33. Courtesy
34. Model to others
35. Environmental exposure
36. Dependable
37. Good follower of himself
38. Capacity to lead the group democratically (Democratic approach)
39. Cooperation
40. Supportive to his members
41. Emotional control

42. Cheerful nature
43. Self-confidence
44. Industrious
45. Honesty
46. Punctuality and regularity
47. Imagination
48. Social Service
49. Tolerance
50. Habits
51. Self-control
52. Self-discipline
53. Consideration for others
54. Social responsibility
55. Humanism and Respect
56. Behaviour as a player in a sport situation
57. Social adjustment
58. Fortitude
59. Sympathetic and friendly a attitude and avoid undue familiarity
60. Impartiality
61. Time-Pursuit
62. Resourcefulness
63. Respect for manual work
64. Physical growth
65. Concentration
66. Sense of accomplishment
67. Alertness
68. Lover of work
69. Desire of name and fame
70. Brotherhood
71. Harmonious life

72. Open-mindedness
73. Balance
74. Courage of his convictions
75. Social awareness
76. Personality

The dimensions listed from 1 to 52 were considered for Leadership Qualities and the dimensions listed from 39 to 76 were considered for Social Attitudes. The dimensions from 39 to 52 were the Common Questions for these two variables.

As suggested by the subject experts the dimensions of Social Attitudes were divided into the following three clusters:

Cluster-I SA1-Attitude to People

53. Consideration for others
54. Social Responsibility
55. Humanism and Respect
56. Behaviour as a player in a sports situation
57. Social adjustment
58. Fortitude
59. Sympathetic and friendly attitude and avoid undue familiarity
60. Impracticality
39. Co-operation
40. Supporting to his members
41. Emotional control
42. Cheerful nature

Cluster-II SA2-Attitude to Work

61. Time Pursuit
62. Resourcefulness
63. Respect for manual work
64. Physical growth
65. Concentration

66. Sense of accomplishment
67. Alertness
68. Lover of work
69. Desire of name and fame
43. Self-Confidence
44. Industrious
45. Honesty
46. Punctuality & Regularity
47. Imagination

Cluster-III SA3-General Life Attitudes

70. Brotherhood
71. Harmonious life
72. Open-mindedness
73. Balance
74. Courage of his convictions
75. Social awareness
76. Personality
48. Social Service
49. Tolerance
50. Habits
51. Self-control
52. Self-discipline

As suggested by the subject experts the dimensions of Leadership Qualities were divided into the following three clusters:

Cluster-I LQ1-Leadership Ability

01. Perseverance
02. Self-Reliance
03. Tactful & Understanding
04. Technical Mastery

05. Creative Ability
06. Intellectual Penetration
07. Communicable
08. Trained body abounding in vitality
09. Administrative ability
10. See a little further ahead of his followers
11. Set the pace
12. Good Judgement
13. Inspiring fellow players to do their best
14. Reciprocal - Reinforcement
44. Industries
47. Imagination

Cluster-II LQ2-Leadership Temperamental

15. Truthful
16. Adaptable
17. Sense of humour
18. Enthusiastic
19. Optimistic
20. Balance in defeat
21. Emotional stability
22. Faith
23. Integrity
24. Sensitive of others and feelings
25. Tough—mindedness
26. Dominant & Authoritative
41. Emotional control
42. Cheerful nature
43. Self-Confidence
45. Honesty

Cluster-III LQ3-Leadership Behavioural

27. Extrovert Tendency
28. Consistency.
29. Sincere
30. Fair-Mindedness
31. Moral outlook
32. Carefulness
33. Courtesy
34. Model to others
35. Environmental Exposure
36. Dependable
37. Good follower of himself
38. Capacity to lead the group democratically (Democratic approach)
39. Co-operation
40. Supportive to his members
46. Punctuality and Regularity
48. Social Service
49. Tolerance
50. Habits
51. Self-control
52. Self-discipline

The investigator with help of the supervisor and a Professor of Psychology from Osmania University had prepared the statements for the dimensions listed on the five point scale (Strongly agree, Agree, Undecided, Disagree and Strong dis-agree) (see annexure).

These 76 statements (including Social Attitudes and Leadership Qualities) were scientifically pruned by the subject experts in the fields of Sociology, Psychology and Education from different Universities like, Osmania University, Andhra University, S.V. University and from Kakatiya University, an English Professor has gone through the statements for trimming of language.

All these statements finally figured in these two scales and was translated into Telugu language by the experts in Telugu.

To test the reliability of scale the pilot study was conducted on 75 students of Participants and Non-participants in Games & Sport at School, Intermediate and Degree level.

The test re-test yielded significant results covering reliability. The results of the test and retest were significant at 1% level of significance.

Thus, the scale constructed for the study was standardized scientifically.

4.1.2.4 DATA COLLECTION PROCEDURE

A total of 690 students (345 Participants, 345 Non-participants in Games & Sports) from Schools, Junior Colleges, Degree Colleges and play fields of different sport centres of Warangal, Hyderabad, Karimnagar, Khammam, Adilabad were considered for the study.

The investigator had faced a hard time in tracing the participants in Games & Sports especially at inter level.

Hence, the researcher had considered the Intermediate completed students appearing for the under-graduate diploma (UGD) course entrance test and the degree completed students appearing for the B.P.Ed. entrance test at Physical Education Common Entrance Test PECET-95 conducted at different centres of State like, Warangal, Rajahmundry, Ananthapur and Tirupati. The scale consisting of both Social Attitudes and Leadership Qualities in a jumbled form (see appendix) with 76 statements (1-52 Leadership Qualities statements, 36-76 Social Attitude Students and 39-52 Common Questions) was used for the data collection. The students asked to give their opinion on five point scale (Strongly Agree, Agree, Undecided, Disagree and Strongly Disagree).

4.1.2.5 STATISTICAL TECHNIQUES USED

The present study sought to find out the relationship between various variables as shown in the following paras:

1. The study sought to find out the significance of difference

of Leadership Qualities developed at various levels of education between participants and non-participants in Games & Sports.

2. The study carried out to find out the significance of difference of Leadership Qualities developed at various levels of education between participants and non-participants in Games & Sports.
3. The relationship between the measure of the Social Attitudes formed at various levels of education and the measure of the Leadership Qualities developed at various levels of education.

To test the above said relations the investigator computed the various **co-efficient of correlations**, and test the significance of difference of any between the variables that are put forth in the study. **The means and standard deviations** of Social Attitudes and Leadership Qualities developed among participants and non-participants and the **t-test** were computed between the participants and non-participants at various levels of education. To find out the inter-relationship between these two variables i.e., Social Attitudes and Leadership Qualities the co-efficient of correlations were computed.

4.1.3.0 SUMMARY RELATED TO CHAPTER-III

Previous chapters were devoted for the presentation of review of literature, for focusing the problem, for the discussion of significance of the study, for the formulation of objectives and hypotheses, for laying out the design of the study, for the construction of tools (Social Attitude Tool, Leadership Qualities Tool and Participation in Games & Sports Tool) and for the selection of the methods of sampling and procedure adopted for data collection and analysis.

The present chapter discusses the results relating to the levels of participation in Games & Sports and their association with the formation of Social Attitudes and the development of Leadership Qualities.

It has been specified that the main objectives of the research under report were to find out the association between the following pairs of variables:

(i) Participation in Games & Sports and formation of Social Attitudes,

(ii) Participation in Games & Sports and development of Leadership Qualities, and

(iii) Interrelationship between the formation of Social Attitudes and the development of leadership qualities among students at various levels of education.

4.1.3.1 PARTICIPATION IN GAMES & SPORTS AND FORMATION OF SOCIAL ATTITUDES

HYPOTHESIS-I

'There will be a positive association between the participation of pupils in Games & Sports and Social Attitudes formed.'

The participation of pupils in Games & Sports at three levels of education i.e., School level, Inter level and Degree level was considered separately and cumulatively and its association with Social Attitude formation was underscored.

(a) *School Level*

The results pertaining to the participation of pupils in Games & Sports at School level and their scores on Social Attitude Scale are presented in the Table 4.1.3.1(A).

TABLE 4.1.3.1 (A)

SHOWING THE SIGNIFICANCE OF DIFFERENCE IN SOCIAL ATTITUDES AMONG PARTICIPANTS (PAG) AND NON-PARTICIPANTS (NPAG) IN GAMES & SPORTS AT SCHOOL LEVEL

Variable	*PAG (n=125)*		*NPAG (n=125)*		*t-value*	*p-value*
	Mean	*SD*	*Mean*	*SD*		
SA1	48.31	5.86	46.06	4.57	3.38	.001*
SA2	55.89	6.42	53.36	5.36	3.39	.001*
SA3	47.50	5.83	45.77	4.47	2.63	.009*
SAT	151.71	16.26	145.20	11.86	3.61	.000*

* *Significant at .05 level*

(Social attitudes are measured in terms of three categories i.e., SA1 = Attitude to people; SA2 = Attitude to work; and SA3 = General Life attitudes).

Even the totals - SAT of these three segments are presented in the said table.

The results presented in the Table 4.1.3.1(A) show the scores on Social Attitude scale. The results yield a significant difference in Social Attitudes of participants in Games & Sports and non-participants in Games & Sports at School Level.

The p-values of all these segments of the Social Attitude variable are found to be significant at 0.05 level (The p-value shown against each segment in the table is lesser than the significant level i.e., 0.05 level).

Thus it can be concluded that the participation of pupils in Games & Sports at School Level develops the Social Attitudes in a significant measure.

(b) ***Inter Level***

The results pertaining to the pupils who participate in Games & Sports at Inter Level and their scores on Social Attitude scale are presented in the Table 4.1.3.1(B).

TABLE 4.1.3.1(B)

SHOWING THE SIGNIFICANCE OF DIFFERENCE IN SOCIAL ATTITUDES AMONG PARTICIPANTS (PAG) AND NON-PARTICIPANTS (NPAG) IN GAMES & SPORTS AT INTER LEVEL

Variable	*PAG (n=110)*		*NPAG (n=110)*		*t-value*	*p-value*
	Mean	*SD*	*Mean*	*SD*		
SA1	47.60	4.76	44.90	4.84	4.15	.000*
SA2	54.38	5.50	52.36	4.73	2.92	.004*
SA3	46.18	5.47	44.69	4.81	2.15	.033*
SAT	148.16	13.82	141.96	11.83	3.57	.000*

** Significant at .05 level*

The results presented in the Table 4.1.3.1(B) reveal the scores on Social Attitude scale. The results show a significant different in Social Attitudes between the participants in Games & Sports and non-participants in Games & Sports at Inter Level.

The results reveal significant difference in Social Attitudes in total as well as in segments between participants and non participants in Games & Sports. The p-values of all these segments of the Social Attitude variable are found to be significant at 0.05 level.

Thus it can be concluded that the participation of pupils in Games & Sports at Inter Level develops the Social Attitudes in a significant measure.

(c) *Degree Level*

The results pertaining to the participation in Games & Sports at Degree Level and their scores on Social Attitudes scale are presented in the Table 4.1.3.1(C).

TABLE 4.1.3.1(C)
SHOWING THE SIGNIFICANCE OF DIFFERENCE IN SOCIAL ATTITUDES AMONG PARTICIPANTS (PAG) AND NON-PARTICIPANTS (NPAG) IN GAMES & SPORTS AT DEGREE LEVEL

Variable	*PAG (n=110)*		*NPAG (n=110)*		*t-value*	*p-value*
	Mean	*SD*	*Mean*	*SD*		
SA1	46.56	4.73	46.10	4.85	0.72	.474
SA2	52.56	5.50	51.96	6.05	0.77	.443
SA3	43.61	5.55	43.57	4.97	0.06	.949
SAT	142.74	13.22	141.63	13.42	0.62	.538

Significant Level is .05

The results presented in the Table 4.1.3.1(C) reveal the scores on Social Attitude scale. The results do not show any significant difference in Social Attitudes between the participants in Games & Sports and non-participants in Games & Sports at Degree Level.

The p-values of all these segments of the Social Attitude variable are not found to be significant at 0.05 level (the p-values shown against each segment in the table is higher than the significant level).

Thus it can be concluded that the participation of pupils in Games & Sports at Degree Level does not develop Social Attitudes in a significant measure.

(d) *All Levels of Education*

The results pertaining to the participation of pupils in Games & Sports at all Levels of Education and their scores on Social Attitude scale are presented in the Table 4.1.3.1(D).

TABLE 4.1.3.1(D)

SHOWING THE SIGNIFICANCE OF DIFFERENCE IN SOCIAL ATTITUDES AMONG PARTICIPANTS (PAG) AND NON-PARTICIPANTS (NPAG) IN GAMES & SPORTS AT ALL LEVELS OF EDUCATION

Variable	*PAG (n=345)*		*NPAG (n=345)*		*t-value*	*p-value*
	Mean	*SD*	*Mean*	*SD*		
SA1	47.52	5.21	45.70	4.76	4.78	.000*
SA2	54.35	5.99	52.60	5.41	4.03	.000*
SA3	45.84	5.84	44.72	4.82	2.74	.006*
SAT	147.72	15.00	143.03	12.44	4.47	.000*

** = Significant at .05 level*

The results presented in the Table 4.1.3.1(D) reveal the scores on Social Attitudes scale. The results show a significant difference between the participants in Games & Sports and non-participants in Games & Sports at All Levels of Education.

The results reveal significant difference in Social Attitudes in total as well as in three segments between participants and non-participants in Games & Sports. The computed p-values of these segments of Social Attitude variable are found to be significant at 0.05 level.

Thus it can be concluded that the participation of pupils in Games & Sports at All Levels of Education generally develops the Social Attitudes in a significant measure.

4.1.3.1 DISCUSSION OF THE RESULTS

The results pertaining to the Social Attitude formation in relation to Levels of Education, Sex, Community Background, Age and intensity of participation in Games & Sports have been furnished. In the following paras the discussion covering the said results is presented under 4.1.3.1(A) to 4.1.3.1(D). The relevant results are furnished in abstract forms.

(a) Educational Level and Attitude Formation

Abstracts of the resulted presented in the Tables 3.1.1 to 3.1.4 showing the association between education levels and attitude formation were presented in the Table 4.1.3.1.1(A).

TABLE 4.1.3.1.1(A)

SHOWING THE P-VALUES OF PARTICIPANTS IN GAMES & SPORTS (PAG) AND NON-PARTICIPANTS IN GAMES & SPORTS (NPAG) AND THEIR FORMATION OF SOCIAL ATTITUDES WITH REFERENCE TO EDUCATIONAL LEVELS

Education Level	*School*	*Inter*	*Degree*	*All level of Education*
PAG & NPAG	.000*	.000*	.538	.000*

** = Significant at 0.05 level*

The result furnished in the Table 4.1.3.1.1(A) cover the significance of difference in Social Attitudes formed between the Participants in Games & Sports and Non-participants in Games & Sports at School, Inter, Degree and At All Levels of Education.

It is found that the differences in Social Attitudes formed at School, Inter and at All Levels of Education are significant at 0.05 level. It is only at the degree level the differences in the Social Attitude formed are not found to be significant.

It can be concluded that the Social Attitudes get formed significantly during the School and Intermediate level and not so much at the degree level. The over all differences in Social Attitudes when taken into consideration cumulatively throughout the period of education concluding with the degree level are found to be significant; the participants in Games & Sports scoring higher on the scale of Social Attitude than the Non-participants in Games & Sports. Thus it can be safely concluded that by and large the Social Attitudes get formed when the pupils participate in Games & Sports.

The review of related researches presented under the caption does not throw any light on this aspect as no researches measuring the association between the participants in Games & Sports at various levels of education and Social Attitude formation are recorded.

Thus it can be concluded that the research under report is a pioneering work undertaken which underscores a significant relationship between the participation in Games & Sports at various levels of education and Social Attitude formation.

(b) Sex and Attitude Formation

Under sex caption three categories were identified, they are:

1. Male and Female participants in Games & Sports.
2. Male and Female non-participants in Games & Sports.
3. Male and Female Total Population.

Abstract of the results presented in the Tables 3.1.1.1 to 3.1.4.3 showing the association between Sex and Social Attitude formation were presented in the Table 4.1.3.1.1(B).

TABLE 4.1.3.1.1(B)

SHOWING THE P-VALUES OF PARTICIPANTS IN GAMES & SPORTS (PAG) AND NON-PARTICIPANTS IN GAMES & SPORTS (NPAG) AND THEIR FORMATION OF SOCIAL ATTITUDES WITH REFERENCE TO SEX OF THE PUPILS

Sex	*School*	*Inter*	*Degree*	*All levels of* Education
Male & Female PAG	.106(NS)	.000*	.020*	.009*
Male & Female NPAG	.000*	.407(NS)	.803(NS)	.000*
Male & Female Total	.120(NS)	.003*	.478(NS)	.001*

** = Significant at 0.05 level; NS = Not Significant*

The results furnished in the Table 4.1.3.1.1(B) show the significance of difference in Social Attitudes formed between Male and Female participants in Games & Sports and non-participants in Games & Sports separately at School, Inter, Degree and at All Levels of Education.

The results clearly reveal that among participants in Games & Sports, the male participants at Inter, Degree and at All Levels of Education have shown greater development of Social Attitudes formation when compare to female participants in Games & Sports. But it is only at their early years of study i.e., at School Level the Social Attitude formation is not much as per the results.

Similarly in the case of non-participants in Games & Sports the formation of Social Attitude is far better at an early age i.e., at School Level but as these non-participants go higher up in studies, the development of Social Attitudes decreases.

Finally, it is concluded that among the non-participants in Games & Sports, the Social Attitudes form rapidly and the same level of growth is not recorded at higher levels of education.

(c) Community Background And Attitude Formation

Like sex, the Community Background is also studied under three headings, viz.,

1. Rural and Urban among participants in Games & Sports.
2. Rural and Urban among non-participants in Games & Sports.
3. Rural and Urban, Total Population.

Abstract of the results presented in the Tables 3.1.1.4 to 3.1.4.6 showing the association between Community Background and Social Attitude formation are presented in the Table 4.1.3.1.1(C).

TABLE 4.1.3.1.1(C)

SHOWING THE P-VALUES OF PARTICIPANTS IN GAMES & SPORTS (PAG) AND NON-PARTICIPANTS IN GAMES & SPORTS (NPAG) AND THEIR FORMATION OF SOCIAL ATTITUDES WITH REFERENCE TO COMMUNITY BACKGROUND OF THE PUPILS

Community Background	*School*	*Inter*	*Degree*	*All level of Education*
Rural & Urban PAG	.186(NS)	.103(NS)	.523(NS)	.882(NS)
Rural & Urban NPAG	.761(NS)	.591(NS)	.238(NS)	.394(NS)
Rural & Urban Total	.546(NS)	.130(NS)	.197(NS)	.598(NS)

NS = Not Significant

The results presented in the Table 4.1.3.1.1(C) clearly indicate that the community background variable has got no impact of its own on Social Attitude formation at any level of education on participants and non-participants in Games & Sports.

Thus it can be concluded that the community background of pupils does not influence development in the formation of Social Attitudes.

(d) Age And Attitude Formation

One of the objectives of the research was to find out the association between Age and Social Attitude formation. Such an association was sought to be found covering the cases of the participants in Games & Sports and non-participants in Games & Sports.

As abstract of the results presented in the Tables 3.1.4.7 to 3.1.4.9 is presented in the following Table 4.1.3.1.1(D).

TABLE 4.1.3.1.1(D)

SHOWING THE ABSTRACT OF THE RESULTS PRESENTED IN THE TABLES 3.1.4.7 TO 3.1.4.9 AND THE ASSOCIATION BETWEEN AGE AND SOCIAL ATTITUDE FORMATION

Variable	*AGE*		
	Participants in Games & Sports	*Non-Participants in Games & Sports*	*Total Population*
SA1 - Attitude to People	.1566*	.0334***	.0741(NS)
SA2 - Attitude to Work	.2325**	.1501*	.1702**
SA3 - General Life Attitudes	.2413**	.2065**	.2081**
SAT - Social Attitude Total	.2414**	.1580*	.1774**

** = Significant at 0.01 level* *** = Significant at 0.001 level*

**** = Significant at 0.05 level* *NS = Not Significant*

The abstract of the results presented in the Tables 4.1.3.1.1(D) reveal that the Social Attitudes get formed with age. All the three segments of the Social Attitudes record an increase significant with the age. The increase is significant in the cases of both participants and non-participants in Games & Sports. Thus, without any reference to the participation in Games & Sports the Social Attitudes increase significantly with age.

Even when the total population including the participants and non-participants in Games & Sports is taken into consideration the results display a similar trend.

The review of the reseaches presented under the caption 1.1.0 does not show any researches conducted in this area. This underscores the fact that the research under report is a pioneering one in this area.

Now it is finally concluded that the Social Attitudes of the pupil studying in Schools and Colleges get formed with Age without any reference to their participation in Games & Sports.

(e) Levels of Participation in Games & Sports and Social Attitude Formation

Through the present research it was intended to find out the association, if any, between the levels of participation of pupils in Games & Sports and Social Attitude formation at various levels of Education.

The results presented in the Table 3.1.4.10 are again presented in the Table 4.1.3.1.1(E).

TABLE 4.1.3.1.1(E)

SHOWING THE RELATIONSHIP BETWEEN THE LEVEL OF PARTICIPATION OF PARTICIPATED GROUP (N = 345) AT ALL LEVELS OF EDUCATION AND THEIR SCORES ON SOCIAL ATTITUDE SCALES

Variable	*Participation level*	*Significant level*
SA1 - Attitude to People	.0172	NS
SA2 - Attitude to Work	.0762	NS
SA3 - General Life Attitudes	.0759	NS
SAT - Social Attitudes Total	.0540	NS

NS = Insignificant

The results do not underline any association between the levels of participation in Games & Sports and the Social Attitude formation.

Out of the three segments of the Social Attitude the first segment i.e., Attitude to People-SA1 alone appear to have significant association with levels of participation and other segments i.e., Attitude to Work-SA2 and General Life Attitude-SA3 do not underscore significant association with the levels of participation in Games & Sports. Even the Social Attitude Total-SAT does not seem to have any significant association with levels of participation.

Thus it can be concluded that by and large the levels of participation of pupils in Games & Sports do not have any association with Social Attitude formation.

4.1.3.2 PARTICIPATION IN GAMES & SPORTS AND DEVELOPMENT OF LEADERSHIP QUALITIES

HYPOTHESIS-II

'There will be a positive association between the participation of pupils in Games & Sports and Leadership Qualities development.'

The participation of pupils in Games & Sports at three levels of education i.e., School Level, Inter Level and Degree Level is considered separately and cumulatively and its association with Leadership Qualities development is underscored.

(a) *School Level*

The results pertaining to the participation of pupils in Games & Sports at School Level and their scores on Leadership scale are presented in the Table 4.1.3.2(A).

The data pertaining to the Non-participants in Games & Sports too is presented along with that of the participants, as non-participation in Games & Sports and measures of participation in Games & Sports fall-in a continuum.

TABLE 4.1.3.2(A)

SHOWING THE SIGNIFICANCE OF DIFFERENCE IN LEADERSHIP QUALITIES AMONG PARTICIPANTS (PAG) AND NON-PARTICIPANTS (NPAG) IN GAMES & SPORTS AT SCHOOL LEVEL

Variable	*PAG (n=125)*		*NPAG (n=125)*		*t-value*	*p-value*
	Mean	*SD*	*Mean*	*SD*		
LQ1	63.13	6.91	59.80	5.54	4.21	.000*
LQ2	58.26	8.08	56.10	5.76	2.43	.016*
LQ3	81.16	8.99	78.11	6.35	3.09	.002*
LQT	202.56	21.38	194.01	14.70	3.68	.000*

** = Significant at 0.05 level*

Leadership Qualities are measured in terms of three categories (i.e., LQ1 = Leadership Ability; LQ2 = Leadership Temperamental and LQ3 = Leadership Behavioural).

The total - LQT of these three segments are presented in the said table.

The results presented in the Table 4.1.3.2(A) reveal the scores on Leadership Qualities scale. The results show a significant difference in Leadership Qualities between the participants and non-participants in Games & Sports at School Level.

The p-values of all these segments of Leadership Qualities variable presented in the table are found to be significant at 0.05 level (the p-value shown against each segment in the table is lesser than the significant level).

Thus it can be concluded that the participation of pupils in Games & Sports at school level develops the leadership qualities in a significant measure.

(b) *Inter Level*

The results pertaining to the participation in Games & Sports at Inter Level and their scores on Leadership scale are presented in the Table 4.1.3.2(B).

TABLE 4.1.3.2(B)
SHOWING THE SIGNIFICANCE OF DIFFERENCE IN LEADERSHIP QUALITIES AMONG PARTICIPANTS (PAG) AND NON-PARTICIPANTS (NPAG) IN GAMES & SPORTS AT INTER LEVEL

Variable	*PAG (n=110)*		*NPAG (n=110)*		*t-value*	*p-value*
	Mean	*SD*	*Mean*	*SD*		
LQ1	62.02	6.01	58.79	5.30	4.23	.000*
LQ2	58.05	6.33	56.55	5.77	1.84	.068
LQ3	79.81	7.48	76.74	6.52	3.25	.001*
LQT	199.90	16.60	192.09	13.74	3.80	.000*

** = Significant at 0.05 level*

The results presented in the Table 4.1.3.2(B) reveal the scores on Leadership scale. The results show a significant difference in Leadership Qualities between the participants and non-participants in Games & Sports at Inter Level.

The p-values of these segments of Leadership Qualities variable except LQ2 (Leadership Temperamental) presented in the table are found to be significant at 0.05 level (the p-value shown against each segment in the table is lesser than the significant level).

Thus it can be concluded that the participation of pupils in Games & Sports at Inter Level develops the leadership qualities in a significant measure.

(c) *Degree Level*

The results pertaining to the participation of pupils in Games & Sports at Degree Level and their scores on Leadership scale are presented in the Table 4.1.3.2(C).

TABLE 4.1.3.1(C)

SHOWING THE SIGNIFICANCE OF DIFFERENCE IN LEADERSHIP QUALITIES AMONG PARTICIPANTS (PAG) AND NON-PARTICIPANTS (NPAG) IN GAMES & SPORTS AT DEGREE LEVEL

Variable	*PAG (n=110)*		*NPAG (n=110)*		*t-value*	*p-value*
	Mean	*SD*	*Mean*	*SD*		
LQ1	61.10	4.96	59.10	5.90	2.71	.007*
LQ2	56.82	5.67	57.08	5.94	0.32	.746
LQ3	77.44	8.60	76.90	8.17	0.47	.636
LQT	195.37	16.36	193.10	17.05	1.01	.314

** = Significant at 0.05 level*

The results presented in the Table 4.1.3.2(C) reveal the scores on Leadership scale. The results do not yield any significant difference in Leadership Qualities among the participants and non-participants in Games & Sports at Degree Level. However, the p-value of LQ1 (Leadership Ability) is found to be significant at 0.05 level.

Thus it can be concluded that the participation of pupils in Games & Sports at Degree Level does not develop the leadership qualities in a significant measure. However, the LQ1 (Leader Ability) segment shows a marginal development.

(d) *All Levels of Education*

The results pertaining to the participation in Games & Sports at All Levels of Education and their scores on Leadership scale are presented in the Table 4.1.3.2(D).

TABLE 4.1.3.2(D)
SHOWING THE SIGNIFICANCE OF DIFFERENCE IN LEADERSHIP QUALITIES AMONG PARTICIPANTS (PAG) AND NON-PARTICIPANTS (NPAG) IN GAMES & SPORTS AT ALL LEVELS OF EDUCATION

Variable	*PAG (n=345)*		*NPAG (n=345)*		*t-value*	*p-value*
	Mean	*SD*	*Mean*	*SD*		
LQ1	62.13	6.09	56.25	5.58	6.46	.000*
LQ2	57.73	6.84	56.55	5.82	2.44	.015*
LQ3	79.54	8.53	77.29	7.04	3.79	.000*
LQT	199.42	18.59	193.11	15.18	4.88	.000*

** = Significant at 0.05 level*

The results presented in the Table 4.1.3.2(D) reveal the scores on Leadership scale. The results show a significant difference in Leadership Qualities between the participants and non-participants in Games & Sports at All Levels of Education.

The p-values of all these segments of Leadership Qualities variable are presented in the table are found to be significant at 0.05 level (the p-value shown against each segment in the table is lesser than the significant level).

Thus it can be concluded that the participation of pupils in Games & Sports at All Levels of Education develops the Leadership Qualities in a significant measure.

4.1.3.2.1 DISCUSSION OF THE RESULTS

One of the major objectives of the research was to find out, if participants in Games & Sports at Various Levels of Education develop Leadership Qualities or not. Even it sought to find out if the sex factor has any association with the Leadership development. Likewise the association between the Community Background and Leadership Qualities developed, Age and Leadership Qualities developed and the Levels of Participation in Games & Sports and Leadership Qualities developed were to be researched into.

The relevant results have been presented under captions 4.1.3.2.1(a) to 4.1.3.2.1(e).

The discussion of the said results is presented variable wise in the following paras.

(a) Educational Level And Leadership Development

A positive association was hypothesized between participation of pupils in Games & Sports at Various Levels of Education and Leadership Qualities developed.

An abstract of the results presented in the Tables 3.2.1 to 3.2.4 is presented in the Table 4.1.3.2.1(a).

TABLE 4.1.3.2.1(A)

SHOWING THE P-VALUES OF PARTICIPANTS IN GAMES & SPORTS (PAG) AND NON-PARTICIPANTS IN GAMES & SPORTS (NPAG) AND THEIR DEVELOPMENT OF LEADERSHIP QUALITIES WITH REFERENCE TO EDUCATIONAL LEVELS

Education Level	*School*	*Inter*	*Degree*	*All level of Education*
PAG & NPAG	.000*	.000*	.314	.000*

** = Significant at 0.05 level*

The results furnished in the Table 4.1.3.2.1(a) cover the significance of difference in Leadership Qualities developed between the Participants in Games & Sports and Non-participants in Games & Sports at School, Inter, Degree and At All Levels of Education.

It is established that barring at Degree level the differences in Leadership Qualities developed between Participants and Non-participants in Games & Sports at School and Inter Levels were found to be significant. The scores on Leadership Qualities scale were found to be significantly higher in the case of Participants than Non-Participants in Games & Sports at All Levels of Education.

Thus it can be concluded that the Leadership Qualities get developed because of Participation in Games & Sports in a significant way.

A perusal of the review of researches presented under caption 1.1.2 does not throw any light on this aspect.

Thus it can be concluded that the research under report is a pioneering effort underlining the need to lay greater premium on Games & Sports Activities which are sure to develop Leadership Qualities among the students.

(b) Sex And Leadership Development

Under sex caption three categories were identified, they are:

1. Male and Female participants in Games & Sports.
2. Male and Female non-participants in Games & Sports.
3. Male and Female Total Population.

An abstract of the results presented in the Tables 3.2.1.1 to 3.2.4.3 showing the association between Sex and Leadership Development were presented in the Table 4.1.3.2.1(B).

TABLE 4.1.3.2.1(B)

SHOWING THE P-VALUES OF PARTICIPANTS IN GAMES & SPORTS (PAG) AND NON-PARTICIPANTS IN GAMES & SPORTS (NPAG) AND THEIR DEVELOPMENT OF LEADERSHIP QUALITIES WITH REFERENCE TO SEX OF THE PUPILS

Sex	*School*	*Inter*	*Degree*	*All levels of Education*
Male & Female PAG	.210	.000*	.084	.029*
Male & Female NPAG	.000*	.256	.178	.000*
Male & Female Total	.025*	.001*	.538	.002*

** = Significant at 0.05 level*

The results furnished in the Table 4.1.3.2.1(B) reveals that while the differences in the Leadership Qualities developed among the boys and girls who participate in Games & Sports are not satisfactorily significant at School and Degree Level, they are found to be significant at Inter level and at All Levels of Education. One significant feature is that the differences which may be satisfactorily significant or not it is the girls who have invariably scored higher on the Leadership Qualities Scale than the boys.

Likewise, while the differences in the Leadership Qualities developed among non-participant boys and girls at Inter and Degree Levels are not found to be significant, they are found to be significant at the School Level and at All Levels of Education.

Even in this case, the most striking feature is that the girls outshined boys in Leadership Qualities development throughout their period of education.

When the total sample of boys and girls is taken into consideration by clubbing the Leadership Qualities scores of Participants and Non-participants in Games & Sports, it is found that the girls score significantly higher than the boys at School, Inter and at All Levels of Education. Only at Degree Level the differences are not found to be significant. Even in this case it is found that the scores of girls on Leadership Qualities scale are higher than that of boys.

Thus, it is established that the girls command Leadership Qualities in a greater measure than the boys. May be better Leadership Abilities are inherent in the female sex.

A review of related literature throws some light amply supporting the findings of this research.

Thus it gets conclusively established that while the Participation in Games & Sports develops the Leadership Qualities in a greater measure, girls display relatively better Leadership Qualities than their counterparts both in the case of Participation and Non-Participation in Games & Sports.

(c) Community Background And Leadership Qualities Development

Like sex, the Community Background is also studied under three headings, viz.,

1. Rural and Urban among participants in Games & Sports.
2. Rural and Urban among non-participants in Games & Sports.
3. Rural and Urban Total Population.

Abstract of the results presented in the Tables 3.2.1.3 to 3.2.4.6 showing the association between Community Background and Leadership Qualities development is presented in the Table 4.1.3.2.1(C).

A perusal of the results presented in the Table 4.1.3.2.1(C) reveals that barring at the intermediate level when the total sample is taken into consideration the differences between the rural and urban pupils at Various Levels of Education are not found to be significant. They are not found to be significant both in the case of Participants and Non-Participants in Games & Sports.

TABLE 4.1.3.2.1(C)

SHOWING THE P-VALUES OF PARTICIPANTS IN GAMES & SPORTS (PAG) AND NON-PARTICIPANTS IN GAMES & SPORTS (NPAG) AND THEIR DEVELOPMENT OF LEADERSHIP QUALITIES WITH REFERENCE TO COMMUNITY BACKGROUND OF THE PUPILS

Community Background	*School*	*Inter*	*Degree*	*All level of Education*
Rural & Urban PAG	.310	.088	.805	.977
Rural & Urban NPAG	.230	.138	.446	.065
Rural & Urban Total	.916	.031*	.475	.217

** = Significant at 0.05 Level*

Thus it can be generally concluded that Community Background has nothing to do with Leadership Qualities development.

(d) Age And Leadership Qualities Development

One of the objectives of the research was to find out the association between Age and Leadership Qualities development. Such an association was sought to be found covering the cases of the participants in Games & Sports and non-participants in Games & Sports.

As abstract of the results presented in the Tables 3.2.4.7 to 3.2.4.9 is presented in the following Table 4.1.3.2.1(D).

TABLE 4.1.3.2.1(D)

SHOWING THE ABSTRACT OF THE RESULTS PRESENTED IN THE TABLES 3.2.4.7 TO 3.2.4.9 AND THE ASSOCIATION BETWEEN AGE AND LEADERSHIP QUALITIES DEVELOPMENT

Variable	*AGE*		
	Participants in Games & Sports	*Non-Participants in Games & Sports*	*Total Population*
LQ1 - Leadership Ability	.1593*	.0808NS	.0850NS
LQ2 - Leadership Temperamental	.1109NS	.0248***	.0403***
LQ3 - Leadership Behavioural	.2201**	.1189NS	.1541**
LQT - Leadership Qualities Total	.1940**	.0754NS	.1151*

** = Significant at 0.01 level* *** = Significant at 0.001 level*
**** = Significant at 0.05 level* *NS = Not Significant*

The results presented in the Table 4.1.3.2.1(D) reveal the results which appear to be categorical in the sense that by and large there is a positive correlation between Age and Leadership Qualities developed particularly in the case of Participants in Games & Sports. The correlations between Age of Participants in Games & Sports and LQ1, LQ3 and LQT were found to be significant while they are not found to be significant in the case of Non-participants in Games & Sports. The only exception was LQ2 in the case of Non-participants in Games & Sports.

Even when the entire population was taken into consideration the correlation were found be significant with regard to LQ2, LQ3 and LQT. It simply signifies that while the correlation between Age and Leadership Qualities development was found to be significant in a generally way, the Age was closely associated with the Leadership Qualities development with regard to the Participation in Games & Sports.

It can be hypothesized that the kind of significant association was found between Age and Leadership Qualities development with regard to total population was mentally because of the presence of the sample which had Participated in the Games & Sports.

Thus it can be concluded that while there is positive association between Age and Leadership Qualities development it is highly significant in case of the sample that has participated in the Games & Sports.

Finally, it gets established that the Participation in Games & Sports is instrumental in developing Leadership Qualities.

(e) Levels of Participation in Games & Sports and Leadership Qualities Development

Through the present research it was intended to find out the association, if any, between the levels of participation of pupils in Games & Sports and Leadership Qualities development at various levels of Education.

The results presented in the Table 3.2.4.10 are again presented in the Table 4.1.3.2.1(E).

The intensity of the participation in Games & Sports is construed to be Participation in Games & Sports at higher levels i.e., the National level, State level, Inter-varsity level etc.

TABLE 4.1.3.2.1(E)

SHOWING THE CORRELATION BETWEEN THE LEVELS OF PARTICIPATION OF PARTICIPATED GROUP (N = 345) AT ALL LEVELS OF EDUCATION AND THEIR SCORES ON LEADERSHIP QUALITIES DEVELOPMENT

Variable	*Participation Level*	*Significant level*
LQ1 - Leadership Ability	.0159	NS
LQ2 - Leadership Temperamental	.0533	NS
LQ3 - Leadership Behavioural	.0276	NS
LQT - Leadership Qualities Total	.0018	NS

NS = Not Significant

It was hypothesized that the intensity of Participation in Games & Sports would have a positive bearing on the development of Leadership Qualities in a significant way.

The results presented in the Table 4.1.3.2.1(E) do not seem to support the hypothesis. The association between the intensity of Participation in Games & Sports and Leadership Qualities development is not found to be significant i.e., the intensity of Participation in Games & Sports does not add to the Leadership Qualities development in a significant measure.

At the first sight it appears to be a contradiction in terms. While it has been established that the Participation in Games and Sports develops the Leadership Qualities in a significant way, the intensity of Participation in Games & Sports does not add to the development of Leadership Qualities. What could be reason? Only a thorough research in this regard could provide an answer.

Meanwhile a tentative hypothesis could be formulated in this regard. The lack of significant association between intensity of Participation in Games & Sports an Leadership Qualities development could be mainly because of the concentrated effort an individual directs in a situation of intensive participation. The entire attention of the participation is probably directed to the development of expertise in a narrow sense which excludes the development of concomitant attributes like Leadership Qualities development and Social Attitude formation. However, this needs to be confirmed by a subsequent research.

III. Relationship Between Social Attitudes Formation And Leadership Qualities Development

HYPOTHESIS

'There will be inter-relationship between the developments of Social Attitudes and Leadership Qualities among pupils at Various Levels of Education.'

4 1.3.3 INTRODUCTION

The inter-relationship between the formation of Social Attitudes and the development of Leadership Qualities among pupils at various levels of education are presented under the following captions:

1. School Level
2. Inter Level
3. Degree Level
4. All Levels of Education

(a) *School Level*

The results pertaining to the relationship between Social Attitudes and the development of Leadership Qualities at School Level are presented in the Table 4.1.3.3(A).

TABLE 4.1.3.3(A)

SHOWING THE RELATIONSHIP BETWEEN FORMATION OF SOCIAL ATTITUDES AND SCORES ON LEADERSHIP SCALE OF PUPILS (N = 250) AT SCHOOL LEVEL

Variable	*SA1*	*SA2*	*SA3*	*SAT*
LQ1	.5878**	.6568**	.5275**	.6782**
LQ2	.6971**	.6770**	.5993**	.7527**
LQ3	.7165*	.7547*	.7351**	.8409**
LQT	.7669*	.7992*	.7171**	.8714**

*** = Significant at .001 level*

The social attitudes are measured in terms of three categories (i.e., SA1 = Attitude to People; SA2 = Attitude to work; and SA3 = General life attitudes).

Even the total—SAT of these three segments are presented in the said table.

Leadership Qualities are measured in terms of three categories (i.e., LQ1 = Leadership Ability; LQ2 = Leadership Temperamental; LQ3 = Leadership Behavioural).

Even the totals—LQT of these three segments are presented in the said table.

The results presented in the Table 4.1.3.3(a) reveal the correlations between Social Attitudes and Leadership Qualities. The results show positive association between the social attitudes and Leadership Qualities among pupils at School Level.

The r-values of all the selected variables shown against each other are found to be significant at 0.001 level.

Thus it can be concluded that there is inter-relationship between Social Attitudes and Leadership Qualities among pupils at School Level.

(b) *Inter Level*

The results pertaining to the relationship between Social Attitudes and the development of Leadership Qualities at Inter Level are presented in the Table 4.1.3.3(B).

TABLE 4.1.3.3(B)

SHOWING THE RELATIONSHIP BETWEEN FORMATION OF SOCIAL ATTITUDES AND SCORES ON LEADERSHIP SCALE OF PUPILS (N = 220) AT INTER LEVEL

Variable	*SA1*	*SA2*	*SA3*	*SAT*
LQ1	.4491**	.4987**	.3767**	.5147**
LQ2	.6219**	.5280**	.4735**	.6295**
LQ3	.6500*	.6119*	.6556**	.7449**
LQT	.7065*	.6713*	.6243**	.7775**

*** = Significant at .001 level*

The results presented in the Table 4.1.3.3(B) reveal the correlations between Social Attitudes and scores on Leadership scale. The results show a positive association between the social attitudes and Leadership Qualities among pupils at Inter Level.

The r-values of all the variables shown in the table are found to be significant at 0.001 level.

Thus it can be concluded that there is inter-relationship between Social Attitudes and Leadership Qualities among pupils at Inter Level.

(c) *Degree Level*

The results pertaining to the relationship between Social Attitudes and the scores on Leadership scale at Degree Level are presented in the Table 4.1.3.3(C).

TABLE 4.1.3.3(C)

SHOWING THE RELATIONSHIP BETWEEN FORMATION OF SOCIAL ATTITUDES AND SCORES ON LEADERSHIP SCALE OF PUPILS (N = 220) AT DEGREE LEVEL

Variable	*SA1*	*SA2*	*SA3*	*SAT*
LQ1	.4640**	.6439**	.4536**	.6260**
LQ2	.6029**	.5994**	.4823**	.6679**
LQ3	.6242*	.6576*	.6664**	.7737**
LQT	.6757*	.7507*	.6515**	.8268**

*** = Significant at .001 level*

The results presented in the Table 4.1.3.3(C) show the correlations between Social Attitudes and Leadership Qualities. The results show a positive association between the Social Attitudes and Leadership Qualities among pupils at Degree Level.

The r-values of all the variables are shown in the table are found to be significant at 0.001 level.

Thus it can be concluded that there is inter-relationship between Social Attitudes and Leadership Qualities among pupils at Degree Level.

(d) *All Levels of Education*

The results pertaining to the relationship between Social Attitudes and the scores on Leadership scale at All Levels of Education are presented in the Table 4.1.3.3(D).

TABLE 4.1.3.3(D)

SHOWING THE RELATIONSHIP BETWEEN FORMATION OF SOCIAL ATTITUDES AND SCORES ON LEADERSHIP SCALE OF PUPILS (N = 690) AT ALL LEVELS OF EDUCATION

Variable	SA1	SA2	SA3	SAT
LQ1	.5144**	.6108**	.4641**	.6181**
LQ2	.6440**	.6043**	.5142**	.6825**
LQ3	.6667*	.6887**	.6925**	.7936**
LQT	.7233*	.7516**	.6688**	.8310**

*** = Significant at .001 level*

The results presented in the Table 4.1.3.3(D) show the correlations between Social Attitudes and Leadership Qualities. The results show a positive association between the Social Attitudes and Leadership Qualities among pupils at All Levels of Education.

The r-values of all the variables shown in the table are found to be significant at 0.001 level.

Thus it can be concluded that there is a positive association between Social Attitudes and Leadership Qualities among pupils at All Levels of Education.

(e) ***All Levels of Education (Participant Group)***

The results pertaining to the relationship between Social Attitudes and the scores on Leadership scale at All Levels of Education (participant group) are presented in the Table 4.1.3.3(e).

TABLE 4.1.3.3(E)

SHOWING THE RELATIONSHIP BETWEEN FORMATION OF SOCIAL ATTITUDES AND SCORES ON LEADERSHIP SCALE OF PUPILS (N = 345) AT ALL LEVELS OF EDUCATION (PARTICIPANT GROUP)

Variable	SA1	SA2	SA3	SAT
LQ1	.5430**	.6507**	.5358**	.6577**
LQ2	.6913**	.6278**	.5997**	.7250**
LQ3	.6860**	.7041**	.7495**	.8120**
LQT	.7473**	.7675**	.7403**	.8580**

*** = Significant at .001 level*

The results presented in the Table 4.1.3.3(E) reveal the correlations between Social Attitudes and Leadership Qualities. The results show a positive association between the Social Attitudes and Leadership Qualities among pupils at All Levels of Education (participant group).

The r-values of all the variables shown in the table are found to be significant at 0.001 level.

Thus it can be concluded that there is a Inter-relationship between Social Attitudes and Leadership Qualities developed among pupils at All Levels of Education (participated group).

(f) ***All Levels of Education (Not Participant Group)***

The results pertaining to the relationships between Social Attitudes and the Leadership Qualities at All Levels of Education (non-participant group) are presented in the Table 4.1.3.3(f).

TABLE 4.1.3.3(F)

SHOWING THE RELATIONSHIP BETWEEN SOCIAL ATTITUDES AND SCORES ON LEADERSHIP SCALE OF PUPILS (N = 345) AT ALL LEVELS OF EDUCATION (NON-PARTICIPANT GROUP)

Variable	*SA1*	*SA2*	*SA3*	*SAT*
LQ1	.4346**	.5355**	.3491**	.5345**
LQ2	.5806**	.5637**	.3810**	.6150**
LQ3	.6238**	.6535**	.5986**	.7549**
LQT	.6718**	.7163**	.5522**	.7826**

*** = Significant at .001 level*

The results presented in the Table 4.1.3.3(f) show the correlations between Social Attitudes and Leadership Qualities. The results show a positive association between the Social Attitudes and Leadership Qualities among pupils at All Levels of Education even in the case of the group that has not participated in Games & Sports.

The r-values of all the variables shown in the table are found to be significant at 0.001 level.

Thus it can be concluded that even in the case of the group that has not participated in Games & Sports there is inter-relationship between Social Attitudes and Leadership Qualities developed among pupils at All Levels of Education.

4.1.3.3.1 DISCUSSIONS OF THE RESULTS

HYPOTHESIS-3

There will be Inter-relationship between the developments of Social Attitudes and Leadership Qualities among pupils at Various Levels of Education.

An abstract of the results presented in the Tables 3.3.1 to 3.3.4 is presented in the Table 4.1.3.3.1.

TABLE 4.1.3.3.1

SHOWING THE INTER-RELATIONSHIP BETWEEN THE VARIABLES I.E., SOCIAL ATTITUDES AND LEADERSHIP QUALITIES AT DIFFERENT LEVELS OF EDUCATION

Levels of Education	*r-Values of Social Attitudes & Leadership Qualities*
School	.8714**
Inter	.7775**
Degree	.8268**
All Levels of Education	.8310**

*** Significant at .001 level*

The results presented in the Table 4.1.3.3.1 underscore a consistently significant association between the two variables i.e., Social Attitudes and Leadership Qualities. The association is found to be significant at School Level, Inter Level, Degree Level and All Levels of Education.

It signifies that the Social Attitudes and Leadership Qualities develop simultaneously among students at Various Levels of Education.

Thus, a positive association between Social Attitude and Leadership Qualities can be underscored.

4.1.4.0 COMPREHENSIVE DISCUSSION OF THE RESULTS

The research under report intended to find out the association between Participation in Games & Sports and the development of concomitant attributes like Social Attitudes and Leadership Qualities among students at Various Levels of Education.

The results have highlighted a significant association between Participation in Games & Sports and development of Leadership Qualities and formation of Social Attitudes. Even though these attributes develop with Age, the development of these attributes is significant in the case of those who participate in Games & Sports.

The most significant finding of this research is the pre-eminents of the female sex in the development of Leadership Qualities and formation of Social Attitudes. These findings are corroborated by the findings of other researches. This spectacular result explodes the myth of masculine superiority in providing leadership. Generally an illusion was hugged all through that males are born leaders and females, followers. But the present findings dismantle such assumptions and demonstrates categorically the superior potential Leadership Abilities of women.

The Community Background does not seem to have any association with either the Leadership Qualities development or the Social Attitude formation and surprisingly one more significant finding of the research is lack of any significant association between the intensity of Participation in Games & Sports and Leadership Qualities development and Social Attitude formation. However, a deeper probe into this aspect is in the order.

Finally, a strong association has been discerned between Social Attitudes and Leadership Qualities among students at Various Levels of Education.

Thus a greater provision of Games & Sports and better participation of the students in them are likely to develop both the Leadership Qualities and Social Attitudes.

Finally, the need for the women to get their due share in the Leadership roles in any sphere of human activity is to be highlighted. In fact, they are inherently better equipped than males for any Leadership role. The absence of women Leadership reflects the inability of the society to exploit the feminine leadership potentialities.

To that extent the human societies have pauperised themselves in a predominantly male Chauvnistic Milieu.

4.2.0 RESULTS IN BRIEF AND CONCLUSIONS

A perusal of the entire presentation with a special reference to the Chapter covering the results and the discussions, would help in arriving at the results in brief which enables in drawing general conclusions which are stated briefly in the following paras.

The results and conclusions are presented Objective/ Hypothesis-wise.

HYPOTHESIS-I

'There will be a positive association between the participation in Games & Sports, and Social Attitude formation.'

I. Participation in Games & Sports and Social Attitudes Formation Education—Level-wise

Results

(a) Participation of pupils in Games & Sports at School level develops the Social Attitudes in a significant measure.

(b) Participation of pupils in Games & Sports at Inter level develops the Social Attitudes in a significant measure.

(c) Participation of pupils in Games & Sports at Degree level does not develop the Social Attitudes in a significant measure.

(d) Participation of pupils in Games & Sports at All Levels of Education i.e., for a prolonged period develops the Social Attitudes in a significant measure.

Conclusion

The participation of pupils in Games & Sports generally helps in the formation of Social Attitudes in them.

II. Participation in Games & Sports and Formation of Social Attitudes—Sex-wise

Under caption (a) the results and conclusions covering the

formation of Social Attitudes among Boys and Girls who participate in Games & Sports are presented.

Results

(a) 1. The difference in the formation of Social Attitudes among the Boys and Girls who participate in Games & Sports at School level is not found to be significant, though the Boys have scored slightly higher on Social Attitude Scale than the Girls.

2. The difference in the formation of Social Attitudes among the Boys and Girls who participate in Games & Sports at Inter level is found to be significant the Girls scoring higher than the Boys on Social Attitude Scale.

3. The difference in the formation of Social Attitudes among the Boys and Girls who participate in Games & Sports at Degree level is found to be significant, the Girls scoring higher than the boys on Social Attitude Scale.

4. The difference in the formation of Social Attitudes among the Boys and Girls who participate in Games & Sports at All Levels of Education is found to be significant, the Girls scoring higher than the Boys on Social Attitude Scale.

Conclusion

Initially though the Girls who participate in Games & Sports score less on the Social Attitude Scale than Boys, they progressively continue to score higher and higher on Social Attitude Scale excelling their male counterparts throughout their educational career.

Under caption (b) the results and conclusions covering the formation of Social Attitudes among Boys and Girls who do not participate are in Games & Sports are presented.

Results

(b) 1. The Girls who do not participate in Games & Sports at School level score significantly higher on Social Attitude Scale than their male counterparts.

2. The difference in the formation of Social Attitudes among the Boys and Girls who do not participate in Games & Sports at Inter level is found to be significant, the Girls scoring higher than the Boys on Social Attitude Scale.
3. The difference in the formation of Social Attitudes among the Boys and Girls who do not participate in Games & Sports at Degree level is not found to be significant.
4. The Girls who do not participate in Games & Sports at All Levels of Education score significantly higher on Social Attitude Scale than their male counterparts.

Conclusion

The Girls who do not participate in Games & Sports generally score significantly higher than their male counterparts on Social Attitude Scale during their period of education.

Under Chapter (c) the results and conclusion covering the Social Attitudes among Boys and Girls (when both the Participants and Non-participants in Games & Sports are taken together) are presented.

Results

(c) 1. The difference in the formation of Social Attitudes among Boys and Girls in general at School level is not found to be significant, though the Girls score slightly higher than the Boys.

2. The Girls in general at Inter level score significantly higher on Social Attitude Scale than the Boys.
3. The difference in the formation of Social Attitudes among Boys and Girls in general at Degree level is not found to be significant, though the Girls score slightly higher than the Boys.
4. The Girls in general at All levels of Education score significantly higher on Social Attitude Scale than the Boys.

Conclusion

Irrespective of their participation and non-participation in Games & Sports the Girls generally score significantly higher than the Boys on Social Attitude Scale.

III. Participation in Games & Sports and Formation of Social Attitudes—Community Background-Wise

Under caption (a) the results and conclusions covering the formation of Social Attitudes among Rural and urban students who participate in Games & Sports are presented.

Results

(a) 1. The difference in the formation of Social Attitude among Rural and Urban pupils who participate in Games & Sports at School level is not found to be significant, though the Rural participants have scored slightly higher than the Urban participants on Social Attitude Scale.

2. The difference in the formation of Social Attitudes among Rural and Urban pupils who participate in Games & Sports at Inter level is not found to be significant, though the Urban participants have scored slightly higher than the Rural participants on Social Attitude Scale.

3. The difference in the formation of Social Attitude among Rural and Urban pupils who participate in Games & Sports at Degree level is not found to be significant, though the Urban participants have scored slightly higher than the Rural participants on Social Attitude Scale.

4. The difference in the formation of Social Attitude among Rural and Urban pupils who participate in Games & Sports at All Levels of Education is not found to be significant, though the Rural participants have scored slightly higher than the Urban participants on Social Attitude Scale.

Conclusion

The difference in the Social Attitudes formation during the period of education among the Rural and Urban participants in Games & Sports is not found to be significant.

Under caption (b) the results and conclusions covering the formation of Social Attitudes among Rural and Urban who do not participate in Games & Sports are presented.

Results

(b) 1. The difference in the formation of Social Attitudes among Rural and Urban pupils who do not participate in Games & Sports at School level is not found to be significant, the Urban students scoring higher than the Rural students.

2. The difference in the formation of Social Attitude among Rural and Urban pupils who do not participate in Games & Sports at Inter level is not found to be significant, though the Urban non-participants have scored slightly higher than the Rural participants on Social Attitude Scale.

3. The difference in the formation of Social Attitude among Rural and Urban pupils who do not participate in Games & Sports at Degree level is not found to be significant, though the Urban non-participants have scored slightly higher than the Rural participants on Social Attitude Scale.

4. The difference in the formation of Social Attitude among Rural and Urban pupils who do not participate in Games & Sports at All Levels of Education is not found to be significant, though the Urban non-participants have scored slightly higher than the Rural non-participants on Social Attitude Scale.

Conclusion

The difference in the Social Attitudes formation during the period of education among the Rural and Urban non-participants in Games & Sports is not found to be significant.

Under caption (c) the results and conclusions covering the formation of Social Attitudes among Rural and Urban (when both Participants and Non-participants in Games & Sports are taken together) are presented.

Results

(c) 1. The difference in the formation of Social Attitudes among Rural and Urban students in general at School level is not found to be significant, though the Rural students score slightly higher then the Urban students.

2. The different in the formation of Social Attitudes among Rural and Urban students in general at Inter level is not found to be significant, though the Rural students score slightly higher than the Urban students.

3. The difference in the formation of Social Attitudes among Rural and Urban students in general at Degree level is not found to be significant, though the Urban students score slightly higher than the Rural students.

4. The difference in the formation of Social Attitudes among Rural and Urban students in general at All levels of Education level is not found to be significant, though the Urban students score slightly higher than the Rural students.

Conclusion

Irrespective of the participation of pupils in Games & Sports the differences in the formation of Social Attitudes among Rural and Urban students are not found to be significant.

IV. Participation in Games & Sports and Social Attitude Formation—Age-Wise

Conclusion

The Social Attitude formation among the pupils who participate in Games & Sports develops with age.

The Social Attitude formation among the pupils who do not participate in Games & Sports develops with age.

The Social Attitude formation among the pupils develops with age.

V. The Intensity of Participation In Games & Sports and Social Attitude Formation

Conclusion

The Social Attitudes do not develop in relation to the intensity of the participation of students in Games & Sports.

The results and conclusions of the Objective/Hpothesis-2 are presented hereunder:

HYPOTHESIS-2

'There will be a positive association between the participation in Games & Sports, and Leadership Qualities development.'

I. Participation in Games & Sports and Leadership Qualities Development—Education Level-Wise

Results

(a) Participation of pupils in Games & Sports level develops the Leadership Qualities in a significant measure.

(b) Participation of pupils in Games & Sports at Inter level develops the Leadership Qualities in a significant measure.

(c) Participation of pupils in Games & Sports at Degree level does not develop the Leadership Qualities in a significant measure.

(d) Participation of pupils in Games & Sports at All Levels of Education i.e., for a prolonged period develops the Leadership Qualities in a significant measure.

Conclusion

The participation of pupils in Games & Sports generally helps in the development of Leadership Qualities in them.

II. Participation in Games & Sports and Development of Leadership Qualities Sex-wise

Under caption (a) the results and conclusions covering the development of Leadership Qualities among Boys and Girls who participate in Games & Sports are presented.

(a) 1. The difference in the Development of Leadership Qualities among the Boys and Girls who participate in Games & Sports at School level is not found to be significant, though the Boys have scored slightly higher on Leadership Qualities Scale than the Girls.

2. The difference in the development of Leadership Qualities among the Boys and Girls who participate in Games & Sports at Inter level is found to be significant the Girls scoring higher than the Boys on Leadership Qualities Scale.

3. The difference in the development of Leadership Qualities among the Boys and Girls who participate in Games & Sports at Degree level is found to be significant, the Girls scoring higher than the boys on Leadership Qualities Scale.

4. The difference in the development of Leadership Qualities among the Boys and Girls who participate in Games & Sports at All Levels of Education is found to be significant, the Girls scoring higher than the Boys on Leadership Qualities Scale.

Conclusion

Initially though the Girls who participate in Games & Sports score less on the Leadership Qualities Scale than Boys, they progressively continue to score higher and higher on Leadership Qualities Scale excelling their male counterparts throughout their educational career.

Under caption (b) the results and conclusions covering the development of Leadership Qualities among Non-participating Boys and Girls are in Games & Sports are presented.

Results

(b) 1. The Girls who do not participate in Games & Sports at School level score significantly higher on Leadership Qualities Scale than their male counterparts.

2. The difference in the development of Leadership Qualties among the Boys and Girls who do not participate in Games & Sports at Inter level is not found to be significant, the Girls scoring higher than the Boys on Leadership Qualities Scale.

3. The difference in the development of Leadership Qualities among the Boys and Girls who do not participate in Games & Sports at Degree level is not found to be significant, Boys scoring slightly higher than the Girls on Leadership Qualities Scale.

4. The Girls who do not participate in Games & Sports at All Levels of Education score significantly higher on Leadership Qualities Scale than their male counterparts.

Conclusion

The Girls who do not participate in Games & Sports generally score significantly higher than their male counterparts on Leadership Qualties Scale during their period of education.

Under capton (c) the results and conclusion covering the Leadership Qualities among Boys and Girls (when both the Participants and Non-participants in Games & Sports are taken together) are presented.

Results

(c) 1. The difference in the development of Leadership Qualities among Boys and Girls in general at School level is found to be significant, the Girls scoring slightly higher than the Boys.

2. The Girls in general at Inter level score significantly higher on Leadership Qualities Scale than the Boys.

3. The difference in the development of Leadership

Qualities among Boys and Girls in general at Degree level is not found to be significant, though the Boys score slightly higher than the Girls.

4. The Girls in general at All Levels of Education score significantly higher on Leadership Qualities Scale than the Boys.

Conclusion

Irrespective of their participation in Games & Sports the Girls generally score significantly higher than the Boys on Leadership Qualities Scale.

III. Participation in Games & Sports and Development of Leadership Qualities—Community Background-Wise

Under caption (a) the results and conclusions covering the development of Leadership Qualities among Rural and Urban students who participate in Games & Sports are presented.

Results

(a) 1. The difference in the development of Leadership Qualities among Rural and Urban pupils who participate in Games & Sports at School level is not found to be significant, though the Rural participants have scored slightly higher than the Urban participants on Leadership Qualities Scale.

2. The difference in the development of Leadership Qualities among Rural and Urban pupils who participate in Games & Sports at Inter level is not found to be significant, though the Urban participants have scored slightly higher than the Rural participants on Leadership Qualities Scale.

3. The difference in the development of Leadership Qualities among Rural and Urban pupils who participate in Games & Sports at Degree level is not found to be significant, though the Urban participants have scored slightly higher than the Rural participants on Leadership Qualities Scale.

4. The difference in the development of Leadership Qualities among Rural and Urban pupils who participate in Games & Sports at All Levels of Education is not found to be significant, though the Rural participants have scored slightly higher than the Urban participants on Leadership Qualities Scale.

Conclusion

The difference in the Leadership Qualities development during the period of education among the Rural and Urban participants in Games & Sports is not found to be significant.

Under caption (b) the results and conclusions covering the development of Leadership Qualities among Rural and Urban students who do not participate in Games & Sports are presented.

Results

(b) 1. The difference in the development of Leadership Qualities among Rural and Urban pupils who do not participate in Games & Sports at School level is not found to be significant, the rural students scoring higher than the Urban students.

2. The difference in the development of Leadership Qualities among Rural and Urban pupils who do not participate in Games & Sports at Inter level is not found to be significant, though the Urban non-participants have scored slightly higher than the Rural non-participants on Leadership Qualities Scale.

3. The difference in the development of Leadership Qualities among Rural and Urban pupils who do not participate in Games & Sports at Degree level is not found to be significant, though the Urban non-participants have scored slightly higher their Rural counterparts on Leadership Qualities Scale.

4. The difference in the development of Leadership Qualities among Rural and Urban pupils who do not participate in Games & Sports at All Levels of

Education is not found to be significant, though the Urban non-participants have scored slightly higher than their Rural counterparts on Leadership Qualities Scale.

Conclusion

The difference in the Leadership Qualities development during the period of education among the Rural and Urban non-participants in Games & Sports is not found to be significant.

Under caption (c) the results and conclusions covering the development of Leadership Qualities among Rural and Urban (when both Participants and Non-participants in Games & Sports are taken together) are presented.

Results

(c) 1. The difference in the development of Leadership Qualities among Rural and Urban students in general at School level is not found to be significant, though the Urban students score slightly higher than the Rural students.

2. The difference in the development of Leadership Qualities among Rural and Urban students in general at Inter level is found to be significant, though the Urban students scoring higher than the Rural students.

3. The difference in the development of Leadership Qualities among Rural and Urban students in general at Degree level is not found to be significant, the Urban students scoring higher than the Rural students.

4. The difference in the development of Leadership Qualities among Rural and Urban students in general at All levels of Education level is not found to be significant, though the Urban students scoring higher than the Rural students.

Conclusion

Irrespective of the participation of pupils in Games and Sports the differences in the development of Leadership Qualities among

Rural and Urban students are not found to be significant, except in the case of Urban Inter level students who have scored significantly higher on Leadership Qualities Scale than the Rural Inter Level students.

IV. Participation in Games & Sports and Leadership Qualities Development—Age-Wise

Conclusions

The Leadership Qualities among the pupils who participate in Games & Sports develops with age.

The Leadership Qualities among the pupils who do not participate in Games & Sports develops with age.

The Leadership Qualities among the pupils develops with age.

V. The Intensity of Participation In Games & Sports and Leadership Qualities Development

Conclusion

The Leadership Qualities do not develop in relation to the intensity of the participation of students in Games & Sports.

'The results and conclusions of the Objective/Hypothesis-3 are presented hereunder.'

HYPOTHESIS-3

'There will be inter-relationship between the development of Social Attitudes and Leadership Qualities among pupils at various levels of education.'

The following are the conclusions drawn from the results. They are presented under captions a, b, c, d, with regards to School Level, Inter Level, Degree Level and At all Levels of Education. The caption 'e' covers the general conclusion for the entire population.

(a) School Level

Leadership Qualities develop positively in relation to Social Attitudes formation among pupils at School level.

(b) Inter Level

Leadership Qualities develop positively in relation to Social Attitudes formation among pupils at Inter level.

(c) Degree Level

Leadership Qualities develop positively in relation to Social Attitudes formation among pupils at Degree level.

(d) At All Levels of Education

Leadership Qualities develop positively in relation to Social Attitudes formation among pupils at All Levels of Education.

(e) Conclusion

Irrespective of the levels of education, the pupils develop in them the Leadership Qualities positively in relation to Social Attitudes formation.

4.3.0 SUGGESTIONS FOR FURTHER RESEARCH

The following problems deserving research attention have been generated by the research under report.

1. Women and Leadership

It has been conclusively established that women at various stages of education display higher levels of Leadership Qualities. It has been so both in the case of Participants in Games & Sports and Non-Participants in the Games & Sports hailing from different Community backgrounds. It appears that the women students are better leaders than men students.

It needs research confirmation. For that a deeper probe into this aspect covering larger populations covering the entire gamut of human pursuits appears to be in order.

2. Women and Formation of Social Attitudes

Further it has been established that the formation of Social Attitudes takes place in a greater measure in Girls than in Boys. A research design covering the male and female population drawn from the entire gamut of human activity seems appropriate. It can be comprehensively tested if the females invariably develop Social Attitudes in an accelerated measure than males.

3. Intensity of Participation in Games & Sports and Leadership Qualities Development

It has been established that the Participation in Games & Sports develops Leadership Qualities in a greater measure than the Non-participation in Games & Sports. Likewise, the intensity of participation in Games & Sports too should have positive association with the development of Leadership Qualities. But surprisingly the association between the intensity of participation in Games & Sports and Leadership Qualities development was not found to be significant.

WHAT COULD BE THE REASONS?

Normally it is assumed that the players at the highest levels including International Level are expected to be better Leaders. But the results do not subscribe to the same.

In this connection a deeper and thorough probe atleast at the doctoral level is in order which would highlight the sluggish growth of Leadership Qualities among the sportsmen at the highest levels of the their participation. Does the concentration of effort at the highest levels of the participants sharp in the skills of expertise of a specific game instead of broadbasing the effort in the area including leadership growth? Is it a convergent effort or a divergent one? Expertise could be convergent while leadership could be divergent. A deeper probe probably would explain the lack of commensurate growth of Leadership Qualities among the participants at the highest levels of Games & Sports.

BIBLIOGRAPHY

Adair, John : "Effective Leadership", London: Rupa & Company Pan Books Ltd., 1988.

Adler. A. : "Understanding Human Nature", Prema Books, 1949.

Airan, J.W. : "The Nature of Leadership", A Practical Approach, Bombay: Lalvani Pub. House, 1969.

Allport, G.W. : "Attitudes in Murchison (Ed.) Hand Book of Social Psychology", Mass : Clark University Press, 1935.

Alverdes : "Social Life in the Animal World", London: Kegan Paul, 1927.

Aurobindo : "The systhesis of Yoga", Pondicherry : Sri Aurobindo Ashram Trust, 1948.

Baldwin, A.L. : "The effects of Home Environment on Nursery School Behaviour", Child Development, XX, 1949.

Baljith Kaur : "A study on Attitude towards school of IX Grade Boys and Girls in relation to Achievement Motivation", Punjab: Punjab University, Ph.D. Thesis (Unpublished), 1984.

Bang, U.S. : "The impact of teacher training programme in physical education on Physical fitness, personality, adjustment and motivity of student teachers", New Delhi: Delhi Univ. (Ph.D. Thesis, Unpub.), 1982.

Bass, B.M. : "Leadership Group Discussion ", Psychological Bulletin, 1954.

Bevelas : "Leadership and Social Power", Abstract from R. O. Lippitt, N. Polansky, F. Redl and S. Rosen "The Dynamics of Power", Human Relations, (1952) 5, 37-64, 1942.

Bird, C. : "Social Psychology", New York: Appliton-Century, 1940.

Bhaskara Rao, D. : "Educational Psychology", Guntur, Nagarjuna Publishers, 2000.

Bogardus, E.S. : "International J of Opinion and Attitude Research", 1947.

Bowlby, J. : "Child Care and Growth of Love", London: Penguin Books, 1953.

Britt, S.H. & : "Jews in Gentle World", Graiber, New York: Mcmillan, 1942.

Brownell, Lee & Hagman, E.P. : "Physical Education—Foundations and Principles", New York: McGraw Hill Book Company, Inc., 1951.

Bucher, Charles A. : "Administration of School Health and Physical Education Programme", St. Luis : The C.V.S. Mosby Company, 1958.

Campbell, D. T. : "Social Attitudes and other acquired behavioural disposition", in Kock (Ed.) Psychology Vol. VI, New York: McGraw Hill Co., 1963.

Cartwright & Zander : "Group Dynamics", New York: Harper & Row, 1968.

Cattell, R. B. : "Description and Measurement of Personality", New York: World Book Co., 1946.

Chopra, BS. KS. : "Leadership for the Indian Manager", Culcutta: Times Research Foundation, 1987.

Christiansen, R.B. : "Attitude towards foreign affairs as a functioning of personality", OSLO University Press, 1959.

Clarke, H. : "The application of Measurement to Health and Physical Education", New York: Prentice-Hall, Inc., 1950.

Cowell, C. Charles & Hazelton, W. H. : "Curriculum Designs in Physical Education", New York: Prentice Hall, Inc., 1955.

Darshan, K. S. : "Construction of an Attitude Scale towards Sports on higher secondary school Child ren", Punjab: Punjab Uni. Ph. D Thesis (Unpublished), 1982.

Deshmukh, C. D. : "Deshmukh Committee Report on Physical Education in Indian Universities, 1967."

Deshpande, S. : "An Analytical Study of Leadership Qualities in Junior College Students in Vidarbha Region of Maharashtra", Nagpur: Ph. D. Thesis, Nagpur University, 1983.

Dhillon, G.K. : "A Comparative study of the personality characteristics, Adjustments, and Motivation level of Participants and non-participants of Secondary Schools in Physical Education", Kurukshetra: Ph. D. Thesis (unpublished), 1979.

Fiedler, F. E. : "A Theory of Leadership Effectiveness", McGraw-Hill, 1967.

Garrison, K. C. : "The Psychology of Exceptional Children", New York: The Ronald Press Company, 1940.

Gibb, C. A. : "Leadership", In International Encyclopaedia of the Social Sciences, New York: The McMillan & The Free Press, 1969.

Gross, N. & Harriott, R. E. : "The EPL of Elementary Principal, A Study of Executive Principal Leadership", The National Elementary Principal, 45:66 to 71, 1966.

Halpin, A. : "The Leadership Behaviour and Leadership Ideology of Educational Administrators and Air Craft Commanders", Harward Educational Review, 25 : 18-31, 1955.

Hardev, S. : "Attitudes of Post Graduate Students towards Religion", Punjab, Ph. D. Thesis (Unpublished), 1978.

Heinicke and Bales : "Development Trends in the Structure of small groups", Sociometry, 16, 1953.

Hemphill, J. K. : "The Leader and his group leadership", Penguin Books, pp. 224-5, 1955.

Hetherington, W.C. : "School programme in physical education", New York: World Book Company, 1992.

Homans, G.C. : "Social Behaviour", New York: Harcourt Brace and World, 1967.

Irwin, W.L. : "The curriculum in Health and Physical Education", St. Louis: The C.V Mosby Co., 1951.

Insko, C.A. : "Theories of attitude change", Prentice-Hall, N.J., 1967.

Itkin, W. : "Relationships between attitudes towards parents and parent attitudes towards children", Journal of Genetic Psychology, LXXXVI, 1955.

Jaimal Singh : "A study of relationship between anxiety adjustment and attitude towards teaching of secondary school physical education teachers", Punjab, Punjab Univ., 1986.

Jugal, P.D. : "A study of socio-psychological make-up of student leaders of Kumaun university in relation to their liking for involvement in college/university administration", Kumaun, 1982.

Koch, H. L.: "The relation of certain family constellation characteristics and the attitudes of children towards adults", child development, XXVI, 1955.

Kothari, D.S. : "Kothari (Education commission report 1964-66)."

Krech, D. & Crutchfield, R. : "Theory and Problems of social psychology", New York, McGraw-Hill, 1948.

Kumar, P. : "Personality Study of student leadership", Allahabad: Univ. of Allahabad, Ph.D. thesis, 1964.

Kuppu Swamy, B.: "An introduction to social psychology", Bombay: Asian Pub. House, 1961.

Lalini, V. : "Rural leadership in India", New Delhi: Gian Pub. House, 1991.

Lasalle, Dorothy: "Guidance of children through physical education", New York: A. S. Branes & Co., 1946.

Lasswell, Harold : et al. (ed) Language of politics: studies in qualitative semantics, MIT Press, 1965."

Lewin, K. : "Group discussion and social change, In newcomb and Hartley", (Ed.) Reading in Social Psychology, New York: Holt, 1939.

Lewis, Oscar : "Village life in north India", Urbana Univ. of Illinois Press, 1959.

Lippitt, R. & White, R.K. : "The social climate of children groups", in R.G. Barker et al. (ed), Child behaviour and development, New York: McGraw-Hill book Co., 1943.

Lott & Lott : "A learning theory approach to interpersonal attitudes, in Greenwald et al (ed.) psychological foundations of attitudes", New York, Academic Press, 1968.

Mahajan, J. M. : "A study of supervisory role of principals of Delhi Schools", Delhi Univ. Ph. D. thesis, 1970.

Mann, R. D. : "A review of the relationship between personality and performance in small groups", Psychological Bulletin, 1959.

Mary, S. Charleen : "Diagnosing the causes of prejudice in school children", National Catholic Education Association Bulletin, 1950.

Mathur, V.A. : "A study of political attitudes and alienation among female college students", Rajasthan: Rajasthan Univ., Ph. D. thesis (Unpub.) 1985.

McGuire, W.J. : "Cognitive consistency and attitude change", J. Ab and social psychology, 60-1960.

Meade, R.D. : "An experimental study of leadership in India", The Journal of Social Psychology, 1967.

Mekeachie, W.J. & Doyle, C. L. : "Psychology", Addition Wesley, 1966.

Merie : "Leadership and social power", Abstract from Lippett, Polansky and Rosen: The Dynamics of power: human relations, 1952.

Moser, R. P. : "A study of effects of superintendents—principals interaction upon Principals—teacher interactions in selected middle sized school systems", Univ. of Chicago, Illinois, Unpub. Doctoral dissertation, 1959.

Mudaliar, A. L. : "Mudaliar committee report on Secondary Education", 1952.

Mulia, R. D. : "An investigation into the leadership behaviour of students in the context of some psycho-social factors", Sagar: 1986.

Nandini, Murali : "A true leaders", Progressive educational Herald Journal, "The Hindu", Young World, 1993. As quoted by Ralph Walso Emerson.

Nash, B. Jay : "Physical Education: Interpretations and objectives", New York, A.S. Barnes & Co., 1948.

Norman, B. N. : "A study of women in leadership position in North California ", The Delta-Kappa-Gamma-Bulletin, 1970.

Oberteuffer, Delbert : "Physical Education", New York: Harper & Bro. 1951.

O'conner, C. : "Leadership in our public schools", School and Community, 1969.

Paramjith Kaur : "A study on attitudes of boys and girls studying in professional and non-professional colleges towards marriages and family size", Lucknow: Ph. D. thesis, 1984.

Pigors, Paul : "Leadership of Domination", Boston: Houghton, Mifflin Co., 1955.

Prabhath, G. Singh : "Comparative study of the social attitudes of the physically handicapped and normal children studying in secondary schools of Punjab", 1973.

Radhakrishnan, S. : "Radhakrishnan committee report on university education", 1948.

Rao, P. S. : "Changing certain attitudes in urban secondary schools children—A study of techniques and effects", Mysore: Ph. D. thesis, 1984.

Rauben, B. Frost, Barbara, Day. L., & Stanley, J. M. : "Administration of Physical Education and Athletics", New Delhi: W. C. Brown publishers, 1990.

Ribble, M. A.: "Infantile Experience in relation to personality Development", in J.M. Hunt (ed.) Personality and the Behaviour Disorders, II New York: The Ronald press company, 1944.

Rizvi, S. A. I. : "A study of attitudes towards religious education in relation to certain value orientation", Amruthsir: 1986.

Roudinesco, J. : "Severe maternal deprivation and personality development in early childhood", understanding the child, XXI, 1952.

Rousseau, J. J. : "The confessions of Jean-Jacques Rcuseau/ training an with an introduction by J. M.Cohem", Hammondsworth: Penguin Books 1953.

Sardari Lal : "A study of physical fitness in relation to school adjustment, Emotional stability, Socio-Economic status and Sex of players and non-players", Punjab Univ. Punjab,1990.

Shailaja, Bhagavat : "Relative effectiveness of logical and wishful thinking on attitude change", Jabalpur: Ph.D. Thesis, 1976.

Sharman, R. J. : "Introduction to Physical Education", New York: A. S. Barnes and Co. 1934.

Sinha, D. : "Indian village in transition", Hyderabad: NICD, 1969.

Singh, H. M. : "A study of leadership behaviour of heads of secondary schools in Haryana and its correlates", New Delhi, E.P.A. Bulletin, 1975.

Snygg and Comb : "Individual behaviour", New York: Harper, 1949.

Sorenson, H. : "Psychology in Education", New Delhi, Tata McGraw-Hill, (TMH Edition), 1977.

Sprott, W.J.H. : "Social Psychology", London: Methuen, 1952.

Stern, M.P. : "The distribution of plasma lipo protein in middle aged male runners, metabolism", 25(11): 1249-1257, Nov., 1976.

Stigdill, R. M. : "Personal factors associated with leadership", A survey of the literature: Journal of Psychology, 1948.

Stogdill, R. M. : "Leadership, membership, organisation", pp.42-23 in leadership edited by G.A. Gibb, Penguin Books, 1948.

Stone, G. : "Appearance and the self concept", London: Kegan Paul, 1962.

Tannenbaum, R. : "Leadership and organisation", A frame of reference, p. 23, London: McGraw-Hill Co., 1961.

Tead, Ordway : "Art of leadership: How to train leaders ", pp. 272-275, London: McGraw-Hill Co., Inc. 1935.

Thirunarayan, C., & Harinarayan, S. : "Methods in physical education", Karaikudi: South India Press, 1966.

Toch, H. : "The social psychology of social movements", New York: Bobb Merril,1965.

Travers, R. M. W. : "Educational psychology", New York: Mcmillan Co., 1973.

Vivekananda, Swamy : "The complete works of Swami Vivekananda", 14th Edition-Culcutta, Ashram, 1972.

Wallerstein, H. : "The Penguin Dictionary of Psychology", Middlesex, England: Harmonsworth, Penguin Books Ltd., 1952.

Whittaker, J. O. : "Introduction to psychology", W.B. Saunders Co. (international students edition), 1970.

Wheeler, W. M. : "The social insects", London: Kegan Paul, 1928.

Williams, R.M. : "The reduction of intergroup tensions", New York: Social Science Research Council, 1947.

Wolman, B.B. : "Dictionary of behavioural science", London: Macmillan, 1973.

Young, Kimball: "Handbook of social psychology", London: Routledge and Kegan Paul, 1948.

EXECUTIVE SUMMARY

THE IMPACT OF PHYSICAL EDUCATION IN DEVELOPING SOCIAL ATTITUDES AND LEADERSHIP QUALITIES

Dr. V. Satyanarayana

Dr. Digumarti Bhaskara Rao

INTRODUCTION

Today Games & Sports have become an important part of human culture throughout the world. In 1962, **Stone** stressed that life must be viewed as a continuous socialization for the child and the adult, that life is a series of careers with each critical turning point marked by a definite change, the new upcoming game being rehearsed immediately prior to entry upon the appropriate field of play. Personality traits and the sportsman spirit are highly correlated with each other. A eminent educational thinker, **Froebel** said, 'Sport or play is the highest phases of child development. Play is the purest, most spiritual activity of mankind at this stage, and at the same time, typical of human life as a whole of the inner hidden natural life in man and all things'. It is full of pleasure, freedom, peace and mental as well as physical activity. According to Stern, 'Play is a voluntary self contained activity'. Sportsman spirit is a natural and universal phenomenon. It is an essential part of the adolescent's personality. It helps the individual in moulding his personality towards appropriate future life. Educationists have since long been interested in the phenomenon of sports as a means for personality development. Sports reduce emotional as well as mental tensions. It trims the mind and provides better physique to an individual.

Physical education is one of the aspects of education. 'Physical education is an integral part of the total education process and has as its aim the development of physically, mentally, emotionally, and socially, fit citizens through the medium of physical activities which have been selected with a view to realizing these outcomes' (Charles Bucher).

The aim of physical education is development of effective citizenship and social efficiency. The objective of physical education is to help in the production and maintenance of health in body and mind. The aims of physical education are not different from those of education. The subject teacher is merely contended with discussing the theory and imparting knowledge whereas the physical education teacher makes a ceaseless and untiring effort to achieve these aims through muscular activities.

Physical education takes care of the most vital aspect of human life which is the very basis of human existence and strength. It is the basis of a healthy, happy and harmonious life. It helps in the development of a well-balanced, well-integrated and vitally alive human personality. It inculcates the habits of self discipline, self-control, toleration and forbearance, fortitude and spirit of sportsmanship that enable a person to withstand life's setbacks and shocks and brave all risks and hazards with a smiling face and quiet graceful demeansour.

The concept of physical education has been braodened, as it should contribute not only to physical fitness but also to physical efficiency, mental alertness and the development of certain qualities like perseverance, team spirit, leadership, obedience to rules, moderation in victory and balance in defeat.

Leadership is a social phenomenon that exists every where throughout the world. Leadership arises only where there is a group with norms triving to reach a goal. Sport, a social psychologist said that 'Any one, who acts as model to other is often called a leader'. Every person who leads a group of people is çalled a leader. Leadership behaviour is in demand in various fields of life situations—social, political, cultural, educational, sports, games, etc. Groups and organizations of all sorts are liable to survive and succeed only under effective leadership. Good leadership is a prime necessity for the promotion and enhancement of physical education in educational institutions. An institution may possess all the other facilities but if there is no adequate leadership and supervision, it will be a ship without a captain, a factory without a manager, a temple without a priest, and rest house without a care-taker. Leadership is therefore the mainspring for the proper conduct of the co-ordinated programmes of physical education in schools and colleges.

Similarly the development of desirable social attitudes or reshaping of undersirable attitudes is a gigantic task. It needs co-operation of all forces of environment. Parents, members of the society, teachers, schools and colleges and government authorities, all need to join hands in this task of desirable attitude formation among the young generation. Physical growth and development of the child plays a significant role in the development of social attitudes. Poor physical health, low vitality and undeveloped somatic structure is responsible for poor emotional and social adjustment and poor social adjustment inevitably exercises an important effect on the formation of attitudes in many different directions.

The main aim of education is to modify the behaviour of the child according to the needs and expectancy of the society. Behaviour is composed of so many attributes. One of these important attributes is attitude. One's behaviour, to a great extent, depends upon one's attitude toward the things—idea, person, or object, in this environment. The entire personality and development of the child is influenced by the nature of his attitudes. Learning of a subject and acquisition of habits, interests and other psychophysical dispositions are all effected by his attitudes. According to **Travers**, 'An attitude is a readiness to respond in such a way that behaviour is given a certain direction'. Whittaker said, 'An attitude is a predisposition or readiness to respond in a pre-determined manner to relevant stimuli'. According to Allports's definition an attitude has at least five aspects. It is 1. a mental and neural state, 2. of readiness to respond, 3. organized, 4. through experience, 5. exerting a directive and or influence on behaviour.

It is obvious that all students are not exposed to physical programmes in our educational institutions in equal measures. But a few pupils are exposed to physical education programmes at school level alone, some at junior college level, and others at degree college level, while others are exposed throughout. Among these participants in physical education programmes some of them get the honour for national level participation, inter-versity level participation, state level participation, inter schools & Junior Colleges level participation and district level participation. So the participants in Games & Sports are exposed in different measures and at different stages of their education. Hence it is assumed that these difference in exposure would result in differences in Social Attitudes and Leadership Qualities formed.

The present study envisages to identify the relationship between the exposure of Games & Sports and the Social Attitudes and Leadership Qualities developed.

Now the present study sought to work with the following objectives:

1. To find out the association between the levels of participation of pupils in Games & Sports and social attitudes formed at various levels of education i.e., school, junior college and degree level.
2. To find out the association between the levels of participation of pupils in Games & Sports and leadership qualities formed at various levels of education i.e., school, junior college and degree level.
3. To find out the inter-relationship between the developments of social attitudes and leadership qualities at various levels of education.

HYPOTHESES

The following Hypotheses were formulated in this connection:

1. There will be a positive association between the participation in Games & Sports, and social attitudes formed.
2. There will be a positive association between the participation in Games & Sports, and leadership qualities formed.
3. There will be inter-relationship between the developments of social attitudes and leadership qualities among pupils at various levels of education.

Methodology

Since the research involved the assessment of both Social Attitudes & Leadership Qualities among students at various levels of education three types of tools were required to measure the impact of physical education in developing social attitudes and leadership qualities.

TOOLS

i. Tool to measure the intensity of participation of pupils in Games & Sports.
ii. Tool to measure the social attitudes at various levels of education.
iii. Tool to measure the leadership qualities at various levels of education.

Since the said tools were not available they were constructed and standardized.

SAMPLE

The following sample was drawn from schools, Jr. Colleges and degree colleges through the method of random sampling from the state of Andhra Pradesh.

Institutional	*Participants*	*Non-Participants*	*Total*
School	125	125	250
Junior Colleges	110	110	220
Degree Colleges	110	110	220

RESEARCH DESIGN

The research design is diagrammatically presented:

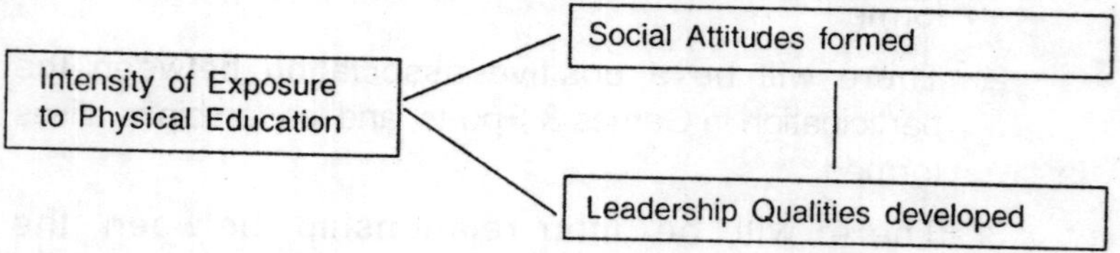

DATA COLLECTION PROCEDURE

A total of 690 students (345 Participants, 345 Non-participants in Games & Sports) from Schools, Junior Colleges, Degree Colleges and play fields of different sport centres of Warangal, Hyderabad, Karimnagar, Khammam, Adilabad were considered for the study.

The investigator had faced a hard time in tracing the participants in Games & Sports especially at inter level.

Hence, the researcher had considered the Intermediate completed students appearing for the under-graduate diploma (UGD) course entrance test and the degree completed students appearing for the B.P.Ed. entrance test at Physical Education Common Entrance Test (PECET-95) conducted at different centres of State like, Warangal, Rajahmundry, Ananthapur and Tirupati. The scale consisting of both Social Attitudes and Leadership Qualities in a jumbled form with 76 statements (1-52 Leadership Qualities statements, 36-76 Social Attitude Students and 39-52 Common Questions) was used for the data collection. The students asked to give their opinion on five point scale (Strongly Agree, Agree, Undecided, Disagree and Strongly Disagree).

STATISTICAL TECHNIQUES USED

The presented study sought to find out the relationship between various variables as shown in the following paras:

1. The study sought to find out the significance of difference of Leadership Qualities developed at various levels of education between participants and Non-participants in Games & Sports.
2. The study carried out to find out the significance of

difference of Leadership Qualities developed at various levels of education between participants and non-participants in Games & Sports.

3. The relationship between the measure of the Social Attitudes formed at various levels of education and the measure of the Leadership Qualities developed at various levels of education.

To test the above said relations the investigator computed the various Co-efficient of correlations, and test the significance of difference of any between the variables that are put forth in the study. **The means & standard deviations** of Social Attitudes and Leadership Qualities developed among participants and non-participants and the t-test were computed between the participants and non-participants at various levels of education. To find out the inter-relationship between these two variables i.e., Social Attitudes and Leadership Qualities the co-efficient of correlations were computed.

RESULTS IN BRIEF AND CONCLUSIONS

The results and conclusions are presented Objective/ Hypothesis-wise.

HYPOTHESIS-I

'There will be a positive association between the participation in Games & Sports, and Social Attitude formation.'

I. Participation in Games & Sports and Social Attitudes Formation—Education Level-wise

Results

(a) Participation of pupils in Games & Sports at School level develops the Social Attitudes in a significant measure.

(b) Participation of pupils in Games & Sports at Inter level develops the Social Attitudes in a significant measure.

(c) Participation of pupils in Games & Sports at Degree level does not develop the Social Attitudes in a significant measure.

(d) Participation of pupils in Games & Sports at All Levels of Education i.e., for a prolonged period develops the Social Attitudes in a significant measure.

Conclusion

The participation of pupils in Games & Sports generally helps in the formation of Social Attitudes in them.

II. Participation in Games & Sports and Formation of Social Attitudes—Sex-wise

Under caption (a) the results and conclusions covering the formation of Social Attitudes among Boys and Girls who participate in Games & Sports are presented:

(a) 1. The difference in the formation of Social Attitudes among the Boys and Girls who participate in Games & Sports at School level is not found to be significant, though the Boys have scored slightly higher on Social Attitude Scale than the Girls.

2. The difference in the formation of Social Attitudes among the Boys and Girls who participate in Games & Sports at Inter level is found to be significant the Girls scoring higher than the Boys on Social Attitude Scale.

3. The difference in the formation of Social Attitudes among the Boys and Girls who participate in Games & Sports at Degree level is found to be significant, the Girls scoring higher than the boys on Social Attitude Scale.

4. The difference in the formation of Social Attitudes among the Boys and Girls who participate in Games & Sports at All Levels of Education is found to be significant, the Girls scoring higher than the Boys on Social Attitude Scale.

Conclusion

Initially though the Girls who participate in Games & Sports score less on the Social Attitude Scale than Boys, they progressively continue to score higher and higher on Social Attitude Scale excelling their male counterparts throughout their educational career.

Under caption (b) the results and conclusions covering the formation of Social Attitudes among Boys and Girls who do not participate are in Games & Sports are presented.

Results

(b) 1. The Girls who do not participate in Games & Sports at School level score significantly higher on Social Attitude Scale than their male counterparts.

2. The difference in the formation of Social Attitudes among the Boys and Girls who do not participate in Games & Sports at Inter level is found to be significant, the Girls scoring higher than the Boys on Social Attitude Scale.

3. The difference in the formation of Social Attitudes among the Boys and Girls who do not participate in Games & Sports at Degree level is not found to be significant.

4. The Girls who do not participate in Games & Sports at All Levels of Education score significantly higher on Social Attitude Scale than their male counterparts.

Conclusion

The Girls who do not participate in Games & Sports generally score significantly higher than their male counterparts on Social Attitude Scale during their period of education.

Under caption (c) the results and conclusion covering the Social Attitudes among Boys and Girls (when both the Participants and Non-participants in Games & Sports are taken together) are presented.

Results

(c) 1. The difference in the formation of Social Attitudes among Boys and Girls in general at School level is not found to be significant, though the Girls score slightly higher than the Boys.

2. The Girls in general at Inter level score significantly higher on Social Attitude Scale than the Boys.
3. The difference in the formation of Social Attitudes among Boys and Girls in general at Degree level is not found to be significant, though the Girls score slightly higher than the Boys.
4. The Girls in general at All levels of Education score significantly higher on Social Attitude Scale than the Boys.

Conclusion

Irrespective of their participation and non-participation in Games & Sports the Girls generally score significantly higher than the Boys on Social Attitude Scale.

III. Participation in Games & Sports and Formation of Social Attitudes—Community Background-Wise

Under caption (a) the results and conclusions covering the formation of Social Attitudes among Rural and Urban students who participate in Games & Sports are presented.

Results

(a) 1. The difference in the formation of Social Attitudes among Rural and Urban pupils who participate in Games & Sports at School level is not found to be significant, though the Rural participants have scored slightly higher than the Urban participants on Social Attitude Scale.

2. The difference in the formation of Social Attitudes among Rural and Urban pupils who participate in Games & Sports at Inter level is not found to be significant, though the Urban participants have scored slightly higher than the Rural participants on Social Attitude Scale.

3. The difference in the formation of Social Attitude among Rural and Urban pupils who participate in Games & Sports at Degree level is not found to be

significant, though the Urban participants have scored slightly higher than the Rural participants on Social Attitude Scale.

4. The difference in the formation of Social Attitude among Rural and Urban pupils who participate in Games & Sports at All Levels of Education is not found to be significant, though the Rural participants have scored slightly higher than the Urban participants on Social Attitude Scale.

Conclusion

The difference in the Social Attitudes formation during the period of education among the Rural and Urban participants in Games & Sports is not found to be significant.

Under caption (b) the results and conclusions covering the formation of Social Attitudes among Rural and Urban who do not participate in Games & Sports are presented.

Results

(b) 1. The difference in the formation of Social Attitudes among Rural and Urban pupils who do not participate in Games & Sports at School level is not found to be significant, the Urban students scoring than the Rural students.

2. The difference in the formation of Social Attitudes among Rural and Urban pupils who do not participate in Games & Sports at Inter level is not found to be significant, though the Urban non-participants have scored slightly higher than the Rural participants on Social Attitude Scale.

3. The difference in the formation of Social Attitude among Rural and Urban pupils who do not participate in Games & Sports at Degree level is not found to be significant, though the Urban non-participants have scored slightly higher than the Rural participants on Social Attitude Scale.

4. The difference in the formation of Social Attitude

among Rural and Urban pupils who do not participate in Games & Sports at All Levels of Education is not found to be significant, though the Urban non-participants have scored slightly higher than the Rural non-participants on Social Attitude Scale.

Conclusion

The difference in the Social Attitudes formation during the period of education among the Rural and Urban non-participants in Games & Sports is not found to be significant.

Under caption (c) the results and conclusions covering the formation of Social Attitudes among Rural and Urban (when both Participants and Non-participants in Games & Sports are taken together) are presented.

Results

(c) 1. The difference in the formation of Social Attitudes among Rural and Urban students in general at School level is not found to be significant, though the Rural students score slightly higher than the Urban students.

2. The different in the formation of Social Attitudes among Rural and Urban students in general at Inter level is not found to be significant, though the Urban students score slightly higher than the Rural students.

3. The difference in the formation of Social Attitudes among Rural and Urban students in general at Degree level is not found to be significant though the Urban students score slightly higher than the Rural students.

4. The difference in the formation of Social Attitudes among Rural and Urban students in general at All levels of Education level is not found to be significant, though the Urban students score slightly higher than the Rural students.

Conclusion

Irrespective of the participation of pupils in Games and Sports the differences in the formation of Social Attitudes among Rural and Urban students are not found to be significant.

IV. Participation in Games & Sports and Social Attitude Formation—Age-Wise

Conclusion

The Social Attitude formation among the pupils who participate in Games & Sports develops with age.

The Social Attitude formation among the pupils who do not participate in Games & Sports develops with age.

The Social Attitude formation among the pupils develops with age.

V. The Intensity of Participation In Games & Sports and Social Attitude Formation

Conclusion

The Social Attitudes do not develop in relation to the intensity of the participation of students in Games & Sports.

The results and conclusions of the Objective/Hpothesis-2 are presented hereunder:

HYPOTHESIS-2

'There will be a positive association between the participation in Games & Sports, and Leadership Qualities development.'

I. Participation in Games & Sports and Leadership Qualities Development—Education Level-Wise

Results

(a) Participation of pupils in Games & Sports at School level develops the Leadership Qualities in a significant measure.

(b) Participation of pupils in Games & Sports at Inter level develops the Leadership Qualities in a significant measure.

(c) Participation of pupils in Games & Sports at Degree level does not develop the Leadership Qualities in a significant measure.

(d) Participation of pupils in Games & Sports at All Levels of Education i.e., for a prolonged period develops the Leadership Qualities in a significant measure.

Conclusion

The participation of pupils in Games & Sports generally helps in the development of Leadership Qualities in them.

II. Participation in Games & Sports and Development of Leadership—Qualities Sex-wise

Under caption (a) the results and conclusions covering the development of Leadership Qualities among participating Boys and Girls in Games & Sports are presented.

(a) 1. The difference in the Development of Leadership Qualities among the Boys and Girls who participate in Games & Sports at School level is not found to be significant, though the Boys have scored slightly higher on Leadership Qualities Scale than the Girls.

2. The difference in the development of Leadership Qualities among the Boys and Girls who participate in Games & Sports at Inter level is found to be significant, the Girls scoring higher than the Boys on Leadership Qualities Scale.

3. The difference in the development of Leadership Qualities among the Boys and Girls who participate in Games & Sports at Degree level is found to be significant, the Girls scoring higher than the boys on Leadership Qualities Scale.

4. The difference in the development of Leadership Qualities among the Boys and Girls who participate in Games & Sports at All Levels of Education is found to be significant, the Girls scoring higher than the Boys on Leadership Qualities Scale.

Conclusion

Initially though the Girls who participate in Games & Sports score less on the Leadership Qualities Scale than Boys, they progressively continue to score higher and higher on Leadership Qualities Scale excelling their male counterparts throughout their educational career.

Under caption (b) the results and conclusions covering the development of Leadership Qualities among Non-participating Boys and Girls in Games & Sports are presented.

Results

(b) 1. The Girls who do not participate in Games & Sports at School level score significantly higher on Leadership Qualities Scale than their male counterparts.

2. The difference in the development of Leadership Qualities among the Boys and Girls who do not participate in Games & Sports at Inter level is not found to be significant, the Girls scoring higher than the Boys on Leadership Qualities Scale.

3. The difference in the development of Leadership Qualities among the Boys and Girls who do not participate in Games & Sports at Degree level is not found to be significant, Boys scoring slightly higher than the Girls on Leadership Qualities Scale.

4. The Girls who do not participate in Games & Sports at All Levels of Education score significantly higher on Leadership Qualities Scale than their male counterparts.

Conclusion

The Girls who do not participate in Games & Sports generally score significantly higher than their male counterparts on Leadership Qualities Scale during their period of education.

Under caption (c) the results and conclusion covering the Leadership Qualities among Boys and Girls (when both the Participants and Non-participants in Games & Sports are taken together) are presented.

Results

(c) 1. The difference in the development of Leadership

Qualities among Boys and Girls in general at School level is found to be significant, the Girls scoring slightly higher than the Boys.

2. The Girls in general at Inter level score significantly higher on Leadership Qualities Scale than the Boys.
3. The difference in the development of Leadership Qualities among Boys and Girls in general at Degree level is not found to be significant, though the Boys score slightly higher than the Boys.
4. The Girls in general at All Levels of Education score significantly higher on Leadership Qualities Scale than the Boys.

Conclusion

Irrespective of their participation in Games & Sports the Girls generally score significantly higher than the Boys on Leadership Qualities Scale.

III. Participation in Games & Sports and Development of Leadership Qualities—Community Background-Wise

Under caption (a) the results and conclusions covering the development of Leadership Qualities among Rural and Urban students who participate in Games & Sports are presented.

Results

(a) 1. The difference in the development of Leadership Qualities among Rural and Urban pupils who participate in Games & Sports at School level is not found to be significant, though the Rural participants have scored slightly higher than the Urban participants on Leadership Qualities Scale.

2. The difference in the development of Leadership Qualities among Rural and Urban pupils who participate in Games & Sports at Inter level is not found to be significant, though the Urban participants have scored slightly higher than the Rural participants on Leadership Qualities Scale.

3. The difference in the development of Leadership Qualities among Rural and Urban pupils who participate in Games & Sports at Degree level is not found to be significant, though the Urban participants have scored slightly higher than the Rural participants on Leadership Qualities Scale.
4. The difference in the development of Leadership Qualities among Rural and Urban pupils who participate in Games & Sports at All Levels of Education is not found to be significant, though the Rural participants have scored slightly higher than the Urban participants on Leadership Qualities Scale.

Conclusion

The differences in the Leadership Qualities development during the period of education among the Rural and Urban participants in Games & Sports is not found to be significant.

Under caption (b) the results and conclusions covering the development of Leadership Qualities among Rural and Urban students who do not participate in Games & Sports are presented.

Results

(b) 1. The difference in the development of Leadership Qualities among Rural and Urban pupils who do not participate in Games & Sports at School level is not found to be significant, the Rural students scoring slightly higher than the Urban students.

2. The difference in the development of Leadership Qualities among Rural and Urban pupils who do not participate in Games & Sports at Inter level is not found to be significant, though the Urban non-participants have scored slightly higher than the Rural non-participants on Leadership Qualities Scale.

3. The difference in the development of Leadership Qualities among Rural and Urban pupils who do not participate in Games & Sports at Degree level is not found to be significant, though the Urban non-

participants have scored slightly higher their Rural counterparts on Leadership Qualities Scale.

4. The difference in the development of Leadership Qualities among Rural and Urban pupils who do not participate in Games & Sports at All Levels of Education is not found to be significant, though the Urban non-participants have scored slightly higherthan the Rural counterparts on Leadership Qualities Scale.

Conclusion

The difference in the Leadership Qualities development during the period of education among the Rural and Urban non-participants in Games & Sports is not found to be significant.

Under caption (c) the results and conclusions covering the development of Leadership Qualities among Rural and Urban (when both Participants and Non-participants in Games & Sports are taken together) are presented.

Results

(c) 1. The difference in the development of Leadership Qualities among Rural and Urban students in general at School level is not found to be significant, though the Urban students score slightly higher than the Rural students.

2. The different in the development of Leadership Qualities among Rural and urban students in general at Inter level is found to be significant, though the Urban students scoring higher than the Rural students.

3. The difference in the development of Leadership Qualities among Rural and Urban students in general at Degree level is not found to be significant, the Urban students scoring higher than the Rural students.

4. The difference in the development of Leadership Qualities among Rural and Urban students in general at All levels of Education level is not found to be significant, though the Urban students scoring higher than the Rural students.

Conclusion

Irrespective of the participation of pupils in Games and Sports the differences in the development of Leadership Qualities among Rural and Urban students are not found to be significant, except in the case of Urban Inter level students who have scored significantly higher on Leadership Qualities Scale than the Rural Inter Level students.

IV. Participation in Games & Sports and Leadership Qualities Development—Age-Wise

Conclusions

The Leadership Qualities among the pupils who participate in Games & Sports develops with age.

The Leadership Qualities among the pupils who do not participate in Games & Sports develops with age.

The Leadership Qualities among the pupils develops with age.

V. The Intensity of Participation In Games & Sports and Leadership Qualities Development

Conclusion

The Leadership Qualities do not develop in relation to the intensity of the participation of students in Games & Sports.

'The results and conclusions of the Objective/Hypothesis-3 are presented hereunder':

HYPOTHESIS-3

'There will be inter-relationship between the development of Social Attitudes and Leadership Qualities among pupils at various levels of education.'

The following are the conclusions drawn from the results. They are presented under captions a, b, c, d, with regards to School Level, Inter Level, Degree Level and At all Levels of Education. The caption "e" covers the general conclusion for the entire population.

(a) School Level

Leadership Qualities develop positively in relation to Social Attitudes formation among pupils at Schools level.

(b) Inter Level

Leadership Qualities develop positively in relation to Social Attitudes formation among pupils at Inter level.

(c) Degree Level

Leadership Qualities develop positively in relation to Social Attitudes formation among pupils at Degree level.

(d) At All Levels of Education

Leadership Qualities develop positively in relation to Social Attitudes formation among pupils at All Levels of Education.

(e) Conclusion

Irrespective of the levels of education, the pupils develop in them the Leadership Qualities positively in relation to Social Attitudes formation.

SUGGESTIONS FOR FURTHER RESEARCH

The following problems deserving research attention have been generated by the research under report.

1. Women and Leadership

It has been conclusively established that women at various stages of education display higher levels of Leadership Qualities. It has been so both in the case of Participants in Games & Sports and Non-Participants in the Games & Sports hailing from different community backgrounds. It appears that the women students are better leaders than men students.

It needs research confirmation. For that a deeper probe into this aspect covering larger populations covering the entire gamut of human pursuits appears to be in order.

2. *Women and Formation of Social Attitudes*

Further it has been established that the formation of Social Attitudes takes place in a greater measure in Girls than in Boys. A research design covering the male and female population drawn from the entire gamut of human activity seems appropriate. It can be comprehensively tested if the females invariably develop Social Attitudes in an accelerated measure than males.

3. *Intensity of Participation in Games & Sports and Leadership Qualities Development*

It has been established that the Participation in Games & Sports develops Leadership Qualities in a greater measure than the Non-participation in Games & Sports. Likewise, the intensity of participation in Games & Sports too should have positive association with the development of Leadership Qualities. But surprisingly the association between the intensity of participation in Games & Sports and Leadership Qualities development was not found to be significant.

Normally it is assumed that the players at the highest levels including International Level are expected to be better Leaders. But the results do not subscribe to the same.

In this connection a thorough probe atleast at the Doctoral level is necessary which would highlity the sluggish growth of Leadership Qualities among the sportsmen at the highest levels of their participation. Does the concentration of effort at the highest levels of the participants sharp in the skills of expertise of a specific game instead of broadbasing the effort in the area including leadership growth? It is a convergent effort or a divergent one? Expertise could be convergent while leadership could be divergent. A deeper probe probably would explain the lack of commensurate growth of Leadership Qualities among the participants at the highest levels of Games & Sports.

INDEX